When Words Collide

A Media Writer's Guide
to Grammar and Style

From the Wadsworth Series in Mass Communication and Journalism

Eighth Edition

When Words Collide

A Media Writer's Guide to Grammar and Style

Lauren Kessler
University of Oregon

Duncan McDonald
University of Oregon

Exercises Prepared by

Duncan McDonald
University of Oregon

Tracy Ilene Miller
University of Oregon

WADSWORTH
CENGAGE Learning™

Australia • Brazil • Japan • Korea • Mexico • Singapore • Spain • United Kingdom • United States

WADSWORTH
CENGAGE Learning™

**When Words Collide:
A Media Writer's Guide to
Grammar and Style, 8/e**
**Lauren Kessler and Duncan
McDonald**

Senior Publisher: Lyn Uhl

Publisher/Executive Editor:
Michael Rosenberg

Development Editor: Mary
Beth Walden

Assistant Editor: Jillian
D'Urso

Editorial Assistant: Erin Pass

Media Editor: Jessica Badiner

Marketing Director: Jason
Sakos

Marketing Communications
Manager: Tami Strang

Content Project Manager:
Aimee Chevrette Bear

Art Director: Marissa Falco

Print Buyer: Justin Palmeiro

Rights Acquisition Specialist:
Katie Huha

Production Service:
S4Carlisle Publishing
Services

Text Designer: Glenna
Collett

Cover Designer: Lisa Kuhn,
Curio Press, LLC

Compositor: S4Carlisle
Publishing Services

For product information and technology
assistance, contact us at **Cengage Learning
Customer & Sales Support, 1-800-354-9706**

For permission to use material from this text or
product, submit all requests online at
www.cengage.com/permissions
Further permissions questions can be emailed to
permissionrequest@cengage.com

Library of Congress Control Number: 2010931697

ISBN-13: 978-0-495-90144-0
ISBN-10: 0-495-90144-X

Wadsworth
20 Channel Center St,
Boston, MA 02210
USA

Cengage Learning is a leading provider of customized
learning solutions with office locations around the globe,
including Singapore, the United Kingdom, Australia, Mexico,
Brazil, and Japan. Locate your local office at:
international.cengage.com/region

Cengage Learning products are represented in Canada by
Nelson Education, Ltd.

For your course and learning solutions, visit
www.cengage.com

Purchase any of our products at your local college store
or at our preferred online store **www.cengagebrain.com**

Printed in the United States of America
2 3 4 5 6 7   14

Contents

CHAPTER 5   Power and Precision: It Begins with the Verb   **45**

CHAPTER 6   The Rest of the Crew   **57**

CHAPTER 7   Are We in Agreement?   **75**

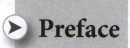

Preface

Online, on paper, on the air. Where will your writing appear?

Blog posts, news bulletins, essays. Documentary scripts, speeches, ad copy. Investigative reports, narrative features, multimedia presentations. What will you write?

You may not know yet, and if you do know (and even if you are *very, very* sure), it's more than likely you will change your mind and the direction of your career many times. What will remain, what is at the core of all of these endeavors, all these "delivery systems," all the new and changing technology that will always be a part of our lives is this: Correct, crisp, compelling prose. Good, solid writing. Writing that sparks discussion, ignites emotions, captures experience, tells stories. And what is at the core of all *that*? Good grammar. This brings us to the book you hold in your hands. Welcome to the new edition of *When Words Collide*, your friendly and authoritative guide to grammar and word use.

Whether you're a veteran writer or a writer-in-training, a would-be, a wanna-be, or a might-be, we welcome you to this book. We also welcome those of you brought kicking and screaming to a book on grammar. However you got here, we're glad to have you. We're glad to share our love of language and our commitment to great writing.

If you want to write well, *When Words Collide* can help you.

There are those who find the study of grammar endlessly fascinating. We wish them well, but we don't number ourselves among them. Rather, we are writers who understand a fundamental concept: The better we know the tools of our trade, the better writers we will be. We don't *love* grammar. We *need* it. We get frustrated, just like you, with its intricacies and inconsistencies, its sometimes finicky rules and occasionally exasperating exceptions. But we know from experience that the reward for mastering grammar is the ability to write with clarity, power and grace—and that's quite a reward.

It is from our perspective as committed writers, avid readers and (we hope) thoughtful teachers that we offer this eighth edition of *When Words Collide*. We want you to stick with us, read the book carefully and use it as a reference while you write. Learn grammar not for its own sake, not—*please*—to pass some test, but rather because grammar is one of the foundations of good writing.

We find ourselves saying this with every edition—and we mean it with every edition: This is the best *When Words Collide* yet. In this edition, we pay particular attention to the dynamic, evolving, cross-platform, multimedia environment in which today's writers function—and how it is more than ever vital to know how to communicate crisply, clearly and powerfully.

We begin this edition with a new chapter (possibly the briefest chapter in textbook history), which we hope will grab your attention and set the tone.

We begin our exploration of language in a different way than in past editions, with a revised chapter on the sentence, to explore the forest before investigating the trees.

We've revamped and combined previous chapters on agreement and case, and omitted our chapter on spelling, moving our advice about this important subject into quickly accessible new appendices.

We've rethought and re-imagined, expanded where we needed to expand, trimmed where we needed to trim, and everywhere added new examples and clear explanations (and dollops of humor).

We hope this book helps you become the best writer you can be. We hope you keep it on your desk for years to come.

ACKNOWLEDGMENTS

We thank the following reviewers for their ideas and comments: Mathew Cabot, San José State University; Rasha Kamhawi, University of Florida; Joel Kaplan, Syracuse University; Becky McDonald, Ball State University; and Gemma R. Puglisi, American University. We especially thank the many teachers around the country who have enthusiastically supported our efforts and have made *When Words Collide* a part of their classes. We thank the thousands of students who have struggled with the complexities of the English language on the road to becoming professional writers. We dedicate this book to them and to our families.

Lauren Kessler
Duncan McDonald
Eugene, Oregon

Preface to Exercises for
When Words Collide

The eighth edition of *Exercises for When Words Collide* challenges you to test yourself and to grow in confidence. This workbook's 36 exercises, which have even greater depth and breadth than those of the previous edition, carefully match the readings in the *When Words Collide* text.

This exercise book has been challenging students and helping instructors for more than 25 years. And with this edition, I am very pleased to introduce Tracy Ilene Miller, a gifted writer, teacher and editor, who joins me in supporting your quest to learn and grow. I'm delighted to have Tracy as a co-author; here are some introductory words from her:

"My in-depth study of grammar came after the first 20 years of a career as a writer, editor and designer. I was asked to teach grammar at the University of Oregon, and at that point, I became intent on figuring ways to unpack the rules and get at logic so as to promote the study of grammar as more problem-solving than tenet. That's what grammar is to me: not so much a set of rules, but rather a major, unseen influence on the front end of my writing to organize my thoughts, and then again during the middle and end cycles of my writing and editing process, when overtly I rely on grammar to check, among other things, that I've successfully and correctly communicated my ideas.

In joining Duncan McDonald, a respected teacher of more than 30 years and a mentor of mine, to craft this new edition of exercises, my hope is that you use these exercises as they were designed: to explore grammar not from a distance, as rules, but instead as a tool that promotes and supports your quest to write and communicate at your best."

We'd like to let instructors know that the answers to exercises 2-36 are available to them at the following Web site: www.cengage.com/masscomm/kessler/whenwordscollide8e

Your instructors will work with you to explain the answers, if needed, and to offer even more challenges as you strengthen your writing skills.

In the belief that more help is usually welcomed, let us offer personal assistance: If you are struggling with a concept or a problem sentence, or you can't make sense out of a particular question in an exercise, please send Tracy an e-mail with your query, at: **miller .wwcworkbook@gmail.com**

You will receive a personal response! (And, as needed, I'll be happy to follow up as well.)

Good luck! Keep on digging and learning—and be sure to write about it!

Duncan McDonald
School of Journalism and Communication
University of Oregon
Eugene, Oregon

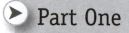
Part One

UNDERSTANDING GRAMMAR AND STYLE

Chapter 1

Hey...

Those of us who love words have our pet peeves. Mr. Hawkey, an aptly named eleventh-grade English teacher who years ago told one of your authors that she might someday be a writer, used to get sweaty and red in the face over collective nouns and their pronouns.

"I don't care how many players are on a team," he would say, pacing the classroom, directing an icy glare at one or another of us offenders of good grammar. "A team is an *it*. That means singular—not plural." Here is where his face would redden. "The team and *its* captain. *Its, its, its*." He would jab his finger with each *its*. We would have laughed had we all not been so terrified of the guy.

Then there was Roy Paul Nelson, our colleague and an otherwise perfectly reasonable man, who went ballistic over *hopefully*. He campaigned tirelessly—well, *he* wasn't tired, but some who have listened to him for two decades were—against the improper use of hopefully. *Hopefully*, Roy Paul would tell you (again and again) means "with hope," as in "She looks to the future hopefully." It does not mean "I hope that" as in "Hopefully, I'll be at the concert tonight." It was a lonely battle for Roy Paul, but that didn't stop him.

This brings us to our own pet peeve. It isn't about the nuts and bolts of grammar. It's about appropriate language use, which is becoming more of an issue the more colloquial we become in our writing. (We'll talk about this in the next chapter.) Colloquial and casual are fine . . . in their place. The trick is knowing their place. When you compose a term paper, you don't use the same tone, the same style, the same vocabulary as when you text a friend. When you write an essay for a job application, you don't—please tell us you don't!—use the same tone, style and vocabulary as when you e-mail your cousin.

Our pet peeve is *hey*. We're not talking about "Hey!" yelled from across the street to a friend, or "Hey" in a text message. *Hey* is okay for friends. It is not okay for employers, future employers, people you are contacting in the act of reporting, people you want to impress with your intelligence and wit or anyone who has the power to give you a grade—or a raise.

There. We've said what we need to say. Congratulations! You have now finished an *entire* chapter of this book. You can pay us back for our amazing brevity by beginning to consider this notion of appropriate language use. And, hey, you might start by deleting *hey* from your professional vocabulary.

Chapter 2

grmr: CWOT?

Is grmr (grammar) a CWOT (complete waste of time)?

Not IRL (in real life).

IRL grammar is the key to effective, powerful, successful communication.

Why start talking about grammar by referencing twitter/ chat/ and text messaging acronyms? Stay with us for a moment as we explain.

Insta-Talk

Grammar and texting go together like peanut butter and eggs. Or ham and jelly. You get the idea. The accepted rules of grammar, spelling and punctuation—the rules that govern the use of language—don't apply to tweeting, IMing, texting or sometimes even e-mailing, which are the most common ways we communicate with each other these days. That means that the way we are comfortable communicating every day, the way members of the Born Digital generation have grown up communicating, conflicts with the way we all must communicate as media professionals.

Consider this simple, accepted rule of grammar: The word that begins a sentence starts with a capital letter. Or this one: A sentence ends with a piece of terminal punctuation. Spelling, of course, is all about rules: doubling or not doubling consonants, possessives and contractions, -ence versus -ance, i before e except after c.

But when you're striding down the street (or, we hate to say it, driving your car) and using your thumbs to click on a tiny touchpad or when you're firing off a 140-character text or tweet, grammatical conventions don't apply. Capitalize a letter to begin a sentence? Why waste that time? In fact, why write a sentence at all? Spell out a word? *Correctly* spell out a word? Y wd u do tht whn u cd abrve8? It's so much faster (and uses fewer characters).

Of course, it's not just the medium that negates the traditional rules. It is also the purpose, the goal of the act of communication. Tweeting, texting and IMing are all about quick, casual, instantaneous connection. The purpose is not to communicate intellectually or emotionally complex material. The emoticon is about as deep as it gets. The purpose is not to have far-ranging discussions or reason out a problem or bring up thought-provoking issues. The purpose is to check in (r u ok?) or to confirm a date (cu @ 10?) or to update a friend (standing in line 4 tickets) or maybe to make a quick comment (BTDT [been there, done that]).

Okay. The lesson thus far is that formal written communication, from college essays to press releases, from corporate reports to online stories, follows certain rules that informal communication like texting and tweeting do not.

Fine. What's the problem?

The problem is not realizing that there are different rules for different kinds of communication. The problem is that when you practice—every day, many times a day—a certain way of writing (the shortcut, no-traditional-rules way of writing), you can get so comfortable with it that you forget how specialized it is. You forget it was created for a narrow purpose—insta-talk—and not for the wider, more important, long-term purpose of communicating thoughts, ideas, issues, information and opinions across time and space. Just because the coded shorthand of the txt msg works when you are text messaging doesn't mean it works when you are writing a blog post, news story or press release. Just because lack of punctuation is fine when you text your friend does not mean it is fine when you write a report for your boss—or, for that matter, when you e-mail your boss.

What Does Your E-mail Say about You?

Compared with texting and IMing, e-mail seems old-fashioned, stodgy even. Although not as impossibly quaint as an actual letter placed in an actual envelope and deposited in an actual mailbox, e-mail is nonetheless comparatively prim and proper. E-mailers spend more time (and use more words) constructing messages than IMers or texters. They are more likely to write in full sentences and less likely to use shortcuts (b4, gr8, g2cu) or abbreviations (gtg) or contractions that may, with enough use, confound correct spelling (thx, ur). Adhering to grammatical conventions makes sense because e-mail is, in fact, more formal than IMing or texting. Although friends certainly e-mail friends in a casual way, e-mail is also an integral part of the business and professional world. In fact, e-mail has almost entirely replaced the phone for workplace communication.

Dependence on e-mail in the workplace combined with its limbo-land status—less formal than the business letters or memos of old, more formal than friend-to-friend text messaging—is creating big problems, say those in the business world. In a lengthy story on the subject in the Wall Street Journal, the headline of which read "Thx for the IView! I Wud (heart) to Work 4 U!!," recruiters and personnel managers railed against too casual communication. One national recruiter quoted in the story said that she had interviewed a particular candidate and thought she had found the perfect intern until she received the candidate's thank-you email. It was laced with words like *hiya* and *thanx* along with three exclamation points and a smiley-face emoticon. The candidate did not get the job. What some think of as casual, business people think of as unprofessional. The laid-back, offhand, short-cut way of communicating that many millions of us use everyday is, when used in the workplace, considered a mark of immaturity and thoughtlessness, an indicator of a more generalized slap-dash attitude.

Other e-mails, according to consultants and writing coaches in the corporate trenches, are just the opposite: inflated and flabby, stuffed with polysyllabic words, cluttered phrasing and tortured sentence structure. And then there are the incoherent e-mails, whose meaning eludes—or, often worse, misguides—their receivers. These e-mails are riddled with incorrect punctuation, misplaced or dangling modifiers, incorrect word choice or syntax so tangled that it would take a machete to cut through it. The grammar—or lack thereof—prevents people from understanding one another.

The lessons to be learned from the corporate experience are important ones. The first one, of course, is that clear written communication matters—not just for those in the communication business but for everyone in the world of work. The second is that the cavalier attitude toward grammatical conventions that comes from and is daily reinforced by, IMing and texting is decidedly not the attitude a media writer (or any working professional) should adopt. And here's a third lesson: Just because you can type fast doesn't mean you should write fast.

Beware the Media Multitasker

Here's a final idea to consider as you navigate the terrain between casual and professional communication: Media multitasking may be dangerous to your (professional) health—and most certainly to your growth as a writer.

In high school or college, you may have become accustomed to media overload. You IM a friend while listening to your iPod, doing a homework assignment and playing an online video game. You check your e-mail while perusing craigslist and talking on your cell phone. That may work for you or you may *think* it works for you, but now that you're on the road to becoming a media writer, it's time to reconsider. Decades of research have shown that the more tasks multitaskers attempt, the worse they do at them. A recent Stanford University study of more than 250 college undergrads reinforced this conclusion, finding that the more media multitaskers used, the poorer their performance. Memory, ability to focus and ability to switch from one task to another all suffered mightily.

In fact, brain research shows that there is no such thing as multitasking. The brain cannot do two tasks simultaneously, unless one is what researchers call a "highly practiced skill." That means—not to worry—you can walk and chew gum at the same time. But the brain cannot simultaneously perform tasks that require focus, like writing, reading or carrying on a conversation. Instead, a kind of toggle mechanism allows the brain to switch from one activity to another. You may think you are talking to a friend and checking out a Web site simultaneously, but your brain is really switching rapidly between one activity and another.

The bad news? When you try to perform two or more related tasks, either at the same time or alternating quickly between them, you not only make far more errors than you would if you concentrated on each task individually, but you also take far longer (as much as double the time) to complete the jobs than if you had focused on each in sequence. Multitasking is not a time saver; it's a time waster.

Learning to use language correctly, crisply, gracefully, powerfully—which is what this book is about—takes focus and concentration. Our advice: Regardless of the habits you may have developed, when it comes to writing, become a unitasker.

In fact, start now.

Chapter 3

Ten Little Secrets Ten Big Mistakes

Here's what grammar is not: It is not a roster of rules meant to confuse or constrain. It is not a catalogue of caveats to be memorized. It is not a litany of lessons to be learned in isolation. No! Grammar is the essence of good, clear, powerful writing. It is the all-important instruction manual that will help you master the tools of the writer's trade: words, phrases, sentences, paragraphs.

We're not saying that knowing grammar will automatically transform you into a great writer any more than knowing the rules of tennis will transform you into Serena Williams. We are saying that the rules underlie the game—and the game is writing well. So, before we start with the rules and rudiments of grammar, let's take a moment to remember why we are learning them in the first place. Let's remember the game. Let's focus for a moment on writing and what it takes to write well.

The Ten Secrets of Writing Well

Are there really 10 secrets to writing well? Maybe there is only one. To paraphrase the great ("It's hard to be humble when you're as great as I am") Muhammed Ali: *You have to have the skill and the will. But the will must be stronger than the skill.* That said, these other "secrets" may help you along the path to your own greatness.

Secret #1: Read

Reading is not just a way to find out about the world or yourself; it is an immersion in language. Whether you read a microbiology textbook or a murder mystery, a news blog or a sci fi story, you are swimming in words, awash in sentences, carried along by a stream of paragraphs. Whether you know it or not, you are learning language along with whatever else you are reading. You are learning vocabulary and syntax, words and how they are put together. You are learning how language flows (or doesn't).

The lessons can be positive and obvious, as when you marvel at a passage that transports you to another time or place, or when, midparagraph, you feel in the grip of ideas or emotions. That's a writer forging a connection with words, and it's a lesson you take with you, consciously or not, after you close the book (or switch off the iPad), exit the Web site or stash the magazine. The more you read, the more you have these experiences, the more embedded becomes the beauty and the precision of language.

Of course, the lessons can be negative as well—the book that puts you to sleep, the news story you don't scroll down to finish reading. You are learning something here, too: You are learning what doesn't work, how not to put words together, how not to tell a story.

Imagine wanting to be a musician and not listening to music. That's as odd and wrongheaded as aspiring to be a writer and not reading.

Secret #2: Have Something to Say

That sounds too obvious, doesn't it? But how many times have you sat in front of your computer screen, mind numb, unable to write a single intelligent sentence? You tell yourself you have writer's block. You don't have writer's block. You are more likely suffering from a dearth of material, a paucity of ideas—the lack of something to say. Perhaps you haven't worked your ideas through in your head. You aren't clear about what you think. Or maybe you haven't done the necessary research. You don't know your subject well enough yet. You can't write well if you are not in command of the material. You can't write well if you don't know what you want to say.

Consider how all of us, at times, are reduced to babbling. Sometimes our lips seem to be moving faster than our brains. Words come out. We sputter, stop and start, ramble, backtrack, circumlocute. The lips keep moving, but there is little sense and less meaning behind the words because we haven't stopped to figure out what we want to say. Friends may indulge us, but readers don't.

Secret #3: Organize Your Thoughts

Without a plan, writing well is much more difficult than it needs to be. It is not, however, impossible. You can write without a plan if you want to rewrite and revise and restructure many times over. But it is much more sensible, more efficient and decidedly less stressful to think about how you will structure the piece—be it advertising copy or a feature article—before you begin writing. Some forms of writing have their own internal structure and provide a kind of template you can use. Basic news stories are like that. So are press releases. Advertising copy also often follows a certain pattern. Personal essays conform to a common shape. But even if the template is provided, you need to organize your thoughts and your material within it. And so, determined to write well, you sit with the material, review everything, scribble notes to yourself, look up missing details, check a few more sites, make a few phone calls. You don't rush to write. You take the time to understand the material. From that understanding can come good ideas about how to structure the piece.

How should you organize? For short pieces, you may be able to keep everything in your head. But most writers who know what they're doing don't trust this method. They depend on notes. Some do fine with phrases scribbled on scraps of paper or key concepts dictated to themselves on their iPhones. Some use the computer to organize, putting their notes into a database that's accessible, and sortable, in countless ways. Others like to use file cards, one idea to a card, which can be shuffled and reshuffled as the writer thinks through the piece. It may take time to figure out what works for you, and what works for you may change as technology and your own habits change.

Secret #4: Consider Your Audience

Unlike your tweets or the e-mails you send to friends, media messages are meant for public consumption. But what public? How can you write well if you don't know who will be reading or listening? You can't—or at the very least you stack the deck against it. If you don't know the audience, you are not sure what your readers or viewers or listeners know or need to know. You are not sure how to approach these folks, what level of vocabulary to employ, what tone to choose, how to structure what you want to say. Should you use humor? Is word play appropriate? Will irony work? Who knows? *You* will know—if you know your audience.

That's why companies fund market research: to see who is out there and how best to reach them. That's why magazines conduct readership studies or run surveys to gauge what their readers think about certain issues. That's why serious bloggers track their readers using various diagnostic tools. Knowing the audience is a key to good writing.

Secret #5: Know Grammatical Conventions and How to Use Them

Here we are, back to the rules of the game. Note that knowing the rules becomes important only when you have something to say, have figured out how you're going to say it, and know to whom you're talking. The rules themselves—memorizing verb forms or knowing when to use a comma—don't exist without a context. The context is writing. You learn the rules for one reason: to play the game. It's worth noting, for those of you who are squirming at our repeated mention of rules, that knowing the rules does allow you to break them, when appropriate, for effect. There's a word for breaking a rule you didn't even know existed, and it is *error*.

Writing well means making countless good decisions, from choosing just the right word (see #6), to crafting phrases, clauses, sentences and paragraphs that say just what you want them to say with precision, clarity and grace (see #7). This lofty but achievable goal is possible only if you understand the architecture of language, the building blocks of prose—if you are at ease with the tools of the trade. Imagine a carpenter who can't use a skill saw, a dancer who doesn't know the steps, a programmer who can't write code. That's a writer without a command of grammar.

Secret #6: Master a Solid Working Vocabulary

Sculptors have clay, painters have paint, writers have words. It's as simple as that. Writers have to figure out how to connect with an audience—spur thought, evoke emotion, inform, educate, entertain, tell a story, set a scene, promote a product, sell an idea—and all they have are words. Yes, words can and do exist within a rich multimedia context. And, of course, sound and image matter. But what the writer has control of, what the writer revels in are words. Words are some of the most potent tools around, perhaps the most potent. (Remember the saying "The pen is mightier than the sword"?) Words carry not only meaning but shades of meaning. What variety, what nuance, what tone! Look up *talk* in a thesaurus and you will find *chatter, mutter, mumble, gossip* and *schmooze,* each with its own connotation, each with its own feel. And words not only have meaning and nuance, but also sound and rhythm.

Building a good vocabulary means reading widely. It means both appreciating the smorgasbord that is the English language and learning to use words with proper respect—that is, choosing the correct word, the word that means exactly what you mean and spelling it correctly. Building a vocabulary does not mean seeking out multisyllabic tongue twisters or collecting fancy or elaborate expressions. It means being able to use words like *chatter, mutter, mumble, gossip* and *schmooze* when called for.

Secret #7: Focus on Precision and Clarity

If you think clear, crisp writing just flows naturally from the fingertips of the writer to the computer screen, you couldn't be more wrong. Good writing (even bad writing) doesn't just happen. Regardless of comments like "the story just wrote itself," believe us, stories do not write themselves. Writing with precision and clarity—saying exactly what you mean, no fuzziness, no confusion, no second or third reading necessary—is hard, purposeful work. But it's work your readers, viewers or listeners expect you to do. If you don't, they click "next" or turn the page or reach for the remote, and whatever you had to say, whatever you thought you were communicating, is lost.

Clear, powerful writing is the result of good decisions, from choosing the right word to crafting just the right construction to relentlessly slashing clutter from your prose. Redundancies? Euphemisms? Jargon? These are obstacles to precision. Misplaced modifiers? Split constructions? Run-on sentences? These are the enemies of clarity. In fact, every grammatical decision you make either enhances or detracts from clarity. That's how important a working knowledge of grammar is to writing well.

Secret #8: Hear Language

"Write for the ear," script writers and broadcasters are told, but this is good advice for all writers. It doesn't matter whether the audience actually hears aloud the words you write or just "hears" your prose when reading silently. In either case, the audience attends to the sound and feels the beat. If you can master the skill of writing for the ear, you are one step closer to writing well.

Listen to the words you use. What meaning is conveyed by their sound? Listen to how words sound together. Do they fight one another? Do they flow? Say your written sentences out loud. Do they have a rhythm? A long sentence can lilt. A short sentence can tap out a staccato beat. Purposeful repetition of words or phrases can add rhythm, as can the emphatic use of parallel structure. Experimenting with and eventually mastering the aural nuances and subtleties of language is one of the joys of writing.

Secret #9: Revise

Think you're finished once you write it all down? Think all you have to do is a quick once-over, a spell check, and it's out the door? Think again. Having the patience and fortitude—and humility—to really revise is what separates the amateurs from the professionals. Revision is much more than tidying up, pruning and polishing prose. It is an opportunity to see if the writing works. It is a chance to rethink what you are trying to say. Consider the word *revision:* re-vision means to look again, to look with new eyes. This is what the revision process should be.

And so thoughtful writers, determined to produce clear, powerful, even memorable prose, take a deep breath after they have "finished" whatever it is they were writing. Now it is time to look at the piece and ask: Does it say what I intended it to say? Will my readers or viewers or listeners learn what I want them to learn? Have I written enough or too much? Do the ideas flow from one to another? Do my transitions work? Does my style fit both the subject and the audience? Taking revision seriously means asking the tough questions and being prepared to spend the extra time to answer them.

Even with the best intentions, it is very difficult to learn the art of revision on your own work. You know what you mean even if you don't write what you mean. Thus, when you read your own work, you read what you know you meant and not necessarily what you have written. A talented and patient editor can help you see what you have and have not accomplished. If you are lucky enough to find one, be attentive, be humble and sponge up all you can.

Here's another idea: It may be that learning how to revise is best accomplished by revising others' writing. It is much easier to see the shortcomings of other people's work, the holes in their logic, the sputtering of their prose, the clutter, the murkiness. It is also true that you often see in others your own problems or shortcomings. With practice and over time, if you stay humble and audience-directed, you can learn to be more clear-eyed about your work.

Secret #10: Apply the Seat of the Pants to the Seat of the Chair

The final secret to writing well is the easiest to state and the hardest to accomplish: Put in the time. Just like mastering a musical instrument or a new sport, learning to write takes practice—lots of practice. This means time—good, concentrated, focused time over weeks and months and, yes, even years. Some people have a natural facility with words (probably because they are voracious readers). Others struggle. But everyone who wants to write well, talent notwithstanding, has to work hard at it. It is easy to get discouraged. It is easy to get distracted. It is easy to talk away your enthusiasm over mochaccinos with friends. Sometimes it feels as if it's easy to do just about anything other than write. You have to rein yourself in. Give yourself a pep talk. As the poet Marge Piercy has wisely written, "A real writer is one who really writes."

Grammar Is Everywhere

We wanted to make the case for writing before we got serious about making the case for grammar. We wanted you to have a reason to care about grammar. You don't have to feel warm and fuzzy about it. You don't have to join a grammar Facebook fan page. But you do have to attend to it. You do have to master it if you want to write well. The good news is that grammar is not rocket science. True, the English language can be challenging. And yes, there is much to learn on the way to mastering the rules that govern how we write. But there is no reason to be intimidated. We human beings are prewired to do this kind of work. Communication is our claim to fame, evolutionarily speaking. We're good at this. It's just that those of us who want to be writers must be *very* good at this.

That's where grammar comes in. Grammar makes communication possible. Without the shared conventions of grammar, without the structure it creates and the patterns it plots, we could not speak to one another across time and space. Grammar is the writer's touchstone. It binds us together whether we write status updates or serious journalism, blogs or bestsellers, whether we are veterans of the craft or mere beginners.

We know that grammar has a bad rap: It's confusing. It's picky. It's fussy. There are almost as many exceptions as there are rules. And it's, well, unnecessary, isn't it? "I never learned grammar in school, but it hasn't hurt me yet," you say. "I don't bother with grammar when I text or IM, and no one seems to care—or even notice. Besides," you say, "I can always write around what I don't know. It's the ideas that count, not the grammar."

Sorry. Wrong on all counts.

First of all, grammar is not all that confusing. In fact, it is mostly logical and orderly, often commonsensical and very accessible (that's right: not rocket science). Most of the rules are straightforward, and, happily, good grammar almost always sounds right to those who read and have the patterns of effective prose embedded in their brains. Second, grammar is absolutely necessary, not only to writing clearly, but also to writing with style, creativity and pizzazz.

On this subject, we never tire of quoting Joan Didion, journalist, essayist, novelist, memoirist, screenwriter and one of the finest prose stylists writing today: "All I know about grammar is its infinite power," she writes. "To shift the structure of a sentence alters the meaning of that sentence, as definitely and inflexibly as the position of a camera alters the meaning of the object photographed. Many people know about cameras today, but not so many know about sentences."

But we must know about sentences, about phrases, clauses, voices, tenses, singulars, plurals—all the patterns and constructions that make our language work. Language is how we spread ideas and information throughout society. The information we have to communicate as writers may be complex; the ideas may be challenging. The message will have to compete with countless distractions for the attention of the audience. It may even have to compete with its own format in multimedia presentations. This puts a tremendous burden on the language: It must be crisp and clear, easy to understand and inviting. It must carry the ideas effortlessly, even gracefully. It must enhance meaning. It must communicate tone and nuance, color and texture, sound and rhythm. But to do all this, the language must be—before all else—correct. It must be grammatical.

All languages depend on rules of grammar, including sign language, where grammar occurs in the eyes, the brows, the tilt of the head, the lips. Just as sentence construction communicates meaning in written

English, a tucked chin, narrowed eyes and raised shoulders act as grammatical signposts in the language of the deaf. Even baby talk has its own simple grammar ("Me want milk!").

Face it: Grammar is everywhere.

Making Mistakes

Learning to write well—and beyond that, to write compellingly, evocatively, gracefully—is a lifelong process. That's the challenge, and it only gets more interesting (and more challenging) the longer we do it. Throughout our lives as writers, we will grow, we will change and, inevitably, we will make mistakes: judgments miscalled, questions unasked and language misused. Errors can be disheartening, not to mention embarrassing. (Egregious errors such as fabricating facts, manufacturing sources or misrepresenting yourself can be career-ending.)

Grammatical errors are particularly hazardous to the health of wannabe writers. "If I see a misspelled word on a résumé or a grammatical error, I look no further. I immediately disqualify the applicant," says the personnel director of a large company. "We look at how much attention a person pays to detail," says the vice president of a major advertising firm. "Things like grammar, spelling and mechanics mean a lot to us. We figure, if the person can't accomplish these things, how can we expect him or her to move on to bigger jobs?" Says a newspaper editor: "If a person can't use grammar correctly, it says either of two things to me—lack of intelligence or extreme sloppiness. Either way, it's not the person I want writing for me." A magazine editor agrees: "We get hundreds of e-mail queries from writers proposing stories for us. For some reason, people think it's okay to write poorly when they write an e-mail. We don't think so at all. We would never hire a writer freelance if that person e-mailed us a query with grammatical or spelling errors. And it's amazing how many of them do."

But mistakes do happen. It is precisely because professional writers know this—and understand the unpleasant consequences of making errors publicly—that they take editing (and editors) so seriously. They begin with a solid understanding of the language and then they edit, edit, edit. Misspelled words, misplaced modifiers, lack of parallelism, shifts in voice—all the little errors that can creep into writing never make it past the editing process. It is during this process that experienced writers turn their uncertain, sometimes ragged prose into the polished material they can proudly present to their audience.

What You Don't Know...

Do you know the expression, "What you don't know won't hurt you"? Forget it. What you don't know *will* hurt you when it comes to grammar. What you don't know will hurt the clarity of your writing, the understanding and respect of your audience, even your ability to land a job in the first place. What is it you don't know? Let's consider 10 of the most common grammatical mistakes and how knowledge of the language (and reading this book) can help you avoid them.

Mistake #1: Thinking You Don't Have to Know Grammar to Write Well

After reading our masterfully persuasive arguments in these beginning chapters, you're not likely to make this mistake again, right?

Mistake #2: Subjects and Verbs that Don't Agree

For a sentence to be grammatically correct and clearly communicative, a verb must agree with the intended number of its subject. That sounds simple, as in: *The laptop* [singular subject] *is* [singular verb] *on sale* or *The laptops* [plural subject] *are* [plural verb] *in the store.* But it gets complicated when you're not quite sure what the subject is. There may be a number of nouns and pronouns in the sentence. Which is the true subject? *A box of books* are/is *on the table.* Is *box* (singular) the subject, or is *books* (plural)? There may be confusion about the intended number of the subject. *Five thousand dollars,* as a subject, looks plural but acts singular; *everyone,* as a subject, clearly implies the plural but acts as a singular subject. To sort this all out, you need to know the parts of speech (Chapters 5 and 6), the parts of a sentence (Chapter 4) and the guidelines for agreement (Chapter 7).

Mistake #3: Subjects and Pronouns that Don't Agree

To communicate crisply and clearly, sentences must have internal harmony. Just as subjects and verbs must agree, so too must subjects and their pronouns. It's a simple rule that depends on your ability to identify the subject, recognize its number and choose a corresponding pronoun. This can be easy, as in: *The musicians* [plural subject] *and their* [plural pronoun] *fans filled the stadium with deafening sound.* Or it can be tougher, as in: *The band made* (their/its) *way to the stage.* But if you understand the parts of speech (Chapters 5 and 6) and the guidelines for agreement (Chapter 7), you should be able to avoid this pitfall.

Mistake #4: Lack of Parallelism

To be both coherent and forceful, a sentence must have parallel structure; that is, its elements must be symmetrical. Consider a construction like *I came. I saw. I conquered.* It is powerful, because it sets out three ideas in three parallel grammatical structures (pronoun–past-tense verb). Consider the same idea expressed this way: *I came. I looked over everything. The enemy was conquered by my armies.* That's lack of parallelism. That's startlingly poor writing. You have to know the parts of speech (Chapters 5 and 6) to understand the concept of parallelism, and you must see parallelism as a form of agreement (Chapter 7), as vital to clarity (Chapter 9), and even as an element of style (Chapter 10).

Mistake #5: Confusing *Who* and *Whom*

Who/whom *did the journalist contact first? She worked for* whoever/whomever *could afford her fee. The blogger* who/whom *broke the story refused to reveal his sources.* Confused? You won't be once you understand the nominative and objective cases (Chapter 7).

Mistake #6: Confusing *That* and *Which*

Did you think these two words were interchangeable? Well, they aren't. Consider this sentence: *The full-body scan* that/which *the doctor recommended showed no abnormalities. That* is used to introduce material that restricts the meaning of the noun; *which* is used to elaborate on meaning. If you know about relative pronouns (Chapter 6) and the role of phrases and clauses in a sentence (Chapter 4), you will use these words correctly.

Mistake #7: Confusing Possessives and Contractions

That's a fancy way of saying that *your* (possessive) and *you're* (contraction) are not interchangeable. They perform very different tasks in a sentence. *Their* and *they're, whose* and *who's, its* and *it's* may sound the same, but they have decidedly different grammatical functions. If you text, you're probably accustomed to omitting apostrophes. Some cell phone keypads don't have this function; others, like the iPhone, insert apostrophes—sometimes incorrectly—themselves. You also may be accustomed to shortcuts: *yr* for *your* (possessive) or *ur* for *you're* (contraction). These are habits you'll have to break (Chapter 2). Learning parts of speech (Chapter 5 and 6) and case (Chapter 7) will help you make the distinction between possessives and contractions and end the confusion.

Mistake #8: Dangling and Misplacing Modifiers

A misplaced modifier (a word, phrase or clause) does not point clearly and directly to what it is supposed to modify. A modifier "dangles" when what it is supposed to modify is not part of the sentence. Both grammatical errors seriously compromise clarity of meaning. If you understand parts of speech (Chapters 5 and 6) and parts of the sentence (Chapter 4), this clarity, conciseness and coherence issue (Chapter 9) will make sense.

Mistake #9: Misusing Commas

Some novice writers liberally sprinkle their sentences with commas as if this important punctuation mark were a decorative tweak. Tweeters, texters and IMers, on the other hand, often eschew commas entirely. But commas have specific functions in a sentence, as do all marks of punctuation. Two specific errors stand out: One is neglecting to use a comma to separate two independent clauses linked by a coordinating conjunction. The other is using only a comma when trying to link two independent clauses (known as the comma-splice error). If some of this terminology is foreign to you, it won't be after you read about parts of speech (Chapter 6), the sentence (Chapter 4) and punctuation (Chapter 8).

Mistake #10: The Dreaded Passive Voice

Passive voice is one of the surest ways to suck the life out of a sentence, a one-way ticket to stilted, falsely formal or bureaucratic prose. Although passive voice construction is not technically a grammatical error and although there are a few defensible reasons for using it, most passive-voice sentences are not written knowingly or purposefully. Both the clarity (Chapter 9) and the liveliness (Chapter 10) of writing are at stake.

All these grammatical hazards—we could list dozens more—may seem daunting. Don't be daunted. Be respectful. Understand that language is alive, complex, fascinating—and full of potential pitfalls. That doesn't mean you should be intimidated. It means you should be careful. It means you should learn the tools of your trade. It means you should study the fundamentals and build your writing from this firm foundation. "When Words Collide" can help.

As you read, never forget that the point of grammar is not grammar. The point is writing well. Please don't lose sight of why you're learning grammar—and why you're reading this book.

The study of grammar is the key to the power of words. Read on. Write on.

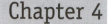

The Sentence

Chapter 4

Yes, we can.

I have a dream.

Let them eat cake.

Behold the power of the sentence, the simple, purposeful, potent ordering of words that can change history. Few of us write (or speak) sentences as momentous as those above, but all good writers work hard to craft their words into meaningful constructions that connect with readers. The sentence is essential building block of memorable prose. To write it well is to know it well.

Learning how to construct a truly worthy sentence—grammatical and graceful, lively and memorable—is a challenge. But learning the basics is not. After all, we *know* sentences. We say them silently to ourselves and out loud to our friends. We write them in e-mails and in notes stuck on the refrigerator door. However, when it comes to studying exactly how sentences are created, it's easy to feel so overwhelmed with definitions, exceptions, rules and regulations that we forget we are already experts.

If you see unfamiliar grammatical terms in this chapter, don't panic. In the two chapters following this one, you will learn all you need to know (well, almost) about parts of speech, the individual building blocks of sentences. In this chapter, we wanted to give you a reason to care about these building blocks—and that reason is the sentence.

You will be reading about all kinds of sentences: simple, compound, complex, compound–complex, incomplete, run-on, subordinated, oversubordinated, passive voice. Don't be put off by these descriptors, and don't obsess about them, either. Just think of them as shorthand or code, a common vocabulary that allows us to talk about how to craft prose, a useful way to explain and categorize the word patterns we call sentences. Learning these terms is not the goal. The goal, as always, is good writing—putting words together with clarity, precision and pizzazz. Should you find yourself caught up in the categories or puzzling over the patterns, remember that when we investigate the sentence, we are investigating a familiar subject, an old friend.

On, then, to the sentence. A *sentence* is a self-contained grammatical unit that ends with a full-stop punctuation mark (period, question mark or exclamation point)—but please, please, take it easy on the exclamation points. A sentence must contain a verb and a subject (stated or implied), and it must state a complete thought.

A sentence can be as concise as a single word: *Go. Stop. Wait.* (The subject *you* is implied.) It can be as expansive (and exhausting) as the 4,391-word sentence James Joyce wrote in "Ulysses." Regardless of length, grammatically correct sentences result from the same procedure: the selection, manipulation and coordination of sentence parts.

Sentence Parts

Predicates and Subjects

A sentence can be divided into two parts: the *predicate* and the *subject*. The *simple predicate* of a sentence is the verb. The *simple subject* is the noun or noun substitute that identifies the "actor" or initiator of action in a sentence, as in:

> **The telemarketer** **called.**
> (simple subj.) (simple pred.)

The *complete predicate* includes the verb plus all its complements and modifiers—words, phrases or clauses that add specificity and meaning.

The *complete subject* includes the noun or noun substitute and all its complements and modifiers:

> **The fast-talking telemarketer** **called at dinner time.**
> (complete subj.) (complete pred.)

We can continue to describe and modify both the subject and the predicate parts of the sentence:

> **The insistent, fast-talking telemarketer** **always called at dinner time.**
> (complete subj.) (complete pred.)

In addition to modifiers and descriptive phrases, action verbs can be complemented by direct objects, indirect objects, and prepositional phrases—all of which are considered part of the predicate. A *direct object* is any noun or pronoun that answers the question *what?* or *whom?* An *indirect object* tells *to whom* or *for what* that action is done. A *prepositional phrase* is a preposition followed by its object. These complements must be in the objective case. Recognizing them will help you avoid making errors in case:

The telemarketer   **was selling <u>satellite dishes.</u>**
                                                         (noun as dir. obj.)

I   **gave the <u>telemarketer</u>   10 <u>seconds</u> of my time.**
        (noun as indir. obj.)   (noun as dir. obj.)

I   **responded <u>with profanity.</u>**
                        (prep. phrase)

I responded to <u>him.</u>
                        (pron. as obj. of prep., objec. case)

The complement of a linking verb is a noun or an adjective describing the subject. These words are also considered part of the predicate:

The telemarketer   was a <u>jerk.</u>
                                (pred. nom.)

I   **was <u>annoyed.</u>**
        (pred. adj.)

Phrases and Clauses

Phrases and clauses are the building blocks of sentences. A *phrase* is a group of related words that lacks both a subject and a predicate. Phrases come in two basic varieties: a *prepositional phrase* (a preposition followed by its object) and a *verbal phrase* (a form of the verb—infinitive, gerund or participle—that does not act as a verb, accompanied by its object or related material). Verbals are also discussed on pp. 54.

<u>During dinner every night that week,</u> a telemarketer called.
(prep. phrase)

My one wish was <u>to enjoy an uninterrupted meal.</u>
                                (infin. phrase, acting as a pred. noun)

<u>Turning off the phone</u> was the obvious solution.
(ger. phrase, acting as a noun... substitute *it* for the phrase)

<u>**Grabbing the phone with one hand,**</u> **I stirred the ramen with**
(pres. participial phrase, acting as adj. modifying *I*)
the other.

<u>**Distracted by the noodles,**</u> **I dropped the phone in the pot of**
(past participial phrase, acting as adj. modifying *I*)
boiling water.

Recognizing phrases and knowing what functions they perform can help you build interesting sentences that not only say what you want them to say but say what you want them to say crisply, clearly, and with style. Understanding phrases can also help you avoid at least two common errors in writing: fragments and dangling participle phrases. If you know that a phrase, however lengthy or complex, is not a sentence, then you will not mistake it for one, punctuate it as one and, in the process, create an ungrammatical fragment. If you understand what a participial phrase is and recognize that its purpose is to modify a noun, then you know the noun must be evident, and the phrase must be placed as close as possible to that noun.

A *clause* is a group of related words that contains a subject and a predicate. An *independent* or *main clause* is a complete sentence:

<u>**My housemate**</u>   <u>**choked**</u> **on her pepperoni pizza.**
(subj.)   (pred.)

A *dependent* or *subordinate clause,* although it also contains a subject and a predicate, does not express a complete thought. It is not a sentence and cannot stand alone:

When she saw my phone slip into the noodle pot
(dep. clause)

<u>**When she saw my phone slip into the noodle pot,**</u> **my housemate**
(dep. clause)   linked with   (main clause)
choked on her pepperoni pizza.

Dependent clauses come in three varieties, according to the function they perform in a sentence. A *noun clause* takes the place of a noun or a noun substitute; an *adjective clause* serves as an adjective; an *adverb clause* acts as an adverb.

<u>**That I was rattled**</u> **did not surprise her.**
(noun clause acting as the subj.)
(*It,* a pronoun, can be substituted for the clause.)

The telemarketers, <u>who had mysteriously managed to get my</u>
<u>cellphone number and had interrupted dinner every night for a</u>
(adj. clause, modifies the noun *telemarketers*)
<u>week,</u> had obviously gotten on my nerves.

<u>After I took a deep breath and ate a pint of Chunky Monkey ice</u>
(adv. clause, modifies the verb by answering *when?*).
<u>cream,</u> I regained control.

When you recognize the variety and the many uses of dependent
clauses, you enhance your ability to craft great prose.

Types of Sentences

Sentences come in four varieties, depending on the number and type
of clauses they contain. Learn—and revel in—this variety. It will add
spark and interest to your prose and help you write with both grace and
rhythm.

Simple Sentences

A *simple sentence* contains one independent clause. The most common
construction is subject–verb–object.

<u>Chickens</u>   <u>lay</u>   <u>eggs</u>.
(subj.)   (verb)   (obj.)

We can add modifiers—single words or phrases or a combination
of both—but regardless of the number of words, the sentence remains
simple if it contains a single, independent clause:

Backyard   <u>chickens</u>   **happily**   <u>lay</u>   **brown** <u>eggs</u>   **in their nesting**
(adj.)   (adv.)   (adj.)   (prep. phrase)
boxes.

Note that a simple sentence can have multiple subjects and/or verbs.
What keeps the sentence simple is that it contains only one independent
clause.

<u>Chickens and roosters</u>   <u>peck and fight</u> **when kept in the**
(multiple subj.)   (multiple verb)
same coop.

Compound Sentences

A *compound sentence* has two or more independent clauses, each containing a subject and a predicate and each expressing a complete thought. The two complete clauses, equal or nearly equal in importance, are linked (coordinated) by a conjunction and a comma, semicolon or colon. *And, but, or, nor* and *yet* are the conjunctions, sometimes referred to as *coordinating conjunctions:*

> **Raising chickens in urban backyards may be a fad,** but
> (indep. clause)   (conj.)
>
> **that doesn't make it any less of a good idea.**
> (indep. clause)
>
> **Chickens are fun to raise; they're also a lot of work.**
> (indep. clauses linked by semicolon)
>
> **The DIY revolution has swept the country, and one thing is clear: Chickens are in our future—and our backyards.**
> (three indep. clauses, linked by comma and conj., and colon)

Punctuation is probably the most common problem associated with compound sentences. Because the two (or more) clauses are independent—actually complete sentences on their own—they cannot be linked by a comma or a conjunction alone. A compound sentence needs both a comma and a coordinating conjunction. If you do not want to use a coordinating conjunction, use a semicolon or, occasionally, a colon. We'll focus on punctuation in Chapter 8.

Complex Sentences

A *complex sentence* contains one independent (main) clause and at least one dependent (subordinate) clause. The subordinate clause depends on the main clause for both meaning and grammatical completion:

> **Before she saw the documentary** *Food, Inc.,*   **she had never**
> (dep. clause)   (indep. clause)
> **considered raising her own chickens.**
>
> **A backyard coop is easy to maintain**   **although sometimes**
> (indep. clause)   (dep. clause)
> **not all that pleasant a chore.**

In the two preceding complex sentences, conjunctions *(before, although)* introduce the dependent clauses. These words, sometimes called *subordinating conjunctions,* establish the relationship between the two sentence parts. Our language has a variety of such words, each with its own precise meaning that expresses a specific relationship between the dependent and the independent clauses. For example:

Relationship	Conjunctions
cause and effect	*because, due to, as a result of, if*
sequence	*after, before, during, while*
time, place	*when, whenever, since, where, until, as long as*

A dependent clause can also be subordinated to the main clause by relative pronouns (*who, whom, whose, which* or *that*). Note that the main clause can be interrupted by the dependent clause:

The farmer **who sold us the baby chicks** **assured us**
(dep. clause)
they were all female.

Compound–Complex Sentences

A *compound–complex* sentence contains at least two main clauses and one dependent clause. The construction seems to invite wordiness, but it also makes rhythm and flow possible if you are careful, precise and grammatical. Here is a four-clause sentence that works:

After the chicks were three months old,
(dep. clause)

the Rhode Island Red started crowing,
(indep. clause)

and we realized the sad truth:
(indep. clause)

We had a non-egg-laying rooster on our hands.
(indep. clause)

If you find that a compound–complex sentence is out of control—so complicated that readers will lose the thread, so long that broadcasters will gasp for breath—break the sentence into two (or more) parts, being careful to maintain the relationship between subordinate and main thoughts.

A Good Sentence

It's craft, but it's also art. It's hard, purposeful work, but there's a bit of alchemy to it. You begin by choosing words, respectful of their meanings, aware of their sounds and rhythms. You fit the words together—carefully, precisely, creatively—to build phrases and clauses. These you link with just the right word, the correct piece of punctuation. You rework, edit, revise.

Then you read what you have written. It says precisely what you want it to say. It has grammatical unity. The idea is coherent; the statement, concise; the language, powerful. You sit back to marvel.

You have written a good sentence.

Sentence Errors

Perhaps you *haven't* written a good sentence. Maybe you've fallen prey to one of the following ungrammatical or sluggish constructions: sentence fragment, run-on sentence, oversubordination, dead construction, passive voice. Don't panic. You can catch this at the editing stage if you know what to look for.

Sentence Fragments

Because fragments are common in casual communication, from text messages to e-mails to blog posts, and because they are so often employed in advertising copy, it's easy to forget that fragments are, in fact, ungrammatical. A *fragment,* literally an incomplete piece, is a group of words sheared off from or never attached to a sentence. The group of words may lack a subject, a predicate, a complete thought, or any combination of the three. No matter what it lacks, it is not a grammatical sentence. If you punctuate it as if it were a sentence, you have created a fragment.

Like this one.

Fragments can be single words, brief phrases or lengthy dependent clauses. The number of words is irrelevant. What matters is that the words do not meet the definition of a sentence. A common mistake is to look only for subject and verb and, having found them, to believe that you have written a complete sentence. Remember, a sentence expresses a complete thought.

Although the blog began as a joke
contains a subject *(blog)* and a verb *(began)*, but does not express a complete thought. It is a dependent clause, a fragment.

Avoiding or rewriting fragments is not difficult. First, recognize that the word, phrase or clause you've written does not meet the requirements for being a sentence. Now you have two choices: (1) Rewrite this fragment to include all the parts it needs (subject, verb, complete thought); (2) add to the fragment, making it a complete sentence. Here's how it works:

Although the blog began as a joke.
(fragment)

The blog began as a joke.
(fragment rewritten as a complete thought)

Although the blog began as a joke, the site now attracts thousands of visitors a day.
(fragment becomes part of a complete thought)

Some accomplished writers will tell you that fragments serve a useful purpose. We agree. In appropriate instances, to achieve particular effects, certain grammatical rules can be broken—and this is one of them. *Purposeful fragments*—consistent with the subject, the audience, and the medium—are a matter of style. *Accidental fragments* are a grammatical error. Put another way: To break the rule, you have to know the rule.

Run-On Sentences

A *run-on sentence* doesn't know when to quit. Rushing forward without proper punctuation, this construction may actually include two or three complete sentences. Length is not the issue here. A relatively short sentence, like this one, can be a run-on:

The concert was sold out for weeks, the promoters didn't add a second date.

This sentence is actually two independent clauses run together with a comma. Using commas to link independent clauses (without the help of a conjunction) almost always results in a run-on sentence. In fact, this comma-splice error is the most common cause of run-on sentences. But if you can recognize an independent clause, and if you understand the limitations of the comma, you can avoid the error.

The most frequently used of all punctuation marks, the comma serves a variety of purposes. But one job a comma rarely performs is linking independent clauses. This function is performed by the semicolon or, occasionally, the colon. When you force the comma to do a job for which it was not designed, you create a grammatically incorrect construction.

Occasionally—and knowingly—a writer might violate the comma-splice rule. When a sentence is composed of two or more brief, parallel clauses, commas might be used:

Be correct, be concise, be coherent.

Comma-splice run-ons, in addition to being grammatically incorrect, almost always lack clarity. A comma signals readers that they are reading one continuous idea interrupted by a brief pause (the comma). Readers expect the words following the comma to augment or complement what they have just read. But in a comma-splice run-on, there is not one continuous idea. New thoughts are introduced without the benefit of connections between them (for example, *but, and* or *or*).

You can easily correct a run-on sentence in four ways:

1. Change the run-on sentence to two (or more) complete sentences by adding periods and capital letters:

   The concert was sold out for weeks. The promoters didn't add a second date.

2. If the relationship between the two (or more) complete thoughts (clauses) is close and equal, insert a semicolon between them to express this. A semicolon shows this connection and allows the reader to move swiftly from the first sentence to the second. But semicolons are somewhat formal and a little stodgy. They may not work in all instances:

   The concert was sold out for week; the promoters didn't add a second date.

3. If the two thoughts are of equal weight and have a connection that can be signaled by a coordinating conjunction (*and, but, or, nor, yet* or *so*), use a comma and the appropriate conjunction to link the clauses:

   The concert was sold out for weeks, but the promoters didn't add a second date.

4. If the relationship between the two (or more) independent clauses is such that one clause depends on the other, rewrite the

"dependent" sentence as a clause and place it in front of or after the main clause. Choose a subordinating conjunction that expresses the nature of the relationship and place it appropriately. Subordinating conjunctions include *after, because, while, when, where, since, if* and *although*.

Although the concert was sold out for a week, the promoters did not add a second date.

Oversubordinated Sentences

Subordination, the fourth way just listed to correct a run-on sentence, is the technique of making one idea less important than, or subordinate to, another. Consider these sentences:

Lizzie Hager won the $200 million Powerball jackpot.

Lizzie Hager purchased only a single Powerball ticket.

Assuming the idea in the first sentence is the more important one, you can subordinate the idea in the second sentence by creating a dependent clause and attaching it to the main clause or inserting it at an appropriate place within the main clause.

Although Lizzie Hager purchased only a single ticket,
(subordinate clause)

she won the $200 million Powerball jackpot.
(main clause)

Lizzie Hager, who had purchased only a single ticket,
(main clause)   (subordinate clause)

won the $200 million Powerball jackpot.
(main clause)

Subordinating one idea to another is a useful sentence-building technique. But do take care. A string of dependent clauses, or one excessively long dependent clause, placed before the main sentence can slow the pace. You make your readers or listeners wait too long to get to the important idea, and you risk losing and confusing them.

After losing her job and having her car repossessed, although she was not a risk-taker and despite the fact that she purchased only a single ticket, Lizzie Hager won the $200 million Powerball jackpot.
(oversubordination)

There are too many ideas here for one sentence. The three subordinate clauses that precede the main idea bog down the sentence and slow the reader's comprehension. The sentence needs to be rewritten, shortening and combining the introductory ideas or giving them a sentence of their own.

Oversubordination can happen at the end of the sentence too. Here's a sentence that just doesn't know when to quit.

> **Lizzie Hager won the $200 million Powerball jackpot, which surprised Powerball experts because she had purchased only one ticket and had never gambled before, which was not the profile of the usual winner who regularly spent at least $20 a week on tickets.**

The solution, as with front-end oversubordination, is to trim and rewrite as several sentences.

The clarity and comprehension (not to mention rhythm) of a sentence can also suffer if the main clause is sandwiched between two (or more) dependent clauses.

> **Although Lizzie Hager purchased only a single ticket, she won the $20 million Powerball jackpot, which surprised experts because she did not fit the winner profile.**
> (front and back subordination)

This sentence is not certifiably awful, but it is certainly not graceful. Two sentences would be best.

Dead Constructions

Perhaps they are holdovers from term paper writing style, but these constructions have a limited place in good writing: *it is* and *there is.* In most cases, these words merely take up space, performing no function in the sentence. They not only add clutter, but also often rob the sentence of its power by shifting emphasis from what could be a strong verb to a weaker construction—a linking verb (*is, was,* and other forms of *to be*):

> <u>There was a</u>   <u>**flood**</u> downtown.
>   (verb potential)

> **Downtown**   <u>**flooded.**</u>
>   (stronger verb)

In addition to strengthening the sentence by using an action verb, avoiding *there is/there are* constructions has another benefit: simpler subject–verb agreement. (See our discussion of there is/there are as "false subjects" in Chapter 7.) *There* is not usually a subject. Whether you use *is* or *are* depends on what follows the verb:

> **There <u>is</u> a <u>sale</u> on laptops at the bookstore.**
>   (subj)

> **There <u>are</u> additional <u>discounts</u> for students.**
>   (subj.)

Looking for the subject after the verb can create agreement confusion. Avoid both the confusion and the dead construction by restructuring the sentence. For example:

> **Laptops are on sale at the bookstore.**

> **Students are eligible for additional discounts.**

It is/there is constructions are not entirely without value. You might purposefully choose this structure to create a particular rhythm and emphasis as in this memorable construction:

> **It was the best of times, it was the worst of times; it was the age of wisdom, it was the age of foolishness; it was the epoch of belief, it was the epoch of incredulity; it was the season of Light, it was the season of Darkness; it was the spring of hope, it was the winter of despair...**

A good rule to follow is this: If *it is/there is* merely takes up space in the sentence, restructure the sentence. Rescue the "hidden verb" and avoid agreement problems. If on occasion you want to emphasize the subject—or have fun parodying Charles Dickens—use *it is/there is,* but do so only sparingly.

Passive Voice

Here's a quiz for you: Would you rather have someone call your writing (a) lively, agile and spirited or (b) listless, stagnant and leaden? If you chose (a), read on. If you chose (b), well, we know you were just kidding....

The adjectives in choice (a) describe *active* writing, which can mean many things. For the purposes of this discussion about sentence pitfalls, we are referring to *active voice.* The adjectives in choice (b) characterize *passive* writing—or *passive voice*—one of the enemies of energetic prose.

> **Awkwardness is caused when passive voice is used. Power is robbed from sentences, and stiltedness is caused. Strong verbs are weakened.**

When writers use passive voice, they create awkward prose and powerless, stilted sentences with weakened verbs.

Read the first example again. Does the language sound clumsy and unnatural, lifeless and detached? We think so. This is passive-voice construction at work. Now read the second example, with the ideas rewritten in the active voice. If you can recognize the improvement— the leaner construction, the faster pace, the straightforward design, the strong, unencumbered verbs—you know why active voice is almost always preferable.

What is passive voice?

Voice refers to the form of the verb. The subject acts when you use the active voice verb form. In the passive voice, the person or thing performing the action becomes instead the object of the sentence; it does not act, but is *acted upon* by the verb:

> **He photographed the homeless teens.**
> (active)

> **The homeless teens were photographed by him.**
> (passive)

> **Photographs were taken of the homeless teens.**
> (passive)

In the first sentence, the actor *(He)* is performing the action *(photographed)* on the recipient of the action *(the homeless teens)*. In the second sentence, the recipient *(teens)* is having the action *(photographed)* performed on it by the actor *(him)*. The second sentence is an awkward inversion of the first. Look at it this way:

Active Construction

who	did what	to whom
actor	performed action	on recipient
He	photographed	teens

Passive Construction

who	had what done to it	by whom
recipient	acted upon	by actor
teens	were photographed	by him

The third sentence is also in the passive voice. Here the actor—who took the photographs—is missing. The recipient *(teens)* is being acted upon *(photographed)*, but we do not know by whom.

Unless something else is structurally wrong with a passive-voice sentence, it is not technically a grammatical error. In fact, all three of the previous examples are grammatically correct. But the first sentence is lean and straightforward, and the second is clumsy and stilted. The third does not do the job we expect of a good sentence. It does not tell us all the information.

Some novice writers mistakenly think that the presence of *is, was* or another form of the verb *to be* always signals the passive voice. Although passive-voice construction does use *to be* forms, many *to be* forms are in the active voice.

She was posting status updates four times a day.
(active)

Here the actor *(she)* performs the action *(posting)*. The order is straightforward: who did what. The *was* does not signal passive voice; it is merely a *helping* or *auxiliary* verb. For this sentence to be in the passive voice, it would have to be constructed like this:

Status updates were being posted by her four times a day.
(passive)

Note that *status updates,* the recipient of the action, is now the subject of the sentence. The actor, *she,* which was the subject of the first sentence, now appears as the object. The order is inverted; the result is clumsy.

In the following sentence, *was* does signal a passive-voice construction:

His "creative accounting" was uncovered.
(passive)

This sentence is passive because *creative accounting* is the recipient of the action (it is what was uncovered), not the one performing the action. The actor, the person responsible for the discovery, is absent from the sentence.

His "creative accounting" was uncovered by a 20-year-old college intern.
(passive, actor supplied)

A 20-year-old college intern uncovered the CFO's "creative accounting."
(active)

Don't try to identify passive voice by the tense of the verb or by the presence of auxiliary verbs. Instead, find the verb and ask: Who or what is performing this action? If the actor (the who) is missing, or if the actor is having the action performed on it rather than directly doing the action, the sentence is passive.

Take another look at one of the sentences from the beginning of this section:

> **Awkwardness is caused when passive voice is used.**
> (Who/what causes awkwardness? Who uses passive voice?)

> **When writers use passive voice, they create awkward prose.**
> (Active voice: who does what to whom)

Remember: Although passive voice is not grammatical error, it is a roadblock on the path to good, strong writing. Here's why:

1. **Passive voice tends to dilute the verb of its power** because the relationship between action and actor is indirect rather than straightforward:

   > **The CFO was ousted by the board of directors.**
   > (passive)

   > **The board of directors ousted the CFO.**
   > (active)

Passive voice can also bury the verb, just as *there is/there are* constructions do. Look at what happens to the strong, direct verb *accused* in the following sentences:

> **The board accused the CFO of criminal behavior.**
> (active)

> **Accusations were made by the board about the criminal behavior of the CFO.**
> (passive)

The passive-voice sentence changes the verb *accused* to the noun *accusations*. The result is a flabby sentence.

2. **Passive voice can make a sentence unnecessarily awkward** by reversing the expected relationship of who did what to whom. Subject–verb–object is almost always the clearest, smoothest construction. It is also the most succinct. Changing the order means adding unnecessary words:

   > **Investigations are being conducted by the attorney general's office into the financial irregularities.**
   > (passive)

The attorney general is investigating the financial irregularities.
(active)

3. **Passive voice creates false formality,** making a sentence sound impersonal, bureaucratic and overinflated.

   It has been revealed by company insiders that "creative accounting" and bookkeeping irregularities are part of a larger pattern of corporate misbehavior.
   (passive, unnecessarily formal)

   Company insiders revealed that "creative accounting" and bookkeeping irregularities are part of a larger pattern of corporate misbehavior.
   (active)

   "Creative accounting" and bookkeeping irregularities are part of a larger pattern of corporate malfeasance, according to company insiders.
   (active)

The tendency to use passive voice to create formality may come from term paper writing or textbook reading, where such stilted sentences often reside. As a favorite construction of politicians and scientists, passive voice is all around us, but as writers, we must strive to communicate simply, directly and unpretentiously.

4. **Passive voice may intentionally or accidentally obscure who or what is responsible for an action** by omitting the identity of the actor from the audience:

   Mistakes were made.

Who made these mistakes? The passive-voice construction masks the identity of the responsible entity, but who or what is responsible for an action may be vital information. It may be the most vital information! Consider the vastly different implications of the following sentences:

   "Mistakes were made," the CFO said at the morning press conference.

   "I made mistakes," the CFO admitted at the morning press conference.

The inclusion of the who makes quite a difference.

Correcting passive voice

Unless you have a specific reason to use passive voice (see p. 53), avoid it by constructing or rewriting sentences in the active voice. Remember: In the active voice, the actor performs the action. That doesn't mean that all sentences will be alike. You can vary sentences by placement of phrases and clauses, by length, by internal rhythm, by any number of stylistic decisions.

Correcting passive voice is simple once you recognize the construction.

Here's how:

1. Find the verb in the sentence.

2. Ask yourself who or what is performing the action of the verb. When you do this, you are identifying the actor in the sentence. Keep in mind that some passive-voice sentences omit the real actor (as in the *Mistakes were made* example.) You may not be able to find the person or thing responsible for the action in the sentence; you may have to add it.

3. Construct the sentence so that the real actor performs the action.

Now let's go through the three steps, beginning with the following passive-voice sentence:

An exposé of the financial scandal is being written by the young intern who first uncovered the irregularities.

1. The verb is *is being written.*

2. Who performed the action? Who is writing? *The intern.* He or she should be the subject of the sentence.

3. Construct the sentence so that the actor performs the action:

The young intern who first uncovered the financial irregularities is writing an exposé of the scandal.

When passive voice is justified

Because passive-voice construction reverses the order of a sentence from actor–verb–recipient to recipient–verb–actor, it can be a useful and justifiable construction when: (1) the recipient is more important than the actor, or (2) the actor is unknown, irrelevant or impossible to identify.

In certain instances, the recipient of the action is more important (in journalism, more newsworthy) than the performer of the action:

The CFO was indicted on three counts of fraud by a federal grand jury.

The verb is *indicted*. Who indicted? The grand jury. But clearly the object of the indictment—the CFO—takes precedence in the sentence. It is the newsworthy element. Passive voice is justified here.

The CFO and his top assistant were arrested this morning after a high-speed chase through the streets of downtown Cincinnati.

The verb is *arrested*. Who arrested? The sentence does not tell us. The person or persons performing the action in the sentence are missing. But because arrests are almost always made by law enforcement personnel, the actor is far less important than the recipients of the action—the CFO and his assistant. Passive voice is allowable, even preferable, in this example as well.

Sometimes the who or what performing the action is unknown or difficult to identify. When the doer cannot be identified, the writer has little choice but to construct a passive-voice sentence. In this case, passive voice is appropriate:

The company's offices were burglarized sometime late last night.

The verb is *burglarized*. Who or what burglarized the offices? The desperate CFO? His mistakenly loyal assistant? A trio of 10-year-old girls? The doer of this action is unknown. The recipient of the action—the object of the burglary—assumes the prominent place in the sentence.

Occasionally, an expert writer might use passive voice as a stylistic device to create a sense of detachment, a sense that no one is taking responsibility for certain actions, a feeling that actions are out of control or mysterious. Purposefully obscuring or removing prominence from the doer might create suspense. Passive voice can be a stylistic element.

Shifting voices

Here's an easy rule: Do not change voice from active to passive, or vice versa, within a sentence. This muddled construction shifts focus and confuses the audience. Active voice emphasizes the doer. Passive voice emphasizes the recipient:

The company president expressed concern over the financial scandal, but the drop in stock prices was not mentioned in his speech yesterday.

The focus of the first part of the sentence is *the company president,* the doer or actor. The focus of the second part of the sentence is *drop in stock prices* (the recipient of the action), resulting in a confusing and awkward shift that adds unnecessary words and robs the second verb, *mentioned,* of its power. (This sentence also lacks parallel structure, which we discuss in Chapter 7.) The sentence would be stronger and clearer if both parts were in the active voice.

The company president expressed concern over the financial scandal in yesterday's speech but avoided any mention of the drop in stock prices.

Pay particular attention to shifts to the passive after an impersonal *one* or *you:*

If you exercise aerobically, mental acuity can be improved.

The first part of the sentence is in the active voice. The second part shifts the emphasis from the actor *(you)* to the recipient *(mental acuity)*. Keep both sentence parts in the active voice for clarity:

If you exercise aerobically, you can improve mental acuity.

Better yet:

Aerobic exercise improves mental acuity.

The Lead Sentence

Let's end this discussion of the sentence with a few thoughts about the single most important sentence you will write: the first sentence. Capturing someone's attention in our media-saturated environment is a tremendous challenge. The competition for attention is staggering: Google indexes more than 4,500 news sites (including the online sites for more than 1,000 daily newspapers); the American Society of Magazine Editors lists 22,000 magazines currently being published in the United States; Radio World estimates more than 14,000 licensed radio stations. As anyone who has been stranded in a hotel room in a strange city can attest, there are more cable channels than even a world-class surfer would care to surf. There are, by conservative estimates, more than 200 million blogs. A writer using any of these conduits and hoping to ensnare a reader, listener or viewer will have to do it in one quick, powerful motion: the first sentence.

That sentence can be a simple but reader-enticing question, like this one that begins a blog post at www.thinhouse.net:

Are you sick of being awash in greenwashing?

It can be a bold, provocative sentence, like this one that introduces an eight-page advertising insert for the famous M. D. Anderson Cancer Center at the University of Texas:

Everything causes cancer.

It can be foreboding, the kind of sentence that compels a reader to keep reading, like this one that began a 5,000-word magazine feature:

Fourteen months ago, Tom McDonald heard the news no one wants to hear.

In a traditional news story (wherever it appears—on newsprint, online, on TV), the first sentence is designed to give the audience a concise, comprehensive summary of the most important elements of the story. With its admonishments to tell everything (who? what? when? where? how?) in one sentence, the summary lead approach can open the door to bad writing. Packing a sentence with all this material increases the chance that you will write an awkward, muddled, rambling or otherwise confusing sentence. Did you hear that? That was the click of a reader exiting your story, the ruffle of a page being turned. That was an opportunity lost, a person who will not be reading (or listening to) your words because you didn't put sufficient thought, energy and grammatical know-how into your very first sentence.

We don't want that to happen to you. You have the power—the obligation!—to construct all your sentences both grammatically and gracefully. Let's get to it. We'll start with the most important word in a sentence, the vibrant core, the verb.

Chapter 5

Power and Precision: It Begins with the Verb

Chapter 4 challenged you to "construct all your sentences both grammatically and gracefully." We'll add to that this we're-not-kidding rule: **You can't write a complete sentence without a verb.** However, you will write a weak sentence if you don't employ the strongest, most focused verb. So, we must understand the nature and roles of verbs in order to construct sentences that give power and precision to our communication.

The verb, in all of its forms, is the first step in understanding the eight parts of speech that are key to mastery of grammar and your growth as a writer. In this chapter, we examine the verb according to function, form, number and person, tense, principal parts, voice and mood. We conclude with a discussion of verbals, which seem to have the power of verbs but in reality are only nouns, adjectives or adverbs. As with all our grammatical lessons, these are intended to bring power and precision to your prose.

In Chapter 6, we discuss the other parts of speech that work with verbs to create sentences that are clear, concise and correct.

Giving Power to Our Sentences

The Latin *verbum* means "the word," with emphasis on *the*. Indeed, the verb is at the core of all writing: It propels, it positions, it pronounces.

A sentence goes nowhere without a verb. As you learned in Chapter 4, a sentence is a group of words that expresses a complete thought. At a minimum, it contains a subject (a starting point, either stated or implied, for the thought) and a verb (which provides the power), as in

Lightning	**struck.**
(subj.)	(verb)

The following is **not** a sentence:

The lightning's damage

Why? These three words contain an image but not a complete thought. They need a verb. *Damage* may seem to suggest action, but it's a label—a noun. So, this is not a sentence but a *phrase*—a group of related words that doesn't contain a verb. With a subject and a verb, that partial thought becomes complete. It becomes a sentence:

Lightning	**damaged**	**10 homes.**
(subj.)	(verb)	(obj.)

The verb is at the heart of all our writing. It focuses, it directs, it commands. Let's examine this powerful tool by focusing on the verb *write*. Note that you will see *write* in various tenses, including the *wrote* and *has written* forms. We'll also employ the nouns *writer* and *writing* to show their roles as subjects and objects.

Verb Functions

In most writing, a verb states an action or effort. Let's examine two examples that reflect two different functions.

She <u>writes</u> seven magazine articles each year.

(Note how *article* receives the action of *writes*.)

He <u>writes</u> too slowly, in the opinion of his editors.

(No recipient of action here, but *writes* is followed by a description of that action.)
What some may consider a "softer" form of a verb indicates a state of being or a condition. These verbs are often a form of *is*:

She <u>is</u> a gifted writer.
His writing <u>is</u> brilliant.

In all of these examples, the verb directs the sentence. Note how the absence of those verbs takes away the power and direction of those sentences.

Verb Forms

The examples in the preceding section illustrate the three forms of verbs: *transitive, intransitive* and *linking*. You'll see that these forms are quite different in how they portray action, show direction or connect a sentence's subject to a description or qualification. Understanding these forms is key to making correct choices of case (discussed in Chapter 7, "Are We in Agreement"), to preventing the use of an adverb where an adjective belongs and to avoiding errors with such troublesome verb pairs as *lay/lie* and *sit/set*. There are many more reasons to understand them, as you will discover.

1. **Transitive verb.** In Latin, *trans* means "through" or "across." Therefore, the transitive verb moves action from the subject to an object, as in:

<u>Tom</u>	<u>wrote</u>	<u>12 letters of complaint</u> **to his landlord.**
(subj.)	(trans. verb)	(dir. obj.)

   Note that transitive verbs are always followed by a *direct object*—the recipient of the verb's action. When you can answer the question *what* or *whom* after a verb, you have a direct object.

   Transitive verbs are considered the most action-oriented of verbs, although our next form—intransitive—has plenty of drive.

2. **Intransitive verb.** As the prefix *in* suggests, this verb form is not transitive. Although there is no recipient of any action from this type of verb, sentences with intransitive verbs do convey action as well as a sense of location or some description of that action. Here is an example, with *write* in the past tense:

<u>He</u>	<u>wrote</u>	<u>promptly</u> **to his frustrated editor.**
(subj.)	(intrans. verb)	(adv. describing the verb)

   Note that in intransitive verb constructions, the words following the verb don't answer the question *what*; they generally reply to *where, how* or *when*. So, intransitive verbs do not take direct objects. And as will be fully explained in Chapter 6, these verbs are generally followed by prepositional phrases or adverbs. In this example, the verb is in the *past perfect tense*, using *has*, often called a *helping verb*:

<u>Tom</u>	<u>has written</u>	<u>to his landlord a dozen times.</u>
(subj.)	(intrans. verb)	(prepositional phrase)

3. **Linking verb.** This verb form may seem less forceful compared with its transitive and intransitive cousins, but it has an important role in linking the subject with a modifier, which enhances the meaning or description of that subject. Most *linking verbs* are a form of the verb *to be (is, are, seems);* here is an example that uses *writing* as a noun:

Writing	**is**	**difficult and time-consuming** for her.
(subj.)	(l. verb)	(pred. adjs. describing *writing*)

Nouns and pronouns can also follow linking verbs. They are called *predicate nominatives,* because they simply restate the subject or connect a related concept to it, as in:

Writing	**is**	her chief **ambition.**
(subj.)	(l. verb)	(pred. nom.)

Here is an example of a linking verb followed by a pronoun that serves as a predicate nominative:

The best **writer** in the class	**is**	**you.**
(subj.)	(l. verb)	(pred. nom.)

The predicate nominative requires that pronouns are in the *nominative case.* Stay tuned for this interesting discussion in Chapter 7.

As we mentioned earlier, the most common verb in these linking constructions is a form of *to be*—as in *is, are, was, were,* etc. However, there are a number of linking verbs that are not *to be* constructions, although they indicate a state of being. These linking verbs include:

appear	become	feel	get	grow	look
remain	seem	smell	sound	taste	turn

Let's use the verb *smell* to make the point that linking verbs connect only nouns and adjectives back to the subject—not adverbs. This sentence would not be correct:

The **corpse**	**smells**	**badly.**
(subj.)	(l. verb)	(adv.)

An adverb, which frequently is an *–ly* word, can characterize (modify) only a verb, an adjective or another adverb. Because a corpse has no sense of smell, you can't modify this verb. And there are no adjectives or adverbs to modify. So, this sentence requires an adjective for the linking verb *smelled,* as in:

> **The <u>corpse</u>   <u>smells</u>   <u>bad</u>.**
> (subject)   (l. verb)   (pred. adj.)

(Put another way, the corpse has a bad smell.)

Some verbs can be used correctly in all three verb forms, which is a good device for understanding the forms' differences:

> **"I <u>smell</u> a rat here," the mayor told the council.**

(*Smell* is a transitive verb—the direct object *rat* follows it. Note that the question *what* is answered.)

> **The diner told the chef that the pasta <u>smelled</u> like dirty laundry.**

(*Smelled* is an intransitive verb; there is no object, just a prepositional phrase following *smelled,* to answer the question *how.*)

Now back to that decomposing body:

> **The bullet-riddled corpse <u>smelled</u> bad.**

(*Smelled* is a linking verb—it connects *corpse* to *bad,* noun to adjective. It has no recipient of action, just a description.)

Okay—enough about foul odors! Let's move on to a preliminary discussion about verb number, which will also be discussed in greater depth in Chapter 7.

Verb Number and Person

We can't talk about verbs without mentioning *agreement*—a key tenet of grammar we'll deal with in Chapter 7. For now, here is the rule: **The number of the verb (singular or plural) must match the number of the subject of the sentence.** This requires that the writer identify the true subject of the sentence. The agreement errors (choosing a plural verb rather than a singular one) in the following sentences show some common areas of difficulty:

> **An elite group of writers <u>are chronicling</u> the first 100 days of his presidency.**

The noun or pronoun that is closest to the verb is not necessarily the subject of the sentence. The true subject here is *group*—a singular noun—so the verb should be *is chronicling*. Yes, a verb can be more than one word!)

> **The American Federation of Advertising Copywriters <u>have failed</u> to represent the interests of its membership.**

The Federation is a union, a collective group, so it is a singular entity. One clue to this is the use of the phrase "its (singular) membership" rather than "their (plural) membership." The correct verb, a singular, should be *has failed*.

> **Among the many reasons for these writing errors <u>are</u> poor proofreading.**

The true subject here is the singular noun *proofreading*. Yes, sometimes the subject can be at the end of a sentence rather than at the beginning. The verb should be *is*.)

What is the *person* of a verb? Person is also an important part of agreement. In our grammar, we have six persons—three singular and three plural. Let's use the verb *is* (derived from *to be*) to show how verbs change their forms depending on the person used. We'll use personal pronouns as the subjects.

First person singular *(I)*

> **I <u>am</u> a struggling writer.**

Second person singular *(you)*

> **You <u>are</u> a terrific writer.**

Third person singular *(he, she, it* or an appropriate noun)

> **She <u>is</u> a gifted editor.**
> or
> **A good writer <u>is</u> not always a good editor.**

First person plural *(we)*

> **We <u>are</u> great fans of her writing.**

Second person plural *(you)*

> **You <u>are</u> wonderful supporters of her writing.**

Third person plural *(they* or an appropriate plural noun)

> **They <u>are</u> writers who remain committed their audiences.**

Note the number of the transitive verb in this sentence:

They <u>enjoy</u> great writing.

The verb *enjoy* is plural. Many third-person singular verbs in the present tense end in *s,* as in

She <u>enjoys</u> great writing.

Verb Tense

A *tense* acts as a "time stamp" in a sentence. Verbs reflect present, past, future or ongoing action or states of being, as well as *perfect* forms of these. Here is a tense-by-tense breakdown of the third-person singular verb *writes:*

Sarah <u>writes</u> beautifully. (*present tense*)
Tom <u>wrote</u> to his landlord this morning. (*past tense*)
The committee <u>will write</u> its report soon. (*future tense*)

In addition, we have six additional tenses, three in the *perfect* form and three in the *progressive* form. Knowing their proper terminology is obviously not as important as understanding how a verb moves through time. Briefly, here are those forms, showing just the verbs. You'll note that two or more verbs are used to create these forms:

has written (*present perfect tense*)
had written (*past perfect tense*)
will have written (*future perfect tense*)

The progressive forms indicate some form of ongoing or continuous action, even if it details some future action:

is writing (*present progressive tense*)
had been writing (*past progressive tense*)
will have been writing (*future progressive tense*)

It is important to keep tenses "in step," or parallel. Changing tenses unnecessarily creates confusion. We examine parallel structure in Chapter 7.

Next we look at a number of verbs that change more than most typical or *regular* ones, as we examine principal parts.

Principal Parts of Verbs

Verbs have four principal parts: the *to* infinitive form to establish its root (as an indicator of the present) and three tenses—past, past participle and present participle. Again, the terminology is less important than your understanding of how verbs change according to their "time stamp."

Let's focus on the verb *appear,* which is considered regular because its infinitive form is *to appear* (we discuss the infinitive in the section on verbals later in this chapter). If a verb is regular, its past tense and past participle form have an *-ed* ending and its present participle has an *-ing* ending.

The team <u>appeared</u> to lose all its confidence.
(past tense)

She <u>has appeared</u> in 200 consecutive performances.
(past participle, creating the present perfect tense)

The playwright <u>is appearing</u> to make a major breakthrough.
(present participle, creating the present progressive tense)

Not all verbs in our language are regular. *Irregular* verbs change their form depending on their tense. The following is a brief list of frequently used irregular verbs; note how the forms change, sometimes dramatically.

Infinitive	Past Tense	Past Participle	Present Participle
to arise	arose	(has) arisen	(is) arising
to begin	began	begun	beginning
to choose	chose	chosen	choosing
to fly	flew	flown	flying
to lay	laid	laid	laying
to lie	lay	lain	lying
to ring	rang	rung	ringing
to rise	rose	risen	rising
to set	set	set	setting
to sit	sat	sat	sitting
to steal	stole	stolen	stealing
to write	wrote	written	writing

You'll find a much longer list of irregular verbs in Appendix C.

The Voice of Verbs

As you discovered in Chapter 4, verbs also have a voice that is either active or passive.

Hannah <u>wrote</u> her college admissions essay in less than an hour.

In the previous example, the action moves from transitive verb to direct object, from *wrote* to *essay*. In active voice constructions, the subject performs the action. Generally this is a more direct and concise form of writing.

In the passive voice, the subject of the sentence is acted upon by the verb:

The <u>report</u> critical of city police <u>was written</u> last week.

The writer of the report is not identified. The result is a sentence with incomplete information.

In most cases, we prefer the active voice because it tends to be clearer, crisper and more complete. In some instances, the subject acted upon may be more important than the initiator of the action, as in this sentence:

The <u>mayor was attacked</u> this morning by an unknown assailant.

In general, however, using the passive voice creates awkward sentences and occasionally a false formality.

The Mood of Verbs

Verbs also have moods. Verbs are *indicative* when they convey a fact or question. They are *imperative* when they issue a command of sorts and they are *subjunctive* when they convey some information that is actually contrary to fact or possibility. Examples:

Six investigative reporters <u>wrote</u> the award-winning series. (*indicative*)

<u>Write</u> that on your blog! (*imperative*)

If only I <u>were</u> the writer Ernest Hemingway was. (*subjunctive*)

Note the use of *I were,* which is the tipoff that the statement is not a likely possibility. The subjunctive mood is often used to express a wish.

Verbals: Don't Be Fooled!

What looks like a verb but doesn't have the horsepower to drive a sentence? It's the confusingly named *verbal,* which is really a noun or adjective (or occasional adverb). The way it is imbedded in a phrase often suggests a strength it simply doesn't have. We hope this brief discussion keeps you from giving such words undeserved power.

Verbals are classified as *gerunds, participles* or *infinitives.* They can be the subject of a sentence, they can be a direct object or they can modify nouns and pronouns to add description—but they can never act as a verb.

1. **Gerunds.** These verbals, which always have an *-ing* ending, have the feel of action but serve only as the subject or object in a sentence:

   <u>Writing</u> for The New York Times is his life's goal.
   (gerund as subj.)

   You can see that *writing* represents an activity, not an action. It cannot carry the requirements of a complete sentence. If you dropped the linking verb *is* from the example sentence above, you would have a sentence fragment—in reality, just a phrase.

   Now here's a pair of gerunds that serves as the object of a transitive verb:

   She really <u>enjoys</u> <u>swimming</u> and <u>weightlifting</u>.
        (verb) (gerunds as direct objects)

   Remember: *Gerunds are always nouns.* They will act in the sentence the same way as nouns (see p. 59). However, because the gerund has an *-ing* ending, it is sometimes confused with another verbal, the participle.

2. **Participles.** These verbals have either an *-ing* or *-ed* ending and are always used as adjectives. As an adjective (see p. 64), the participle generally will modify (give extra meaning to) a noun or a pronoun. Examples:

   <u>Writing under the pen name of Currer Bell,</u> Charlotte Bronte gained literary fame with "Jane Eyre."

   Here, *Writing* modifies the proper noun and subject, Charlotte Bronte. The only verb in this sentence is *gained.* If you merely wrote, "Writing under the pen name of Currer Bell," you would have a sentence fragment.

3. **Infinitives.** These are verbals that are formed by *to* plus (in most cases) the present tense of a verb. Infinitives generally are easy to identify; their place as a part of speech (noun, adjective or adverb), however, is not always so easy to determine. Let's look at three examples.

Good <u>writers</u> <u>need</u> <u>to write</u> frequently.
      (subj.) (verb) (infin.)

In this sentence, *to write* is an infinitive acting as a noun, the object of the transitive verb *need*. The object *to write* answers the question *what.*, In the next example, an infinitive works as an adjective modifying a noun that functions as a direct object:

Good <u>writers</u> <u>have</u> three overarching <u>principles</u> <u>to keep</u> in mind.
    (subj.) (verb)   (dir. obj.) (infin.)

And in a final example, the infinitive is used as an adverb modifying the predicate adjective *eager*:

The cub <u>reporter</u> <u>was</u>   eager   <u>to write a prize-winning story.</u>
    (subj.) (l. v.) (pred. adj.)   (infin.)

These, then, are our three verbals. Remember that a verbal is not a verb. (You can walk like a duck and talk like a duck, but that doesn't mean you're a duck!) Verbals are only nouns, adjectives or adverbs.

A final thought before we wade into the remaining parts of speech in Chapter 6: If you recognize verbs and use them well, you have a powerful tool at your disposal. You are on your way. If you understand that a phrase has no verbs and that clauses do, you are on your way to solid sentence construction. If you know that this one word

Stop!

is not only a verb but also a complete sentence and if you agree that

A brief stop for gas and oil

has no verb and is just a simple phrase, you are ready to move on.

Got it?

Go!

Chapter 6

The Rest of the Crew

Consider the verb as the captain of a mighty ship that rules the byways of your communication. The verb commands and guides. It directs and connects.

While every vessel needs a captain, where would it be without the rest of the crew? Indeed, where would our sentences be without these seven characters?

The NOUN: It can be the actor who initiates or receives action. With its partner the pronoun, it can serve as the subject, direct object, predicate nominative or the object of the preposition of its sentence. Of course, the noun goes nowhere without its verb.

The PRONOUN: Consider it a "noun substitute." It steps in for a person, place or thing that has already been stated or implied in your writing.

The ADJECTIVE: What a colorful and creative part of speech! We can describe and focus nouns and pronouns with this ambitious character.

The ADVERB: Whereas the adjective is tightly bound to nouns and pronouns, the adverb provides descriptions and limits for the verb, which strengthens your sentences.

The PREPOSITION: This versatile part of speech is a navigator of sorts. That is, words such as *in, on, under, up* and *down* provide a location or direction that a verb will suggest.

The CONJUNCTION: This vital part of sentence construction connects and coordinates both phrases and clauses. It's remarkable how seemingly simple words like *and, but , that, which* and *although* can give clarity and context to a sentence.

The INTERJECTION: This part of speech brings fun to sentence writing. It deserves a mighty "Wow!"

Before we discuss these "crew members" in greater detail, we'll offer some reasons you need to understand these important components of the sentence. But first, here's a sentence that contains each of the the parts of speech. Can you identify all of them?

Wow—you really like writing crisp sentences and paragraphs for us!

Why You Need to Understand Parts of Speech

How will a solid understanding of parts of speech help you master the challenges of grammar and of good writing—the reason you are trying to master grammar in the first place? Here are several examples.

- Proper recognition of a verb helps you distinguish a *phrase* from a *clause,* which will help you use both to craft crisp sentences. As Chapter 4 points out, a phrase does not contain a verb. A clause, however, does contain a verb. Therefore, a construction such as

  the dark, windswept sky

  is merely a phrase composed of several adjectives and one noun. It has no verb and cannot stand alone. It becomes a clause with the insertion of an action word:

  The dark, windswept sky <u>warns</u> us of an approaching storm.

  Now we have a clause and, because this one can stand independently, a complete thought. We have a verb. We have a sentence.

- Identifying a sentence's subject prevents errors in subject–verb agreement. Not all nouns are subjects of a sentence, as in this example:

  The <u>rate</u> of automobile *thefts* <u>is</u> startling.
      (singular subj.)   (singular verb)

  As you will see in Chapter 7, the noun *thefts*—the object of the preposition *of*—cannot be the subject of a sentence. It helps to recognize prepositions!

- Proper recognition of how a pronoun functions in a sentence helps you to correctly select the case of a pronoun (Chapter 7). For example, a decision about the use of *I* or *me* in the following sentence requires that you understand what prepositions and pronouns do:

  Everyone <u>except</u> Billy and <u>me</u> got job offers.
           (prep.)   (obj. of prep)

  Get the point? These are just a few of the many examples that show why understanding parts of speech is so critical to writing well.

Nouns

We hope that you've known for a long time that a *noun* can be a person, place or thing—and that it can appear in many parts of a sentence. Here are a few nouns that we'll use in several examples:

scientists

Amanda (called a *proper noun*)

collecting

unemployment

company's (*possessive* form)

These are not action words, although they can be the activators or receivers of some action from a verb. Because a noun is such a common component of a sentence, it has many roles.

1. As the **subject** of a sentence:

   <u>Scientists</u> **are excited about the discovery of water on Mars.**

2. As the **direct object** of a transitive verb:

   The dean named <u>Amanda</u> to the scholarship committee.

3. As the **predicate nominative** of a linking verb:

   His favorite pastime is <u>finding</u> old hubcaps. (*Finding* is not a verb—remember the gerund?)

4. As the **object of a preposition:**

   Your story about <u>unemployment</u> was well-written.

5. As a **possessive or modifier** of another noun:

   The <u>company's</u> stock is in trouble.

You'll find that recognizing and properly using nouns will help you to make correct decisions about agreement and case (Chapter 7).

Pronouns

Like an eager understudy, a *pronoun* stands in for a noun. Also known as a *noun substitute*, a pronoun adds flexibility and variety to a sentence by not restating the earlier noun.

Pronouns can be more confusing to use than nouns, however. Some of the most common grammatical problems relate to the use of pronouns in such areas as antecedent agreement, case and selecting the proper pronoun to introduce a dependent clause.

First, let's review these types of pronouns: *personal, indefinite, relative, interrogative* and *demonstrative*. Identifying and using them well will help you write with more focus and rhythm.

Types of Pronouns

1. **Personal pronoun.** The most common pronoun type, the personal pronoun, takes distinct forms in three cases: nominative (subjective), objective and possessive. To show you how different each pronoun is in its three cases, we'll review each one, from first-person singular to third-person plural.

Nominative	Objective	Possessive
I	me	my/mine
you	you	your/yours
he	him	his
she	her	her/hers
it	it	its
we	us	our/ours
you	you	your/yours
they	them	their/theirs

Because personal pronouns change their forms depending on their location in a sentence, it is important to be aware of these roles. Here is an example of three proper uses of *we*, which is a first-person plural pronoun:

We almost missed the final exam.
(*We* is the subject—nominative case.)

Please send this report to us tomorrow.
(*Us* is the object of the preposition *to*—objective case.)

Our presentation won first place.
(*Our* modifies *presentation*—possessive case.)

An important note about *its* and *it's*

The personal possessive pronoun often lures an unnecessary apostrophe from the unwary writer. The most common problem is confusion between *its* and *it's*, which, of course, sound alike. Sadly, this type of error—which is mortifying if it makes it to publication—seems to be cropping up more and more frequently:

The river has reached it's highest level in the last 25 years.
(Remember: *It's* means *it is.* This is called a *subject-verb contraction.* Personal pronouns in the possessive case do not require apostrophes.)

This is correct usage for *it's*:

It's just a matter of time before this story is published.

Whereas *it's* and *your's* are often used incorrectly as pronouns (and, by the way, there is no such word as *your's*), noun possessives do use an apostrophe, as in:

Tommy's record collection
(*proper noun*)

the nation's loss
    (*common noun*)

So, here's a sentence that will either effectively illustrate this issue or propel you to further confusion (we hope it's the former):

It's apparent that the company's success has a
(It is)   (possessive noun)

great deal to do with its commitment to fair trade.
                (possessive pronoun)

2. **Indefinite pronoun.** Pronouns such as *anyone, enough, many, most, none* and *several* reveal little if anything about their gender or number. As such they can cause troublesome subject–verb and antecedent agreement problems. It's important to understand the sense of the sentence so you can properly match subject, verb and *antecedent* (a previous word to which a pronoun refers).

   The good news is that only a handful of indefinite pronouns can take either a singular or a plural verb, depending on the sense of the sentence. If the pronoun refers to what is a singular unit, the verb will be singular. The plural connotation should be equally obvious in the construction. These indefinites include:

   all   most   none   some

   All of the candy **has** been eaten.

   All of the passengers **have** been rescued.

   See our comments in Chapter 7 and in Part II about *none,* which can be a bit vexing.
   Some indefinite pronouns, such as *both, few, many* and *several,* are obviously plural:

   Both of those cars **are** overpriced.

Indefinite pronouns and gender choice

Indefinite pronouns such as *anybody* and *somebody* can be vexing when it comes to gender identification—and they can cause awkward writing. So, which of the four choices of personal possessive pronouns is correct?

   Anybody can enter **his** photograph in the competition.

   Anybody can enter **her** photograph in the competition.

   Anybody can enter **his or her** photograph in the competition.

   Anybody can enter **their** photograph in the competition.

The only grammatically incorrect choice is *their; anybody* (any one person) is obviously singular, so you can't connect a plural possessive pronoun to it. We prefer the most inclusive (and grammatically correct) choice: *anybody . . . his or her.* A writer also has the option of using the plural throughout, changing *anybody* to *people.*

3. **Relative and interrogative pronouns.** Pronouns such as *that, which* and *who* are easy to recognize, but they can be difficult to use properly. Examine the next four sentences and note the correct choices (underlined):

Who/<u>Whom</u> did the police arrest?

She is the type of leader that/<u>who</u> commands unwavering loyalty.

The aircraft carrier Stennis, that/<u>which</u> is now heading toward the Persian Gulf, is an intimidating spectacle.

This is one of those pens <u>that</u>/which <u>write</u>/writes over bacon grease.

Using these pronouns correctly requires an understanding of antecedent agreement, case and restrictive and nonrestrictive clauses, which we examine in Chapter 7. This, however, is an ideal point to cite a common error with relative pronouns—the use of *that* to avoid a *who/whom* selection:

The police officers <u>that</u> stopped my car were polite but firm.
(The correct pronoun choice is *who*.)

The candidate <u>that</u> the voters elected has been arrested for fraud.
(The correct pronoun is *whom*.)

Who or *whom*, rather than *that*, must be selected when the antecedent (in these cases, *officers* and *candidate*) is human or has human qualities. In an earlier sentence, the relative pronoun *that* correctly substituted for the noun *pens*.

Note that the relative pronoun *who* has a separate possessive form (Remember the *it's/its* issue?) The possessive of *who* is *whose*—not the subject–verb contraction *who's* (*who is*). Consider this sentence:

Helen Thompson, <u>whose</u> purse was snatched this
                (possessive)

morning, is a plucky former teacher <u>who's</u> determined not to
                (*who is*—subj.-verb cont.)

let the incident get her down.

4. **Demonstrative pronoun.** These pronouns are "pointers"—their specificity leaves little room for doubt. They include *this, that, these* and *those.* They can stand alone, as in:

<u>This</u> is your opportunity to excel.
(refers to a specific opportunity)

All of these demonstrative pronouns can be adjectives if they modify a noun rather than substitute for one. We turn to that colorful part of speech now.

Adjectives

The *adjective* describes, limits and otherwise qualifies nouns and some pronouns. It cannot modify verbs; that is the realm of the adverb. Adjectives are sometimes called "picture words", because they provide color and dimension. But like many aspects of writing, they can be overused and misapplied. Given their many nuances, adjectives challenge the writer to be on target with meaning and intent.

There are two basic types of adjectives: descriptive and limiting.

Types of Adjectives

1. **Descriptive.** In adding detail, the descriptive adjective expands images in a sentence. Consider the differences in these two sentences (adjectives are underlined in the enhanced sentence):

   The nation's economy continued its plunge yesterday, reflecting anxiety about the growing national debt.

   The nation's battered economy continued its perilous plunge yesterday, reflecting mounting anxiety over escalating national debt.

   Which sentence paints a more detailed and colorful picture?

   Skilled writers use adjectives carefully. They are concerned more with focused content rather than with flashiness. Properly employed, adjectives don't add glitz or fluff; they provide information to create a more complete picture.

2. **Limiting.** Whereas the descriptive adjective is colorful and artistic, the limiting adjective is more spartan. In jeans parlance, if the descriptive adjective is designer label, the limiting adjective is plain-pockets. This adjective sets boundaries and qualifies (limits) meaning. Compare the following two examples:

   Hikers lost in the Mount Hood National Forest met their rescuers after walking out of the wilderness.

   Six teenage hikers lost in the Mount Hood National Forest for three days met their rescuers today after hiking 15 miles out of the wilderness.

   (The number *15* tells us specifically how far the teenagers had to hike. Much can be inferred from this, although in this case, the writer did not choose to add more descriptive detail, such as *tortuous* or *snow-clogged* miles. The number of hikers and of days they were lost also provide important detail.)

More examples:

"<u>This</u> turnover cost us the game," the coach said sadly.

(*This,* which often can be a pronoun, becomes an adjective when it modifies a noun, such as *turnover.* Again, the adjective limits [focuses] the meaning of the sentence. The coach is referring to one specific turnover.)

Do you know <u>any</u> ways to improve your writing?

Although the boundaries set here in specifying *ways* are very broad, *any* is seen as a limiting adjective because it provides no description or other helpful context. *Each* and *either* also fit into the category of limiting adjectives.

Degrees of Adjectives

Many adjectives and adverbs have three forms that show degree, intensity or comparison. For example, the trio of

smart   smarter   smartest

moves from the *base* level *(smart)* to a *comparative* level *(smarter)* and then to the *superlative* level *(smartest).* Obviously, at the superlative level no higher comparison can be made—that is, it makes no sense (and is ungrammatical) to characterize an individual as "most smartest."

Most adjectives take either the *-er* or *-est* suffix to indicate degree. Some, however, retain their base form and merely add the adverbs *more* and *most* to show a change in degree:

controversial   more controversial   most controversial

The use of *more* with an adjective in its comparative form, such as *richer,* creates a funny-sounding (and ungrammatical) construction: *more richer* (!). See further discussion of comparatives and superlatives later in this chapter in the section on adverbs.

The Predicate Adjective

An adjective that follows a linking verb is called a *predicate adjective.* It modifies the subject, which can be either a noun or a pronoun:

The company's advertising <u>campaign</u> is <u>offensive</u>.
                         (subj.)   (pred. adj.)

(*Offensive* is a predicate adjective. The verb *is* links the quality of being offensive to the noun *campaign*—thus creating the meaning of an *offensive campaign* [adjective modifying a noun].)

<u>She</u>	**is <u>upset</u> about the committee's decision.**
(subj.)	(pred. adj.)

The adjective *upset* describes the condition of the subject *she*. This is one of few instances in which an adjective modifies a pronoun.

Adjectives as Verbals

Two verbals, the participle and the infinitive (see pp. 54–55), can be classified as adjectives. Whereas the participle is always an adjective, the infinitive is an adjective only when it modifies a noun. An infinitive can also act as a noun or an adverb, depending on its role in a sentence.

<u>Climbing</u> over the barbed wire fence, the robber tore his pants.
(*Climbing*, a participle, modifies the noun *robber*.)

A quick note about the dangling modifier: An often-humorous error occurs with the misplacement of a noun and its participle (modifier), as in this sentence:

Climbing over the barbed wire fence, the robber's pants tore.

As you can see, the pants didn't do the climbing! This is what we call a *dangling* or *misplaced modifier*.

Here is an example of an infinitive that acts as an adjective:

The senator announced her decision <u>to vote</u> against health care reform.

The infinitive *to vote* modifies the noun *decision; to vote* characterizes or helps describe *decision*.

Adverbs

Although *adverbs* also perform descriptive and limiting functions, their uses in sentences can be more complex. For example, this is what an adverb can do:

• **Modify a verb**

   The marathoner trained <u>faithfully</u> throughout the long winter.

The adverb *faithfully* describes or modifies the verb *trained;* in this type of construction, an adverb often answers the question *how.*

• **Modify an adjective**

This coffee is <u>really</u> hot!

Really modifies the predicate adjective *hot;* pardon the pun, but it states a degree.

• **Modify another adverb**

The rock star formerly known as Roadkill took his concert review <u>very</u> badly.

Very modifies the adverb *badly* and together they modify the verb *took;* again, these adverbs answer the question *how.*

• **Introduce a sentence**

<u>Why</u> do fools fall in love?

Why is an interrogative adverb; it modifies the verb *fall.*

• **Connect two clauses**

I don't agree with your conclusions; <u>however</u>, I admire the passion of your argument.

Because it links two clauses that could stand alone as two sentences, *however* is called a *conjunctive adverb.*

Many adverbs end in *-ly,* but don't always count on that for proper identification. Examine a sentence carefully to be sure. For example, *slow* can be both an adjective and an adverb, depending on how it is used in a sentence, but *slowly* can be only an adverb.

As you can see, an adverb can provide the how, where, when and why of a sentence, which shows its close connection to the verb.

In addition to selecting the most appropriate and descriptive adverbs for a sentence, writers should be concerned about the proper positioning of an adverb. Although an adverb can be moved to provide a change in emphasis, it's a good idea to position the adverb as closely as possible to the word it is supposed to modify. Position alters meaning, as in:

<u>Only</u> I love you.
or
I love you <u>only</u>.

Comparatives and Superlatives

An adverb can indicate a comparison between two units; it can also express the highest degree of quality among three or more units.

Here's an example of the adverbial *comparative,* with the sufix *-er:*

Health insurance costs are rising <u>faster</u> than the Consumer Price Index.

Comparative: Two items are being compared, through modification (degree) of the verb *are rising.*

And here is an example of the *superlative,* with the suffix *–est:*

Her time in the 10,000 meter race is the <u>fastest</u> this year.

Superlative: There is no higher degree of comparison available.

Remember that not all adverbs use the *–er* and *–est* suffix. Many, like words such as *fearful* and *dangerous,* use extra adverbs such as *more* to indicate the comparative and *most* to show the superlative. Obviously, we don't employ both *most* and the *–est* characterization: It is redundant (and silly) to describe someone as the "most smartest" in the class.

A cautionary note

Be sure that your meaning is clear when you employ a comparative or superlative. Consider these errors:

High blood pressure is <u>more</u> dangerous than any chronic disease in the world today.

Besides being an amazingly sweeping (and arguable) statement, this sentence implies that high blood pressure is also more pernicious than itself, because it, too, is a chronic disease. The last part of the sentence should read *than any **other** chronic disease in the world today.*

This is the <u>most</u> unique piece of art I have ever seen.

Certain words, called *absolutes,* defy comparisons. *Unique,* an absolute, is already a superlative. So are *perfect, excellent, impossible, final* and *supreme.* This says it all:

This is a <u>unique</u> piece of art.

There's more on this issue in the context of clarity and conciseness in Chapter 9.

Prepositions

Prepositions have a heavy work ethic as both navigators and locators. They connect nouns and pronouns to create phrases, linking these phrases to the rest of a sentence, as in these two examples:

Police found the suspect hiding <u>*behind*</u> <u>the kitchen door.</u>

and

Your kind words mean a lot _to_ Tom and me.

Like many other parts of speech, prepositions can have tightly focused meanings. Writers sometimes make the wrong choices with such prepositional pairs as *among/between, beside/besides, beneath/ below, because of/due to* and *on/upon.* Part 2 of this book discusses the differences between these pairs.

The prepositions we most frequently use in our writing include:

about   at   by   down   for   from   in   of   on   to   up   with

Here is a partial list of the prepositions. Note that some are more than one word while others such as *but, like* and *since* can serve as another part of speech, depending on the sense of the sentence.

above	beyond	past
according to	but	per
across	despite	prior to
after	during	since
against	except	through
ahead of	in back of	throughout
alongside	in front of	till
along with	in lieu of	toward
amid	in place of	under
among	in spite of	underneath
apart from	instead of	until
around	into	unto
aside from	in view of	up
as of	like	upon
at	near	with
atop	nearby	within
because of	next to	without
before	off	
behind	on top of	
below	out	
beneath	out of	
beside	outside	
besides	owing to	
between	over	

Prepositions and Case

Prepositions link with nouns and pronouns to form *prepositional phrases,* as in *to him and me.* Remember that a pronoun must be in the objective case when it is the object of the preposition (nouns don't have an objective case change). So, it would not be correct to write (or say):

Between you and I, this plan won't work.

The personal pronoun *I* changes to *me* in the objective case; the sentence should begin with:

Between you and me . . .

The same is true for such phrases as:

according to <u>her</u>   for <u>us</u>   to <u>them</u>

Indeed, prepositional phrases always have objects. The English poet John Donne understood this more than 400 years ago when he wrote:

"never send to know for <u>whom</u> the bell tolls . . ."

For a discussion of case, see Chapter 7.

Objects of Prepositions Are Not Subjects!

In addition to proper selection of case, writers should pay attention to subject–verb agreement. Consider this sentence:

Each   **of these bicycles**   **is custom-made.**
(subj.)   (prep. phrase)   (l. v.)

Some writers are tempted to use the plural verb *are,* thinking that the noun *bicycles* is the subject of the sentence. It's not—*bicycles* is the object of the preposition and that is the only role it has in this sentence.

Writers should also avoid excessive or unnecessary use of prepositions. Consider this bloated sentence (prepositional phrases underlined):

<u>In the matter of your convention presentation</u>, I think that it was rambling and confusing.

Using these prepositional phrases creates an unnecessary introduction. This sentence is more concise and direct:

I thought your convention presentation was rambling and confusing.

One final point about prepositions, long a part of grammatical lore: What is this business about not ending a sentence with a preposition?

If it was good enough for the writer of the hit song "Devil with a Blue Dress On," why can't you end with *with, to* or *on?* We feel the same way about this as we do about cracking open fresh eggs with just one hand: Do it as long as you don't make a mess. Scrambling a sentence to move around a preposition can sometimes be awkward:

> **This is a sentence <u>up with which</u> a good writer will not put.**

You're looking for clarity, right? Isn't that what effective writing is *about?*

Conjunctions

Conjunctions are strong, helpful bridges. They help us maintain rhythm and coherence, in addition to creating needed transitions in thought. Let's examine how conjunctions work in sentences. We introduced these ideas in Chapter 4 when we talked about compound and complex sentences. Remember these sentence types are we move through this discussion.

Coordinating and Subordinating Conjunctions

In its primary role, a conjunction coordinates (balances) clauses and phrases of equal weight. A *coordinating conjunction* can link two independent clauses, which could stand alone as separate sentences:

> **The bank approved his loan, <u>but</u> he will need two acceptable co-signers.**

A coordinating conjunction can also link simple words and phrases that are combined to show a relationship:

> **She enjoys baseball <u>and</u> chess.**

> **In a stressful situation, avoid jumping out of the frying pan <u>and</u> into the fire.**

The most common coordinating conjunctions are:

and	but	for	nor	or	yet	while

When conjunctions are used to join clauses of unequal weight (that is, one clause clearly takes precedence and can stand by itself if necessary as a complete sentence), they are called *subordinating conjunctions.*

They often are used to introduce some material or to provide context or counterpoint to the main part of the sentence:

> **Although the bank approved his loan, Tom must find two acceptable co-signers.**

> **I will cancel my appearance <u>unless</u> you can meet my contract demands.**

The most common subordinating conjunctions are:

after	although	as	as if	before	how
if	since	so	through	unless	while

Pay careful attention to use of the subordinating conjunction *as if*. Be wary of substitutes for it; a common error is to use the preposition *like*:

> **It looks <u>like</u> it will snow today.**

Remember that prepositions cannot link a clause—only a phrase or single word. In the previous sentence, a writer has two correct choices:

> **It looks <u>as if</u> it will snow today.**

> **It looks <u>like</u> snow today.**

Correlative Conjunctions

This group of conjunctions, operating in pairs, are called *correlative conjunctions*, because they pair words, phrases and clauses to provide balance:

> **Our vacation was <u>both</u> refreshing <u>and</u> exhausting.**

> **<u>Neither</u> the players <u>nor</u> the coach has met with the media.**

(Note: In *either/or* and *neither/nor* constructions, the noun closest to the verb controls the number of the verb, as in *coach has . . .*)
The most common correlative conjunctions are:

both . . . and	not only . . . but also
either . . . or	whether . . . or
neither . . . nor	

Adverbs That Look Like Conjunctions

Words such as *accordingly, consequently, however, moreover, nevertheless* and *therefore* appear to have linking qualities. However, they are adverbs inserted between two independent clauses to provide transition or a change in flow, which is why they also are called *conjunctive adverbs.* Understanding this should help you punctuate correctly.

Our meeting lacks a quorum; <u>therefore</u>, we will adjourn until next Friday.

(Note the use of the semicolon after *quorum.* We discuss this and other punctuation in Chapter 8.)

Interjections

If a preposition is a low-key part of speech, the *interjection* is easily the most manic. Also called the *exclamation,* it gives emotion and outburst to a sentence. It frequently stands alone and has its own punctuation, the exclamation point:

Wow!

Whew!

and one of our favorites,

Mama mia!

Note that a sentence may have a concluding exclamation point while not including an interjection:

Good luck with your writing!

Chapter 7

Are We in Agreement?

This is a chapter about harmony and balance. It's also about logic and rules. Together, they are keys to improving the flow of your writing by avoiding errors in agreement, case and parallelism.

Let's pinpoint some common errors and then discuss how to avoid them.

When the subject and verb don't agree

Here's a classic error:

The rate of mortgage foreclosures and credit defaults <u>have risen</u> dramatically in the last five years.

The subject of this sentence is the singular noun *rate*, so the verb must match its number—*has risen*.

When the pronoun is in the wrong case

We see this error a lot:

Between <u>you and I</u>, this plan may not succeed.

Pronouns that are the objects of a preposition take the objective case; the sentence should begin with Between *you and me*.

When sentence parts aren't parallel

Note the lack of balance:

Her writing is <u>clear</u> and <u>of a concise nature</u>.

This sentence mixes a precise adjective with a long and unnecessary prepositional phrase. This is more direct and parallel:

Her writing is <u>clear and concise</u>.

In this first section, let's examine subject–verb and antecedent agreement.

Subject–Verb Agreement

This rule is firm:

➤ **A verb must agree with the intended number of its subject.**

This requires that you

1. Identify the actual subject of the sentence and
2. Decide the subject's number—singular or plural.

Knowledge of parts of speech and of sentence elements is vital to mastering subject–verb agreement. For example, you now know that a subject of a sentence can be either a noun or a pronoun. A subject, of course, is the actor or key starting point of a sentence; it directly connects to the action or state of being of a verb.

Let's recall what a subject is *not*.

- It is not the object of a preposition.

  <u>**Each**</u>   <u>**of these photos**</u>   <u>**has**</u> **a special place in her heart.**
  (subj.)   (prep. phrase)   (verb)

  The real subject is *Each*, a pronoun. *Photos*, the object of the preposition *of*, is plural; although it is physically close to the verb, *photos* has no effect on the verb's number.

  Of course, a subject isn't always located at the beginning of a sentence. Look at this next example, which begins with three prepositional phrases:

  <u>**Around the corner and next to that shop with all those delicious**</u>
  <u>**cookies**</u>   <u>**is** a delightful</u>   <u>**bookstore**</u>**.**
  (prep. phrases)   (verb—sing.)   (subject)

Here the subject is at the end of the sentence. If you re-cast the sentence as "A delightful bookstore is . . .," you can see that *bookstore* initiates the idea or activity of this sentence. *Bookstore*, singular, requires a singular verb, *is*.

- It is not the expletive *there* or *here*.

There are several new items on the agenda.
(expl.) (verb)   (subject)

In this usage, an expletive such as *here* or *there* "anticipates" the subject that follows it. That is why such words are sometimes called *anticipatory subjects.* However, they have no standing as a subject and in fact, their use can be a sign of weak or indirect writing. In most cases, it should be obvious that the subject resides after the verb in these constructions.

- It is not the object of a gerund.

Running two marathons is her goal this year.
(gerund as subject)   (verb)

Running, a gerund, is the real subject. As such, *running* is an act, not an action, so it is not a verb; all gerunds are nouns. Remember our discussion on p. 54. *Marathons,* the gerund's object, does not influence the verb's number.

- It is not a predicate nominative.

My biggest concern today   is   health care issues.
          (subject)   (verb—sing.) (pred. nominative)

This an example of how a writer needs to "parse" a sentence to properly connect a subject to its verb. Keep in mind that a predicate nominative, although linked to the subject, does not control the number of the verb. *Concern,* the subject, is singular.

- It is not a phrase that is parenthetical to the true subject.

The welfare bill,   as well as two resolutions on medical aid,
          (subj.)   (parenthetical phrase)

was sent to the subcommittee for hearings.
(verb)

Phrases such as *along with* and *as well as* merely modify the real subject of a sentence. They do not turn that subject into compound or plural, construction.

Now that we have focused on what a subject is *not*, let's turn to what a subject *is*. Let's examine this area in three ways: (1) when the subject is always singular, (2) when the subject is always plural and (3) when it could be both.

The Always-Singular Subject

- **As the subject of a sentence, the pronouns *each, either, anyone, everyone, much, one, no one, nothing* and *someone* always take singular verbs.**

  <u>Each</u> of these wines <u>has</u> a special personality.

  Note that *wines*, the object of the preposition *of,* cannot control the number of the verb.

- **When *each, either, every* or *neither* is used as an adjective, the noun it modifies always takes a singular verb.**

  <u>Every</u> package of chocolate chip cookies <u>has</u> been sold.
      (noun)

- **When used as the subject of a sentence, the personal pronoun *it* always takes a singular verb.**

  As President Harding said, <u>it</u> <u>wasn't</u> his enemies who brought him down; <u>it</u> <u>was</u> his friends.

- **When the phrase *the number* is the subject of a sentence, it always takes a singular verb, no matter the number of the noun in the prepositional phrase.**

  <u>The number</u> of university applications <u>is</u> rising.

  Note that *the* is more definite than *a. The number* implies an organized unit, which we can take to be singular. *A number* refers to an undefined amount; we don't know how many, but we do know that it is more than one. Therefore, this sentence would be correct:

  <u>A number</u> of masked protestors <u>have arrived</u> at the convention site.

- **Definable units of money, measurement, time, organization, food and medical problems always take singular verbs.**

  <u>Two million dollars</u> <u>is</u> still a lot of money.

Three million board feet of redwood **has been destroyed** in the fire.

Consider this large amount of lumber as one giant package.

Six hours of waiting has turned anxious parents into angry customers.

The American Federation of Teachers is opposed to this legislation.

This is a labor organization, a singular unit.

Eight ounces of cold cereal is his usual breakfast.

Measles wears down parents as well as children.

- A singular subject followed by such phrases as *together with* and *as well as* always takes a singular verb because those phrases are merely a modification of their subjects.

  The **tax reduction bill**, together with several amendments, **has been sent** to the president for his signature.

  In some cases, *together with* and *as well as* constructions can be awkward. There could be more direct ways to say the same thing.

- When all parts of a compound subject are singular and refer to the same person or thing, the verb is always singular.

  The **president** and **board chair**   **is**   Christie Newland.
       (compound subj.)   (verb)

In this sentence, both of these titles apply to Christie. A plural verb choice would indicate two people, not one.

The Always-Plural Subject

- When a compound subject is joined by the conjunction *and,* it always takes a plural verb if (1) the subjects refer to different persons or things and (2) the subject cannot be considered a unit.

  Ten Boy Scouts and their scoutmaster are missing in a winter blizzard, according to police.

Although the part of the compound subject closer to the verb is singular, the entire subject still takes a plural verb. If it doesn't hurt sentence flow, placing the plural subject closest to the verb may help.

- **As the subject of a sentence, indefinite pronouns such as** *both,* *few, many* **and** *several* **always take a plural verb.**

  Many <u>**are**</u> **cold, but** <u>**few**</u> <u>**are**</u> **frozen.**

- **Well-recognized foreign plurals require plural verbs if they do not represent a singular unit.**

  Your <u>**criteria**</u> **for grading my report** <u>**are**</u> **unfair.**

  Criteria, the plural form of *criterion,* means "standards or rules." This word has origins in the Greek language. *Phenomena,* the plural of the Greek *phenomenon,* is another example of plural usage.

  Her upper <u>**vertebrae**</u> <u>**were**</u> <u>**crushed**</u> **in the accident.**

  The singular of the Latin-derived *vertebrae* is *vertebra.*

  Other so-called foreign plurals include *alumni/alumnae, data, media, memoranda* and *strata.* Your dictionary is helpful in distinguishing singular from plural.

- **The phrase** *"a number"* **as the subject takes a plural verb because it does not represent a singular or cohesive unit.**

  <u>**A number**</u> **of counterfeit $100 bills** <u>**have appeared**</u> **in downtown stores this week.**

  Because the actual number is unknown, it can't be considered—or treated grammatically—as a unit. Therefore, it takes a plural context.

The Singular or Plural Subject

In a few cases, your decision about verb number will be based on the following guidelines, which fortunately have the force of logic behind them.

- **When a compound subject contains the conjunction** *or* **or** *but* **or contains an** *either . . . or* **or** *neither . . . nor* **correlative, the subject closest to the verb determines the number of the verb.**

  Your <u>**nose rings**</u> **or your** <u>**eyebrow stud**</u>   <u>**has**</u> **to be removed.**
  　　(pl. subj.)　　　　(sing. subj.)　　　　　　(sing. verb)

The writer might have listed nose rings first to indicate a priority. If no such ranking was intended, then it might have been better to put the singular subject first and the plural one second in order to use a plural verb.

Neither <u>Sam</u> nor   <u>his sisters</u> <u>are coming</u> to the reunion.
     (sing. subj.)   (pl. subj.)   (pl. verb)

- **Depending on their meaning in a sentence, collective nouns and certain words that seem plural in form may take a singular or a plural verb.**

Once again, the test of a unit must be applied. If a word indicates that persons or things are working together as an identifiable unit, it must take a singular verb.

Here are some examples of the proper use of the singular verb. We'll follow each example with a plural use when appropriate.

<u>Politics</u> <u>is</u> a topic to avoid at parties.

But note:

The mayor's <u>politics</u> <u>are</u> offensive.

"Practiced political principles" is the meaning here, not the concept of "politics." If you think of this politician as spreading offensive political practices, the meaning becomes clearer.

<u>Acoustics</u> <u>is</u> the scientific study of sound.

But note:

The <u>acoustics</u> in this auditorium <u>are</u> terrible.

Typical collective nouns include *audience, board, group, herd, public* and *team*. Their intended meanings determine whether such words are intended as singular or plural.

- **Pronouns such as *any, none* and *some* and nouns such as *all* and *most* take singular verbs if they refer to a unit or a general quantity. They take plural verbs if they refer to amount or individuals.**

<u>All</u> of the county's <u>farmland</u> <u>is</u> under water.
(unit)

<u>All</u> of the theater <u>receipts</u> <u>are</u> missing.
(amount)

None of the prosecution **witnesses is** expected to testify today. (In this sense, *none* means "not one.")

None of the stolen **goods were** recovered. (The sentence cannot mean that no one good was recovered; it means that "no goods were recovered.")

None is a particularly maddening pronoun and its use causes a great deal of debate. We believe that the word *none* (meaning "not one") is almost always singular. In the following sentence, however, a writer's selection of plural predicate nominative (*women*) makes the intended number of *none* clear (we hope):

None of the indicted stockbrokers **are** women.

• **When a subject is a fraction or when it is a word such as *half, part, plenty* and *rest,* its intended number is suggested by the object of the preposition that follows it.**

Yes, we told you on p. 76 not to let the object of the preposition determine the number of the subject. However, the subject still remains half of, part of, etc., rather than the object of the preposition itself.

Three-fourths of **the new apartment complex is flooded.**
(subj.)   (obj. of prep.)   (verb)

Three-fourths of **payroll checks have been stolen.**
(subj.)   (obj. of prep.)   (verb)

Half of the **rent money**   **is** missing.
(subj.)   (obj. of prep.)   (verb)

Half of the **rent receipts**   **are** missing.
(subj.)   (obj. of prep.)   (verb)

Remember: If your sentence seems awkward when you properly employ a rule of agreement, you may want to rewrite it. The use of *none* and of a number of collective nouns may fall into this category. Clarity is your goal.

Your goal is simple: Identifying subjects by their numbers helps you avoid unnecessary errors. (Quick quiz: Why did we use the singular verb *helps* in the previous sentence? <u>Clue</u>: Remember gerunds?)

Pronoun Reference: The Antecedent Search

As noun substitutes, pronouns can provide helpful economy to sentences. However, writers must be careful not to send readers scrambling to find a pronoun's antecedent. So, what is an antecedent? Simply put, it is a noun, either stated or implied, to which that pronoun refers.

> **The president has threatened a <u>veto</u>, but the senators don't seem to fear <u>it.</u>**

In the above example, the pronoun *it* obviously refers to *veto,* the antecedent. If the writer had intended to say that the senators feared the president, the appropriate pronoun would have been *him.*

Now. To whom does the pronoun *she* refer in the following sentence?

> **Just seconds after the <u>officer</u> told the <u>reporter</u> and the <u>photographer</u> about a bomb scare, she dashed to her car radio.**

In this example, you may think it's logical that *she* refers to the officer, who appears to be the main actor in this sentence. However, logic and clarity don't always rule the day in writing. Without a clear connection between pronoun and antecedent, clarity suffers. If your readers search in vain for a clear reference for the pronoun, you have engaged in a false economy. It's time to for more detail:

> **Just seconds after <u>Officer Tom McCarthy</u> told the reporter and the photographer about a bomb scare, <u>the reporter</u> dashed to her car radio.**

A more difficult problem with pronouns is number and person agreement with antecedents. Consider these sentences:

> **Billy Bob is the only one of Universal Tech's <u>quarterbacks</u> who <u>has</u> <u>made</u> it in pro football.**

In this sentence, the proximity of the noun *quarterbacks* to the relative pronoun *who* might suggest that *who* refers to quarterbacks. In fact, only one quarterback—Billy Bob—has "made it." Hence, we use the singular verb *has made.*

> <u>Calculus</u> is <u>one</u> of those <u>subjects</u> <u>that</u> <u>frustrate</u> him.

A logical analysis of this sentence tells us that there is more than one subject that will frustrate him. Hence, a plural verb is needed. And, yes, in this case the object of a preposition (*subjects*) suggests the number of the relative pronoun *that*, which is the subject of its clause.

The <u>logic</u> of his arguments cannot support <u>itself</u>.

Support of the arguments' logic, not the arguments themselves, is the topic of this sentence. Hence, the singular *logic* is followed by the singular pronoun *itself*, rather than *themselves*.

The sales manager's <u>presentation</u> was flashy, but not many buyers
(antecedent)

were swayed by <u>it</u>.
(pronoun)

Don't be fooled by the possessive *manager's*. Obviously, it modifies *presentation*. Most likely the buyers weren't impressed by the manager either!

<u>Neither</u> of the men has admitted <u>his</u> involvement in the burglary.
(subj.)   (pron.)

As you recall, *neither* takes a singular verb. It follows that the possessive pronoun *his*, referring to *neither*, would have to be singular as well.

Remember: A pronoun must agree with its antecedent in both number and person. Stay consistent and make your references clear. We'll add this piece of advice, though: If following the rules creates a clunky, awkward sentence, rewrite it!

Case: It's All About Relationships

Is it *he, him* or *his?* Is it *who, whom* or *whose?*

These questions deal with *case*, the forms that pronouns take depending on their role in a sentence. Case contributes to sentence harmony by maintaining proper grammatical relationships. These relationships require a change in form for pronouns in three instances and for nouns in only one.

We're fairly confident that you understand the theory of case from your study of other languages. Lots of rules there, too!

We focus primarily on pronouns in this section, with a brief mention of the one area of case that affects the noun. Chapter 8 (on punctuation) features a thorough discussion of nouns in the possessive case.

Pronouns have three forms: *nominative* (also known as *subjective*), *objective* and *possessive*. The relative pronoun *who* and the personal pronoun *she* illustrate these forms.

- Nominative, as the subject of the sentence:

<u>Who</u> ate all the leftovers?

<u>She</u> and Sarah are going to the news conference.

- Objective, as the object or receiver of action:

<u>Whom</u> did the committee select as its treasurer?
Remember—subjects aren't always at the beginning of a sentence. Here, the subject is *committee,* which makes *whom* the direct object of the verb *select.*

This should be an easy assignment for <u>her</u>.
In this sentence, *her* is the object of the preposition *for.*

- Possessive, to modify a noun:

It's uncertain <u>whose</u> essay will win the competition.
Whose (not *who's*), the possessive form of *who,* modifies the noun *essay.*

The expedition leader said the decision to proceed was <u>hers</u>.
Hers (not *her's*) modifies the noun *decision.*

All this seems fairly straightforward, but unfortunately, errors in case usage are distressingly common. For example:

Between you and <u>I</u>, this is going to be a tough game.

Here the writer fails to use objective case *me* as object of preposition *between.*

<u>Her</u> and I are going to the mall today.

Her is in the objective case in this erroneous sentence, yet it is acting as a subject—and so, of course, it must be in the nominative case, *she.* This not-uncommon error reflects a lack of understanding of subject and object in a sentence.

Nouns Change Only in the Possessive Case

Case is less complicated for nouns because they change only in their possessive form. When a noun changes to a possessive, it requires an apostrophe; that is not the case for most pronouns. Here is an example of the correct use of both a noun possessive and the possessive of the pronoun *it:*

> The **mayor's** speech was notable for <u>its</u> warning to tax dodgers.
>   (noun—poss.)   (pronoun—poss.)

Nominative Case

The nominative case relates directly to the subject of a sentence and to any pronoun that refers to that subject. So, a subject, the predicate nominative of a linking verb (p. 48) and a subject's *appositive* (a word, phrase or clause related to the subject) all are in the nominative case.

The nominative case of the personal pronoun includes *I, you, he/she/it, we, you* and *they.* The relative pronoun *who* is also in the nominative case.

Look at these examples, beginning with the noun as subject:

> The **mayor** has asked striking firefighters to return to work.
> The noun *mayor* is used as the subject.

> **She** refuses to change her vote on the tax measure.
> The pronoun *she* is used as the subject.

> It was **he** who called the police.

The pronoun *he* is in the nominative case as the predicate nominative of the linking verb *was.* This sounds pretty formal, we know, but you can understand the meaning that *he* called the police.

> **We** dreamers still have to work.

The pronoun *we* is supplemented or "complemented" by *dreamers,* which makes that noun an appositive. So, both *we* and *dreamers* serve as subject of the sentence. Therefore, *we* is in the nominative case.

The nominative case can be used more than once in a sentence: It appears in every clause. Here is an example of a compound–complex sentence (see p. 29), with pronouns serving as both a subject and a predicate nominative of a linking verb:

> **We** must fight this tyranny at every turn; it is **we** who must
> (subject)   (pred. nominative)

> **fight the oppression of this regime.**

Note that the relative pronoun *who* (in the third clause) refers to *we*. That is why *who* stays in the nominative case, rather than changing to *whom* (objective) or *whose* (possessive).

Use of Nominative with Linking Verbs

It's me.

That's him.

These sentences have been acceptable in colloquial speech for years and so you may be unhappily surprised to learn that they are ungrammatical.

It is I is the correct construction. Don't worry: We are not suggesting that you start talking this way. We are suggesting, however, that writing demands an adherence to grammatical rules that casual speech does not.

The following sentence is precise—and correct:

It was <u>he</u> who refused to testify.

Because the pronoun *he* follows a linking verb, you might be tempted to think it belongs in the objective case. It doesn't. *He* is renaming or further defining the subject, *it*. Keep in mind that such a construction is not a paragon of clear, concise writing; it is more direct to say:

<u>He</u> refused to testify.

or, for more precision and detail:

Harold Thompson, who is facing prosecution in another trial, refused to testify yesterday in the racketeering trial of Samuel Robertson.

Selecting *Who* in Complex Constructions

Although there are pressures to make the *who/whom* choice more liberal, we believe that writers should be precise with these choices. Most of us have little difficulty recognizing the correct use of *who* when it is the simple subject of a simple clause:

The Mountaineers, <u>who</u> were undefeated prior to tonight's game, looked disorganized in their 42-0 loss.

But when the true subject *who* is separated from its verb, the possibility of case error increases. Note this incorrect example:

> **The adviser <u>whom</u> the president said had leaked the confidential report has resigned.**

Whom is not the object of *the president said*. The sentence can be analyzed this way to show why the correct choice is *who*:

> **The adviser . . . has resigned** (*independent clause*)
>
> **who . . . had leaked** (*dependent clause*)
>
> **the president said** (*parenthetical information to provide a source*)

As you recall from our earlier discussion, you must match the number of the subject to the proper verb. You must also select the right case if the subject is a pronoun:

> **<u>Who</u> did he say won the race?**

Who won the race, he did say.

Who/Whom in Prepositional Phrases

A pronoun in a prepositional phrase is always in the objective case because it is generally the object of a preposition, as in "To whom did you wish to speak?" But there are exceptions when a preposition controls an entire clause.

Sometimes a preposition will be a linking device, much like a conjunction or a relative pronoun. Look to the clause that follows to determine whether the pronoun is acting as subject or object:

> **The radio station will award $5,000 in cash <u>to whoever</u> submits**
> (independent clause)   (pronoun in nom. case)
>
> **the first correct answer to its "mystery question."**

Although the object of a preposition takes the objective case in a simple phrase, the presence of an entire clause connected to the preposition changes the rules. All clauses need a subject, either stated or implied. Hence, we use *whoever* in the preceding sentence as the subject of the clause (using the preposition *to* as a linking device).

You can be more direct, however, by starting the sentence with *whoever*:

> **<u>Whoever</u> answers the radio station's "mystery question" first will win $5,000.** (Note that we trimmed eight words from the original!)

Here's another example:

He discussed the end of the world <u>with whoever</u> would listen.

Note the two clauses:

<u>He</u> discussed/<u>whoever</u> would listen.

Case in *Than* Clauses

Remember our discussion of comparatives in Chapter 6? Case is an important component in certain clauses when these comparisons are being made, as in this sentence:

He is smarter <u>than I</u>.

Than is frequently a conjunction. As you'll recall, conjunctions connect whole clauses and phrases. Because the second clause in a comparison is often implied, you must mentally complete the thought to determine proper case:

He is smarter than I (am smart).

In this sentence, the nominative case *I* is required because that pronoun is the subject of the implied clause. *Than* can also be a preposition, however, as in this example:

There is no better snowboarder than <u>her</u>.

You can see that *than* is not a conjunction here because in this sentence the comparison ends with *her*. Remember that you can give comparative and superlative degrees to adjectives and adverbs, but not to nouns. So, it doesn't make sense to complete the thought:

There is no better snowboarder <u>than she is a snowboarder</u>.

Tacking on *than she is a snowboarder* doesn't make sense, because the writer is actually expressing a superlative, not a comparative.

Yes, this is another example of why good writers must master the parts of speech!

Objective Case

Personal pronouns (*I, you, he, she, it, we, you, they*) and the relative and interrogative pronoun *who* also change form when used in the objective case.

	Personal Pronouns	Relative or Interrogative Pronoun
Singular:	me, you, him/her/it	whom
Plural:	us, you, them	whom

The Personal Pronoun in the Objective Case

Personal pronouns in the objective case have the following uses:

- As the direct or indirect object of a verb or verbal:

  Oprah accompanied <u>him</u> to the premiere.
                   (dir. obj.)

  County commissioners gave <u>her</u> a   <u>10 percent raise</u>.
                       (indir. obj.) (dir. obj.)

  Giving <u>Tommy and her</u> all those gifts was a big mistake.
       (object of verbal)

  Giving Tommy and her all those gifts is a gerund phrase (a verbal) that acts as the complete subject of the sentence. *Tommy and her* is the object of the gerund *Giving*. It receives the so-called action of the gerund, however and therefore must be in the objective case. We can understand any confusion about this—how can a subject have an object? In the "Tommy" example, it might help to temporarily replace *her* with *them,* to show that it would sound even more incorrect to instead write "Giving Tommy and *they.* . . ." In any case, remember that pronouns that follow a gerund in its phrase must be in the objective case.

- **As the object of a preposition:**

  <u>Between</u> <u>you and me</u>, he won't be around here for long.
  (prep.)   (obj. of prep.)

  Tommy says there is no better lacrosse player than <u>her</u>.
  (preposition and object)

  Remember that while adjectives and adverbs can be compared, nouns can't.

- With an appositive that is in the objective case:

  Guards dragged <u>us reporters</u> out of the convention hall.
  The pronoun *us* and its appositive *reporters* function as one unit—the direct object.

She gave the cleaning job <u>to us students</u>.
The pronoun *us* and appositive *students* are part of the object of the preposition *to*. This construction does seem awkward, but the grammar is correct.

The Proper Use of *Whom*

The relative and interrogative pronoun *who* changes to *whom* in the objective case. The *who/whom* choice is one of the more confusing ones in grammar, but it becomes easier if you carefully analyze the sentence. Let's look at a few examples.

<u>Whom</u> did the grand jury indict today?
(dir. obj.)   (subj.)

Remember that a direct object doesn't always follow the subject and verb. It can appear before the subject, as in the preceding example. To make the *who/whom* choice easier, mentally reorder the sentence as a statement rather than a question:

The grand jury did indict <u>whom</u> today.

Now consider this sentence with two clauses:

She is the only candidate <u>whom</u> the union supports.

First, identify the two subjects, two verbs, one predicate nominative and one direct object in this sentence:

<u>She</u>   is the only <u>candidate</u>/   the <u>union</u> <u>supports</u> <u>whom</u>
(subj.) (verb)   (pred. nom.)   (subj.) (verb)   (dir. object)

So, we have two clauses—one independent, one dependent. The second clause as rewritten clearly shows *whom* (objective case) as a direct object.

However, here's an issue of conciseness to consider: It would be even smoother (and equally correct) to write:

She is the only candidate the union supports.

Another example:

Students can't agree on <u>whom to send</u> to the dean to present
                    (object of verbal—an infinitive)

their demands.

(See p. 77 for information on objects of verbals.)
    So—do you know whom to contact in the event of a grammatical crisis?

Possessive Case

Personal pronouns have these possessive forms:

my	mine	our	ours	your	yours
his	her	hers	its	their	theirs

As you can see, an apostrophe is not used with personal pronouns. However, some indefinite pronouns, such as *another, anyone, everyone, everybody, one* and *someone* do require an apostrophe in their possessive forms.

Here are two examples, all connected with the noun *book*:

Is it <u>your</u> book?

Yes, it <u>is</u> mine.

And note the punctuation, however, with the indefinite pronoun *someone:*

This must be <u>someone's</u> book!

"Possessing" a Gerund

When a personal pronoun modifies a gerund in a sentence, the possessive case is used to show possession or ownership by the gerund, which always acts as a noun.

I certainly understand <u>his</u>   <u>supporting the company's budget</u>
                        (pron.) (gerund phrase as direct object)

<u>priorities</u>.

In this sentence, *his* modifies the gerund *supporting,* which is part of the direct object. Because a gerund is a noun, it is necessary to use its pronoun in the possessive case. The rule makes sense because nouns are linked with possessive pronouns to show modification.

The *Who/Whose* Relationship

The relative pronoun *who* also has a possessive form: *whose.* It does not take an apostrophe even though it modifies a noun:

I can't decide <u>whose</u> exhibit should win top honors.

The interrogative pronoun *who* also uses *whose* as its possessive form:

<u>Whose</u> film will be screened tomorrow?

Some writers struggle with the *who's/whose* distinction. Like *it's, who's* is a *contraction*—a compression of two words (in this case, *who is*). It is a subject and a verb, not a possessive. If you can read *to whom* into a sentence with your *whose* selection, you're on the right track:

Whose tofu is this?
(To whom does this tofu belong?)

Who's cooking the tofu tonight?
(Who is cooking the tofu tonight?)

More About Contractions

Contractions can be troublesome with personal pronouns as well. Some of the most common errors involve misuse of *its/it's, your/you're* and *their/they're*. Note these correct usages for this trio:

The price of oil has hit its highest level in five years.
(possessive)

Voters believe it's time for a change.
(contraction of *it* and *is*)

Your complimentary tickets are at the box office.
(possessive)

You're going to love this new musical!
(contraction of *you* and *are*)

Their poetry readings will be repeated next weekend.
(possessive)

Paul and Paula say they're ready to take the plunge.
(contraction of *they* and *are*)

You can add the expletive *there* to the *their/they're* confusion:

The junta said there would be no elections this year.

Be sure to keep this sentence in mind as you consider these *they're/there/their* choices:

They're convinced there are no obstacles to their success.

We hope you can see how case is connected to agreement—and to harmony. Proper use of case adds clarity to your writing. It reflects a polish, an attention to detail. This area may take time to master, but it's worth the effort!

Parallel Structure

Harmony and order in writing go beyond subject-verb and antecedent agreement and case issues. Parallel structure is also an important component of this area of grammar. A sentence is considered *parallel* when its various units are in grammatical balance. When a sentence lacks parallelism, its focus softens and its rhythm falters.

Parallelism is both a grammatical concern and a stylistic issue. (You'll read more about parallelism and style in Chapter 10.) For now, let's examine the most common of these problems. Note how each of these errors injures harmony and order.

Common Errors in Parallelism

1. **Creating a series that is unbalanced and awkward**

   He enjoys <u>football</u>, <u>movies</u> and <u>driving around in his dune buggy</u>.

   Why is this sentence unbalanced? It contains three nouns in a series, but the third noun is a verbal (gerund). It throws off the meter; it lacks parallel structure. This sentence could easily regain its rhythm by using three gerund phrases:

   He enjoys <u>playing football</u>, <u>watching movies</u> and <u>riding his dune buggy</u>.

   In the next example, an adjective clashes with a prepositional phrase in a brief series:

   Your essay is <u>compelling</u> and <u>of the utmost thoughtfulness</u>.
             (adjective)   (prepositional phrase)

   Using two adjectives with the linking verb makes it parallel:

   Your essay is <u>compelling</u> and <u>thoughtful</u>.
             (adj.)   (adj.)

2. **Mixing verbals**

   Generally speaking, different verbals don't co-exist peacefully in the same sentence, as in

   This is another example of selectively <u>using favorable statistics</u>
             (gerund phrase)

   and then <u>to write a report</u> around that biased selection.
         (infinitive phrase)

Here, the gerund and infinitive phrases conflict. The sentence would be parallel if the writer stuck with gerunds. Note how the rhythm seems more natural in this version:

This is another example of selectively <u>using favorable statistics</u> and <u>writing a report</u> around that biased selection.

3. **Unnecessarily changing voice**

Verbs can have active or passive voices. Writers choose a voice according to the need to have the subject perform the action or to have it acted upon. Generally, it is best to be consistent in voice. Shifting voice can disrupt the flow of a construction, as in this example:

Burglars <u>stole</u> all the jewelry, but the silverware and china
    (active voice)

<u>were not taken</u> by them.
(passive voice)

This awkward sentence uses two subjects and switches unnecessarily from active to passive voice. It is much simpler to stay with one subject and one voice:

Burglars <u>stole</u> all the jewelry but <u>left</u> the silverware and china.

Both verbs are in the active voice now. Another benefit of this change is that the sentence is more concise.

4. **Unnecessarily changing subjects**

<u>One</u> never should argue with a referee; <u>people</u> should know that.

Besides creating a stilted construction with both singular and plural subjects, the writer is also wasting words. The sentence would read better with one focused subject:

<u>People</u> should know never to argue with a referee.

5. **Unnecessarily changing tenses**

In general, verb tenses should agree within a sentence or a paragraph. But it's unreasonable to think that you cannot shift verb tenses in the same sentence or paragraph. In fact, you may need to change tenses to show correct sequence and historical context:

Although she <u>was</u> a reserve guard last year, Lizzie now <u>rides</u> the
           (past tense)   (pres. tense)

bench only after her deadly three-pointers <u>have given</u> her
                                      (pres. perfect tense)

basketball team a comfortable edge.

This is a correct tense sequence. The two shifts make sense because they permit us to understand a chronology. Words such as *although* and *after* help us shift tense smoothly. That smooth flow, however, does not exist in this sentence:

Billy <u>is</u> a poor basketball player and no amount of practice <u>was going</u> to make him any better.

This is a confusing shift. The time-warping verbs cause the reader to lose a sense of chronology.

Remember that tense agreement is an attempt to preserve historical sequence and context. Avoid abrupt and illogical changes in tense. Above all, be consistent.

A Final Note

Yes, this has been a long chapter! We hope you will refer to it often, because harmony and agreement are key to clear, direct and honest writing.

Chapter 8

Punctuation: Graceful Movements, Confident Stops.

What is it about punctuation that prompts some authors to write thoughtful and witty books about it?

Well, we'd like to think that these folks—people such as Lynne Truss, who wrote "Eats, Shoots & Leaves," are fascinated by the coded messages that our punctuation marks send to readers. Indeed, it's amazing how a series of tiny dots and dashes and a variety of intuitive strokes can help direct our reading and comprehension.

We do know these folks understand that proper punctuation brings order and coherence to writing and that its misuse will sabotage it. Just as composers use a system of marks to note the speed and rhythm of music, writers use punctuation. It provides a system of stops and starts, of controlled pauses and of forward motion. The right amount of punctuation works quietly in the background, with grace and elegance, to clarify ideas and determine content exactly as the writer intends. Indeed, punctuation marks establish a proper relationship between words and their meter, guiding the reader from one idea to the next.

Some Basic Guidelines

Let's begin with a quick overview of our punctuation system.

- A *period* ends a sentence.

- A *comma*, however, creates a short pause within a sentence.

- A *semicolon* slows the reader within the sentence; it isn't powerful enough to signal a complete stop.

- A *colon* announces the following: a list, a fragment, a sentence or a quotation.

- A *dash*—maligned by purists but used frequently in journalism—creates a more abrupt break than the comma.

- *Quotation marks* are dedicated "record keepers." They announce somebody's exact words, signify titles of short works and indicate nicknames, among other things.

- A *hyphen* is well-used in our language. It joins modifiers that belong together.

- An *apostrophe* can't be praised enough for being grammar's helper with subject–verb contractions and with the possessive case.

- An *ellipsis* warns us . . . something is missing.

- *Parentheses* (they look like this) are used to clarify a point or add an aside without (we hope) hampering sentence rhythm. We'll also include a discusion [**sic**] of brackets in that section.

- Do you really need an explanation of the *question mark?*

- If you do, we shall indicate our astonishment with another way to end a sentence—the *exclamation point!*

Punctuation marks prevent confusion and create rhythm. Although writers may debate their usage, there are logical, consistent rules to follow. Here we go!

Period

The period is the "closer." It signals that the action of one sentence has stopped before the next begins. Imagine how confusing sentences would be without periods:

> **An eight-car collision stopped traffic for seven hours on the northbound side of Interstate 5 near Portland snow and ice on the overpass caused two drivers to lose control of their vehicles transportation officials say the debris will be cleared by tomorrow**

Proper periods would have created three simple, concise sentences here. Without them, we have trouble sorting out concepts as well as complete thoughts.

The period has two main uses in writing.

1. Use a period to end a sentence that is neither interrogative (?) nor exclamatory (!).

   His boss persuaded Nathan to take a vacation.

2. Use a period to create certain abbreviations and to indicate decimals.

   The $2.5-million package arrived C.O.D. at the home office.

Abbreviations are space savers and periods help signal these shortcuts. Not all abbreviations, however, require periods. Acronyms (abbreviations without punctuation, which are pronounceable words—for example, *UNESCO* and *AIDS*), names of certain organizations and government agencies (*NBC, UAW, FBI* and *CIA*) and abbreviations of technical words (*mph* and *rpm*)—do not require periods. To learn which abbreviations use periods and which ones don't, consult a dictionary or your publication's stylebook.

When Not to Use a Period

Do not use a period outside quotation marks or outside an ending parenthesis if the information forms a complete sentence.
Note these correct uses of periods:

The defendant replied, "I did not see him on the night of the murder."

The incumbent has a memorable history of vetoes. (She rejected more than 75 bills in the last legislative session.)

Comma

The comma is crucial to sentence rhythm and sense. A sentence stumbles with too many commas; with too few, it outpaces comprehension. Let's examine proper use of the comma and then look at some of its inappropriate uses. **Note:** The comma is notorious for its misuse, so please examine this section carefully!

➤ **Use a comma to separate two independent clauses connected by a coordinating conjunction.**

   The senators approved the health bill, but they rejected several of its amendments.

Coordinating conjunctions include *or, and, nor, but, yet* and *so.* A comma is placed before the coordinating conjunction to link two independent clauses that can stand alone as complete sentences. Journalistic style favors dropping the comma if both independent clauses of the sentence are short and uncomplicated (with no long prepositional or dependent clauses, for instance) and meaning is unambiguous:

Wilkins lost a shoe but kept running.

➤ **Use a comma to set off long introductory clauses and phrases and some shorter clauses and phrases that would be confusing without it.**

After three weeks of daily one-hour visits to the hot springs, he had cured his problem of chronic cold feet.

To Tom Hanks, Oscar is a familiar name.

You can omit the comma for some short clauses and phrases if no run-on occurs in the sentence—that is, if the meaning of the introductory segment remains distinct from the rest of the sentence. For example, a comma would be unnecessary here:

In winter we often dream of Hawaii.

➤ **Use commas to set off nonrestrictive (nonessential) clauses, phrases and modifiers from the rest of the sentence.**

Nonrestrictive (Nonessential)

Nonrestrictive clauses, phrases and words require commas because they are incidental to the sentence. That is, those elements could be removed from the sentence with little if any loss to meaning or context.

The electronic games company, <u>which was founded in 1998,</u> is shifting most manufacturing work to three overseas locations.

Sentence meaning remains the same when the underlined subordinate clause is removed. (The company's founding date is not essential to understanding its overseas work.) The underlined phrase is called an *appositive*—a word or phrase that further defines the word or phrase that precedes it. It is not essential to the sentence but adds information and context.

> **The incumbent, <u>who travels on her own plane</u>, will visit nine senior centers in three states this weekend to talk about medical insurance.**

Any other nonessential, amplifying pieces of information could have been substituted for the subordinated clause, such as *who depends on the senior citizen vote*. The existing clause could be removed and an understandable, complete sentence remains.

Restrictive (Essential)

Clauses, phrases or words that are essential to the meaning of the sentence are called *restrictive*. They need not be set off with commas from the rest of the sentence. Notice how this example differs from the nonrestrictive constructions:

> **The three men <u>who hijacked a city bus</u> died when they crashed it into a police blockade.**

The subordinate clause *who hijacked a city bus* limits the meaning of the sentence. One test to determine restrictive meaning is to read the sentence without the clause in question. If you find yourself trying to fill in the meaning of the sentence, that clause is essential. Consider the preceding example:

> **The three men died when they crashed it into a police blockade.**

This clearly requires its accompanying clause to make the sentence more complete, more understandable. (What men? What did they do?) For this reason the clause *who hijacked a city bus* should not be set off by commas.

Here's another example:

> **The water main <u>that broke last night</u> flooded the entire southeast side of the city.**

Not all water mains broke last night. Because the subordinate clause *that broke last night* is essential to the meaning of the sentence, no commas should be used.

Note that in a restrictive clause the pronoun *that* is used instead of *which*. If the clause is not essential to the meaning of the sentence but simply provides added detail, use *which* and set off the clause with commas. (See the entry in Part 2 for *that/which/who*.)

➤ **Use commas to separate items in a series.**

Samantha stuffed seven pebbles, three cookies and two frogs in her pocket.

Journalistic writing favors this rule for use of the *serial comma*: When the last item in a series is connected by a coordinating conjunction, the comma should be omitted before that conjunction. This is especially true when the series is short or uncomplicated. If the series is made up of more than simple adjective–noun combinations, however, the comma can be inserted before the conjunction to eliminate confusion:

Union officials this morning said they would bargain vigorously for the right to negotiate pension fund investments, for an expanded process of grievance procedures and for binding arbitration of all contract matters not settled within 90 days of the start of negotiations.

Although rare in journalistic writing, the serial comma appears more frequently in formal composition, novels and academic texts.

➤ **Use commas to separate coordinate adjectives.**

When a noun is preceded by a string of adjectives, apply this two-part test to determine whether those modifiers are of equal rank and need to be separated by commas: Can you use these adjectives interchangeably? Can you successfully insert the conjunction *and* between them and have the sentence make sense? If so, these adjectives are coordinate and require a comma.

Given this test, the modifiers in the following sentence need a comma:

Her talk show turned into a frantic, irrational gabfest.
You can read "frantic *and* irrational" into this sentence, so the comma is necessary.

Meteorologists forecast another cold, dreary Midwestern night.
You can read "cold *and* dreary" into this sentence. They modify *Midwestern night* equally, so they are considered coordinate. The comma is necessary.

But what about this sentence?

Meteorologists forecast another <u>cold Midwestern</u> night.
You can't read "cold *and* Midwestern night" into this construction, so the adjectives need not be separated by a comma. In fact, *cold* actually modifies *Midwestern night*.

➤ **Use commas to set off parenthetical expressions.**

A *parenthetical expression* is an addition or "aside" to the main thought. It gives extra information without disrupting the flow of the sentence:

> **The first day of the bird-watching season, <u>often a flurry of activity</u>, was unusually quiet this year.**

> **The snow, <u>encrusted with a thin skin of ice</u>, crunched lightly under her boots.**

The underlined phrase could be put in parentheses, but that might be too formal and stilted. Commas create shorter pauses while maintaining the flow.

➤ **Use commas when the absence of a pause can cause confusion.**

> **<u>For the senator</u>, going fishing for three hours is vacation enough.**

> **<u>Sitting below sea level</u>, the city obviously needed a complicated system of sump pumps.**

In the preceding examples, it would be a false economy to waive comma use. The pause is necessary for clarity.

➤ **Use commas to set off participial phrases that modify some part of the independent clause.**

> **The Senate adjourned today, <u>having defeated an attempt to</u>**
> (participial phrase modifies *Senate*)
> **<u>extend the session</u>.**

Various stylebooks list many other examples of comma use (and nonuse). Some may be obvious to you:

- To separate numbers in the thousands and above: 7,240 entries.

- To distinguish a city from its state: He lives in Cleveland, Ohio.

- To separate direct address from a sentence: McGee, will you please clean out that closet?

Comma Misuse

Comma misuse causes rhythm problems in sentences. The comma is designed to improve the flow of prose, not impede it, but poor construction and comma overuse often combine to create staccato passages characterized by disconnected parts and sounds. Writers and editors must be careful to avoid excessive use of the comma. Here are some helpful rules.

▶ **Do not use a comma to separate two independent clauses that are not joined by a coordinating conjunction.**

Violating this rule produces the *comma splice,* one of the most common errors in punctuation. It looks like this:

Voters rejected a proposal for a new library, they have signaled interest in a less costly facility.

Using a comma to link two independent clauses (which could stand alone as separate sentences) offers an inadequate pause in thought and causes a *run-on sentence.* We recommend that you either break the sentence in two or do one of the following:

1. Use a semicolon to link the clauses.

   Voters rejected a proposal for a new library; they have signaled interest in a less costly facility.

2. Use a coordinating conjunction with a comma.

   Voters rejected a proposal for a new library, but they have signaled interest in a less costly facility.

▶ **Do not use a comma to separate a compound predicate.**

A compound predicate (two or more verbs that serve the same subject) does not need a comma because it is part of the same clause:

The <u>judge</u>   <u>fined</u> the men $500 and   <u>ordered</u> them to perform
   (subj.)   (verb #1)   (verb #2)

40 hours of community service.

As you can see, "The judge" has performed two actions within the same clause, making this construction a simple sentence.

▶ **Do not use a comma to introduce a subordinate clause.**

The use of a comma before *because* is one of the biggest offenders. *Because* is a *subordinating conjunction*—it introduces a dependent clause:

The studio executive rejected the movie idea because she wanted a guaranteed blockbuster.

No comma is needed here because the conjunction does not coordinate equal clauses. (Did you notice the lack of a comma in the previous sentence as well?) That is why *and, but* and *or* often require commas; they are called *coordinating conjunctions* because they link clauses of equal weight. (See "Conjunctions" in Chapter 6 for a list of conjunctions that do not coordinate.)

Note that if the subordinate clause is used at the beginning of the sentence, a comma is required:

Because he wanted a guaranteed blockbuster, the studio executive rejected the movie idea.

Can you detect a difference in rhythm between *because* at the beginning of a sentence and *because* in the middle of it?

➤ **Do not use a comma to separate a subject from its predicate or object.**

This is one of the most common errors made by inexperienced writers. Sentences with restrictive clauses, phrases or words between the subject and the predicate sometimes confuse writers into putting a comma before the predicate. Even relatively simple subjects fall prey to this error.

The dangerous inmate, escaped today in a delivery truck.

Knowing rules of grammar, will ensure your credibility as a writer.

In the preceding examples, the comma is unnecessary. Always be sure the subject of the sentence has a clear, unobstructed route to its predicate when restrictive (essential) elements mark the pathway.

➤ **Do not use a comma to separate a noun or a pronoun from its reflexive.**

A *reflexive* is any of the "self" pronouns (*myself, himself*) used to intensify or accent the noun or pronoun preceding it. A comma is not needed to set off the reflexive:

The coach himself will kick off the first ball of the season.

➤ **Do not use a comma between a word and a phrase that amplifies it if it will create a "false series."**

This sentence, as punctuated, is bound to cause confusion:

> **Rescuers discovered seven bodies, four office workers, two firefighters and one police officer.**

Unless the writer meant to say that 14 people were discovered and that seven of them were dead, the comma use after *bodies* is wrong. A colon or dash would be more effective in separating the two ideas:

> **Rescuers discovered seven bodies—those of four office workers, two firefighters and one police officer.**

➤ **Do not use a comma to precede a partial quotation.**

> **The mayor says his opponent is "a rat dressed in weasel's clothing."**

No comma is needed after *is* because the quoted material is the predicate nominative of the verb *is*. Because the quoted material depends on the rest of the sentence for its context, that material should not be set off by a comma.

If the quotation is a full sentence, however, it should be preceded by a comma:

> **The counselor said, "The camper with the best-made bed is excused from kitchen detail for a week."**

Remember: Good writers use commas for clarity and meter. If your sentences contain a clutter of commas, take heed. Perhaps the sentences are too long and too busy. There is grace and order in simplicity and conciseness.

Semicolon

The *semicolon* indicates a longer break than a comma but not the full stop of a period. It is more inflexible than the comma or the period and carries a grammatical formality that some writers like to avoid. For this reason, perhaps, the semicolon is rarely used in media writing.

Writers sometimes opt for two separate and shorter sentences rather than joining two independent clauses with a semicolon. They may choose to break up a series of thoughts normally punctuated by semicolons to avoid long clauses and phrases. They equate the full stop with simplicity and clarity. But the semicolon works when the writer wants the chime of one idea to fall away for a beat before the next rings out—a lingering that is absent with a period.

Here are four guidelines to help you properly employ the semicolon.

➤ **Use a semicolon to join independent clauses not connected by a coordinating conjunction.**

Note: This is a proper rule, but there are more graceful ways to present coordinated or "equal" thoughts.

Sarah will contest the election <u>results</u>; <u>she</u> says she will accept the outcome of a "properly supervised" recount.

If those two clauses had been connected with the coordinating conjunction *but,* a comma would have sufficed:

. . . election results, but she says she . . .

Some writers prefer the use of the coordinating conjunction because it gives more specific direction to the reader. Others would look at these two long clauses and break them into two sentences.

Words like *however, moreover, nevertheless* and *therefore* are not coordinating conjunctions. They are *conjunctive adverbs.* They do not perform the linking function of a conjunction and cannot coordinate clauses of equal rank. When a conjunctive adverb separates two independent clauses, a semicolon is required.

I understand the main points of your argument; however, I don't agree with your conclusion.

As we mentioned in the "Comma Misuse" section, using a comma here to separate the two clauses would create a comma splice.

Before we continue, we must issue a word of caution: We urge you to avoid using a semicolon to connect two independent clauses, even though it is grammatically correct. If you must use it, be sure that the two clauses actually need some connection and that they wouldn't be better off as separate sentences. For example, don't write:

The car slid off the narrow roadway into a muddy embankment; police arrived hours later to find that no one had survived.

when you could write:

> **The car slid off the narrow roadway into a muddy embankment. When police arrived hours later, they found three bodies in the overturned vehicle.**

As you can see, merging two strong thoughts into one construction can be economical, but it may not give you the completeness and creativity that two sentences can. Think of the semicolon as a clarifier, not an economizer.

➤ **Use a semicolon to link more than two independent clauses in a series.**

Semicolons are needed in compound sentences when more than two independent clauses are linked in a series—even when the last part of the series is connected by a coordinating conjunction:

> **We will find proper funding for our <u>schools; we</u> will not abandon our commitment to greater access to higher <u>education; and</u> we will press for a new income tax measure to fully fund our programs.**

➤ **Use a semicolon to separate internally punctuated independent clauses joined by a coordinating conjunction.**

When you punctuate a clause internally with commas, you can't use a comma to separate that clause from another. A semicolon is needed to create a more abrupt stop:

> **The city council has approved the proposed levy, which will go to voters in May; but the mayor has indicated that she will campaign against it.**

➤ **Use a semicolon to set off parts of a series that also contain commas.**

> **Survivors of the early-morning crash are Stan Sarsgaard, 42, of San Francisco; his brother-in-law, Martin Fedler, 40, of Boise, Idaho; and their guide, Deb Walters, 30, of Fairbanks, Alaska.**

The main function of the semicolon in this example is organization. It is helpful because it clarifies boundaries in a series better than a comma so that the parts remain distinct.

To recap: The semicolon is generally used in more formal writing. However, in all forms, the semicolon creates a more distinct break in thought without bringing the sentence to a complete stop. It is essential in joining independent clauses that are not connected with a coordinating conjunction.

Colon

The *colon* presents ideas with a flourish: It announces. It ushers in complete sentences, lists, quotations and dialogue.

Proper Use of the Colon

When the colon is used to introduce a lengthy sentence, the first word of that sentence should be capitalized:

> **This is what reporters apparently agree on: The governor is adamant about not appointing lobbyists to state advisory committees.**

When a colon is used to introduce a word, phrase or clause that is not a lengthy sentence, the first word following the colon should not be capitalized:

> **In the movie classic "The Graduate," Dustin Hoffman learned the one word that would guarantee a successful future: *plastics*.**

> **Here is another thing you should never do: hang-glide in Somalia.**

Note these other functions of the colon:

➤ **Use a colon to introduce a quotation that is longer than one sentence.**

> **The judge eyed the defendant and told him in words dripping with disdain: "Your disgusting conduct in my courtroom has mocked everything that is justice. I now invite you to accept our jail hospitality for the next 90 days."**

➤ **Use a colon to end a sentence that introduces a quotation in the next paragraph.**

> **Here is the text of the president's speech:**

> **"Good evening, my fellow Americans. I appear before you tonight to report on the state of our nation. . . ."**

➤ **Use colons to show the text of questions and answers.**

This can take two forms:

Q: And then what happened?

A: She put the meat cleaver down and called the cops.

Sneed: **Senator, I have done my best to contribute to this discussion.**

Ervin: **Somebody told me once when I was representing a case; he said, "You put up the best possible case for a guilty client!"**

As you can see, the colon eliminates the need for quotation marks unless the dialogue itself quotes other material.

➤ **Use colons to show times and citations.**

Galen ran the mile in 3:53:42.

Psalm 101:5 warns of the danger of slander.

When Not to Use the Colon

➤ **Do not use a colon when introducing a short list without the words the *following*.**

The voters have elected Larry, Curly and Moe.

➤ **Do not use a colon when introducing a direct quotation of one sentence or less. A comma is sufficient.**

Bogie wanted to tell her, "I'll see you when I see you."

➤ **Do not use a colon to separate an independent clause from a prepositional phrase that begins with *including*.**

Please have all of the junior executives report to me, including that no-good Billy Smithers.

The proper punctuation mark to use before *including* is a comma.

Dash

The primary uses of a *dash* are to change direction and create emphasis. Journalists, however, can be rightfully accused of using the dash to excess or of using it when a comma, a colon or parentheses might be more skillfully employed. We believe that the dash should be used sparingly because it is a startling mark of punctuation. If used too often, it loses its impact. Let's look at the two main uses of the dash in all writing.

➤ **Use a dash to end a sentence with a surprising or ironic element.**

> **The tall, distinguished-looking man entered the country with a valid passport, two pieces of leather luggage, an antique Leica camera around his neck—and 16 ounces of uncut heroin in the heels of his alligator boots.**

A comma here would not be as effective in changing meter and warning the reader of a break in thought. Using this reasoning, you would not want a dash in this less surprising sentence:

> **The ice cream parlors competed for customers with discount coupons, free sundae dishes and generous samples.**

That series contains ordinary, unsurprising information. Adding a dash would give the sentence false drama.

➤ **Use dashes to set off a long clause or a phrase that is in apposition to the main clause, when it makes the information clearer and more distinctive.**

> **The closing ceremonies of the Olympics—a dazzling spectacle of unabashed self-promotion—set off an explosion of self-congratulations at the network.**

A comma usually suffices with a shorter appositive:

> **Barry Nelson, heir to the Smoothware fortune, is not noted for his philanthropy.**

Dashes could also be used to set off both parenthetical expressions and a series of items in the middle of a sentence. We recommend restraint with these uses, however and that you concentrate on the two main uses of the dash. The dash should be used only infrequently— make sure your reader will notice it!

Quotation Marks

Quotation marks have several identities. They offer truthfulness when they give a faithful reproduction of what was said. They can also be a weapon that belittles. For example, what impressions do quotation marks create in these sentences?

> **"I believe we can correct this situation," the accountant said.**
> This seems to be a straightforward recounting of what was said.

> **The company spokesperson said her firm could correct the "situation."**
> Placement of quotation marks around *situation* makes us suspicious. What is so strange about this so-called situation? The quotation marks alert us to the possibility of another meaning.

Let's look at the appropriate use of quotation marks in writing and then see how other marks of punctuation are used with quotations.

Proper Use of Quotation Marks

➤ **Use quotation marks to enclose direct quotations and to capture dialog.**

> **"Next quarter's earnings will tell us whether we will survive this economic story or declare bankruptcy by the end of the year," company president Bill Barnett declared.**

> **"So, did you actually see a weapon?" the defense attorney asked.**

> **"No. Well, I thought I did," the defendant replied.**

> **"I'll take that as a no."**

Avoid the unnecessary use of partial quotations. Sometimes a paraphrase will do. So, instead of:

> **Board President Gloria Olson said completion of a new power plant is necessary "to maintain our high bond rating."**

you might write:

Completion of a new power plant is necessary to preserve the board's high bond rating, according to Board President Gloria Olson.

The partial quotation works best if the language or style of what is quoted is distinctive or colorful. For example, it would be difficult to paraphrase this effectively:

Sen. Paul Nelson, D-Hood River, compared the higher-education system to a dinosaur that's "going to fall in the tar pits and become a fossil."

Avoid putting quotation marks around single words if their use results in an inaccurate representation. We generally put these marks around unfamiliar terms on first reference, around slang words and around words used sarcastically or ironically. But don't overdo it!

A wage freeze is in effect.

but

His luck ran into a "freeze" at the track.

Jericho Truett's dreams are a $10-million business.

but

Tom Anderson's "dreams" have ruined those of elderly investors who spent their life savings on his worthless pyramid scheme.

➤ **Use quotation marks for titles of lectures, movies, operas, plays, poems, songs, speeches, television shows and works of art. Do not use these marks for names of magazines, newspapers, reference books or the Bible.**

"Jane Eyre"

"Avatar"

But note:

The New Yorker

The Foundation Directory

➤ **Use quotation marks for nicknames.**

Bob "The Dog" Newland

"Bad Moon Rising" Davis

Use of Other Punctuation with Quotation Marks

One of the most frequently asked questions about quotation marks involves the placement of other punctuation marks with them: "Does the question mark go inside or outside?" Like so many aspects of grammar, that depends. (Remember, coping with uncertainty makes you stronger!) Here are your guidelines.

Punctuation that goes inside quotation marks

A bit of dogma first:

➤ **The period and comma always go inside quotation marks.**

> **The defendant replied, "I refuse to answer on the grounds that it may incriminate me."**

The preceding sentence actually contains a full-sentence quotation, which is why a comma is used to introduce it. If the quotation was longer than sentence, we would use a colon. However, if the sentence contains just a partial quotation (not a complete thought), no introductory punctuation is needed. Example:

> **Karen called her former roommate "a sloppy, thoughtless parasite."**

Here is an example of placing the quoted material first, with the comma following:

> **"I have nothing to hide," she said.**

➤ **Question marks, exclamation points and semicolons go inside quotation marks if they are part of the quoted material.**

> **The surgeon asked, "How did you get seven quarters in your stomach?"**

> **"Give me my dignity!" the prisoner pleaded.**

Punctuation that goes outside quotation marks

➤ **Question marks, exclamation points and semicolons go outside if they are not part of the quoted material.**

> **Have you read the chapter titled "Being Your Own Best Friend"?**

> **Whatever you do, don't see "The Resurrection of Freddy"!**

Hyphen

Whereas the dash creates a break, the *hyphen* is a joiner. It is a tiny bridge that links words to indicate compound constructions and modifiers. Unfortunately, the hyphen can be as frustrating as it is useful. If you use it to join words that need to work as a unit and if you use it to avoid confusion, the hyphen will serve you well.

➤ **Use a hyphen to join compound modifiers that precede a noun unless that modifier is preceded by *very* or an *-ly* adverb.**

Compound modifiers belong together. They are not part of a series of adjectives and adverbs that can separately describe the word they are modifying. The components of a compound modifier actually modify themselves as they describe the noun:

a fair-weather friend

This is a compound modifier. *Fair* doesn't modify *friend*. It modifies the other modifier, *weather*. Together they modify *friend*. The friend is fair-weathered, not fair and weathered, so we use the hyphen.

a sluggish, unresponsive economy

This is not a compound modifier. The economy is both sluggish *and* unresponsive. *Sluggish* doesn't modify *unresponsive*. No hyphen is needed.

If you can insert the conjunction *and* between the modifiers and make sense of the new construction, you do not have a compound modifier. A *sluggish and unresponsive economy* sounds right, but a *fair and weather friend* does not. That should be your signal for a hyphen under this rule, unless the beginning of the compound modifier is *very* or an *-ly* adverb. These words are a clear signal to the reader that a compound modifier is coming.

No hyphen is needed with phrases such as these:

very wealthy philanthropist

warmly received speech

Most compound modifiers are also hyphenated when they follow a form of the linking verb *to be*. In that sense they continue to modify the subject. So, it is proper to write:

Samantha is a well-known anthropologist.

This punctuation is also correct:

Samantha was well-known.

Be sure to make a distinction between a compound modifier and the same words used slightly differently but that don't modify anything. It will prevent the improper use of the hyphen:

Last-minute election returns propelled her to victory.

Last-minute modifies *election returns*. Note, however:

He filed for election at the <u>last minute</u>.

Last minute is the object of the preposition *at*. *Last* modifies only *minute*. Be sure to identify all parts of a compound modifier. For example, it's not a *300 year-old* map. It's a *300-year-old* map.

➤ **Use a hyphen for certain prefixes and suffixes.**

You'll need to consult a dictionary or stylebook in some cases. There are so many exceptions that you will never guess right all the time! For example, the Associated Press stresses that writers hyphenate between the prefix and the following word if the prefix ends in a vowel and the next word begins with the same vowel (for example, *extra-attentive*; exceptions are *cooperate* and *coordinate*). Also hyphenate between the prefix and the following word if that word is capitalized (such as *super-Republican*).

Prefixes that generally take a hyphen include *all-, anti-, ex-, non-* and *pro-*. If you check a dictionary or a stylebook, however, you will find plenty of exceptions.

➤ **Use the hyphen for combinations when the preposition is omitted.**

first-come, first-served basis

a 98-94 squeaker

the push-me, pull-you dilemma

Apostrophe

The *apostrophe's* role isn't difficult to demonstrate. In fact, we just did it in the previous sentence! The apostrophe is used to indicate the possessive case of nouns and pronouns and to create a contraction of several words. Examples:

Sarah's mastery of punctuation is enviable. (*possessive noun*)

Everyone's favorite subject these days is health insurance. (*possessive pronoun*)

Who's going to wake up the professor? (contraction for *Who is*)

You can't do that with a semicolon! (contraction for *cannot*)

Nouns as Possessives

We'll focus first on the use of the apostrophe with a variety of nouns, because the placement of the apostrophe and the letter *s* can be confusing.

There are more than a few rules for possessive nouns, but they are not difficult. Here are eight simple ones, consistent with wire service style, for forming possessives of singular and plural nouns.

➤ **If a singular noun does not end in *s*, add *'s*.**

the **president's** cabinet

Harold's circle of friends

Some guides argue that nouns ending in *ce, x* or *z* (and carrying an *s* or *sh* sound) should have an apostrophe at the end of the word without an *s*. However, it is more common for such words to take an *'s* for simple possession:

science's effect on the environment

the **fox's** den

Hertz's rental rules

Note the exception in the following rule for those possessives that precede a word beginning with *s*:

➤ **If a singular common noun ends in *s*, add *'s* unless the next word begins with *s*. If the next word begins with *s*, add an apostrophe only. (This includes words with *s* and *sh* sounds.)**

the **boss's** evaluation

but:

the <u>boss'</u> swagger

the <u>witness's</u> testimony

but:

the <u>witness'</u> story

<u>science's</u> discoveries

but:

for <u>science'</u> sake

➤ **If a singular proper noun ends in _s_, add an apostrophe only.**

Palin's book deal

but:

<u>**Prentiss'**</u> **autobiography**

➤ **If a noun is plural in form and ends in _s_, add an apostrophe only, even if the intended meaning of the word (such as _mathematics_) is singular.**

<u>poems'</u> meanings

<u>measles'</u> misery

<u>Marine Corps'</u> spirit

➤ **If a plural noun does not end in _s_, add _'s_.**

<u>women's</u> rights

<u>oxen's</u> yoke

<u>media's</u> missteps (_media_ is the plural of _medium_)

➤ **If there is joint possession of a noun (both modify the same word), use the correct possessive form for the possessive closest to that noun.**

Mutt and <u>Jeff's</u> friendship

her husband and <u>children's</u> trust fund

➤ **If there is separate possession of the same noun, use the correct possessive form for each word.**

<u>Billy's</u> and <u>Tom's</u> DVD collections

<u>Zambia's</u> and <u>Paraguay's</u> governments

➤ **In a compound construction, use the correct possessive form for the word closest to the noun. Avoid possessives with compound plurals.**

<u>Society of Friends'</u> gathering

<u>father-in-law's</u> friendship

<u>attorney general's</u> opinion

Other Uses of the Apostrophe

We also use apostrophes to indicate that something has been omitted from a word or a number, as in

I love rock <u>'n'</u> roll.
(*'n'* replaces *and*)

I love the music of the <u>'90s.</u>
(*'90s* means *1990s*)

Here's an interesting use of the apostrophe: to create a plural of a single letter, as in

Tommy got four <u>A's</u> on his report card

However, this rule does not apply with multiple letters, as in

Brenda is going to write a song about the <u>ABCs</u> of love.

Ellipses

We use the *ellipsis mark* (. . .) to alert the reader that something has been removed from the original or quoted material, that the speaker has hesitated or faltered or that there is more material than is actually cited or used:

"We must fight this closure . . . we must save this factory."

The original statement was "We must fight this closure by a management that is bent on saving money with no regard for this town; we

must save this factory." In the interest of economy and impact, the writer
condensed this statement but preserved its accuracy.

> **Facing the hostile audience, Baker tried to frame his thoughts.
> "Under these circumstances," he said, "I feel I can no longer
> serve this community as superintendent. I have tried my best
> . . . I have always wanted. . . ." Unable to continue, he left the
> crowded meeting.**

Note from this example that a period precedes the ellipsis if it ends the
sentence. Ellipses should be used sparingly in journalistic writing because
they can raise reader suspicion about the importance of the missing phrase
and how it affects meaning. Also, too many ellipses can bleed energy away
from the content by forcing readers to follow the breaks. Sometimes it's better to paraphrase and present the idea more succinctly, with more impact.

➤ **Other punctuation marks, if needed, come after the quoted
   material but before the ellipsis.**

> **"How would you feel? . . ."**

> **"We can't stand for this! . . ."**

Parentheses

The characteristics of journalistic writing—brevity, crispness and clarity—
imply that parentheses are not welcome, but they can be effective. Two
of the most common uses are to signify the addition of needed information and to mark an aside to the main thought.

> *Caveat emptor* **("let the buyer beware") should be every
> consumer's mantra.**

> **The swimmer deflected any questions about his health.
> (Some reporters had noted his slight limp.)**

Avoid inserting lengthy or complicated material in parentheses, as a
general rule.

➤ **If the material inside the parentheses is not a complete
   sentence, put the period outside the parentheses.**

> **She likes decaffeinated coffee (the cold-water extract type).**

➤ **If the parenthetical material is a complete sentence but it depends on the sentence around it for context, put the period outside the parentheses.**

He whispered, "Carpe diem" ("Seize the day").

➤ **If the parenthetical material is a complete sentence and can stand alone, put the period inside the parentheses.**

The incumbent refused his opponent's invitation to a debate. (During his last campaign, everyone agreed, he was severely unprepared for impromptu questions.)

A short note about brackets

It's not true that the bracket is a medieval form of the parenthesis. We use brackets (but not often) in these situations:

➤ **To add explanatory material within parentheses**

He will serve as acting dean (for a three-year period [actually 30 months] starting April 1).

➤ **To add explanatory material or a correction within quoted material**

Her husband said, "She will teach at Washington State University [the Vancouver campus] when she returns from Iraq."

The mayor said, "Him [sic] and I go way back and I trust him still."

The term *sic* [from Latin for "thus,"] is used to indicate a grammatical or spelling error in quoted material. It is not used frequently these days, but that doesn't mean that errors are disappearing!

Question Mark and Exclamation Point

➤ **If you are asking a *direct question,* you must use the question mark.**

Why did you sleep through the exam?

➤ **If your question is *indirect*, no question mark is needed.**

Voters want to know when the bond issue will be on the ballot.

➤ **The exclamation point should be used only to express surprise or a strong emotion.**

In most writing, you probably will employ it only in direct quotation because of the exclamation's sensational nature.

After receiving his award, the actor said, "I've never been so honored in all my life!"

➤ **Both the question mark and the exclamation point should be included inside quotation marks if the question or exclamation is part of the quoted material.**

In direct quotations, remember that the comma is not necessary if the exclamation mark or the question mark is part of the quoted material that precedes attribution:

"Give me a break!" the young man pleaded.

"Do you call this chocolate?" the customer asked.

As you can see from this detailed chapter (honestly, this was a brief as we could be), punctuation is more than basic mechanics. It is your tool for grace and rhythm. It provides clarity, flow, emphasis—even drama. Use punctuation marks wisely and naturally. Properly used, they will speak to your readers.

Just in case you're interested, you can join a special "march of marks" once a year on National Punctuation Day. What the heck—celebrate it every day!

Chapter 9

Clarity and Conciseness

If you are a word wonk—and what good writer isn't?—you might find yourself one otherwise gloomy winter afternoon googling "the worst sentence" just for kicks. We did, and the links we found provided hours of great entertainment. It's fun to read bad writing unless you are (a) its humiliated author or (b) the poor editor who has to fix it. Truly bad writing, not just your run-of-the-mill dull prose, is blatant in its badness: clunky, sluggish, dense, overwrought, underrealized, confusing and both downright unreadable and (often) downright laughable. It's also instructive to read bad writing. It so obviously shows little respect for language. It so obviously lacks the two qualities essential to successful communication, the same two qualities this chapter trumpets: clarity and conciseness.

Let's spend a happy moment with some real stinkers.

"Hmm . . ." thought Abigail as she gazed languidly from the veranda past the bright white patio to the cerulean sea beyond, where dolphins played and seagulls sang, where splashing surf sounded like the tintinnabulation of a thousand tiny bells, where great gray whales bellowed and the sunlight sparkled off the myriad of sequins on the flyfish's bow ties, "Time to get my meds checked."

This silly, gloriously verbose sentence was runner-up for the "First Sentence of a Bad Novel" award conferred annually by the Department of English at San Jose State. The writer of that sentence wrote badly on purpose. The writer of the following sentence, whose prose one critic called "not just bad"... but "staggeringly, clumsily, thoughtlessly, almost ingeniously bad," did *not* create this verbal monstrosity on purpose:

> He could taste the familiar tang of museum air—an arid, deionized essence that carried a faint hint of carbon—the product of industrial, coal-filter dehumidifiers that ran around the clock to counteract the corrosive carbon dioxide exhaled by visitors.

For the record, that was Dan Brown, writing in "The DaVinci Code." Ouch.

Lest you think that to lack clarity and conciseness prose must be wordy, consider this:

> The lure of imaginary totality is momentarily frozen before the dialectic of desire hastens on within symbolic chains.

Okay, that wasn't fair. The preceding sentence was written by an academic, and finding professorial prose like this is, shall we say, not a challenge. But here's one written by an ordinary human being:

> When the entire world unites under one flag, people find it very difficult to watch the world cup.

Yep. It can get pretty crowded under that flag.

What's common to all these examples is the (near comical) lack of clarity that comes from careless, uncontrolled use of language. What is common, whether it occurs in the 66-word first example or the 18-word final example, is lack of conciseness: the inability of the writer to communicate keenly, crisply and directly—not to mention sensibly. In this chapter, we'll take a careful look at what it means to write with clarity and conciseness.

Keep in mind that good writing doesn't just happen. Stories don't "write themselves." Skilled writers, talented writers, professional writers work hard at writing well. They struggle and strain. In fact, contrary to the clichéd admonition, they *do* sweat the small stuff. It's all about the small stuff. Behind, or underneath, clear, concise prose is a series of conscious choices that transform the ideas inside their heads into the prose we want to read.

Good writers care about each word they choose, each clause they construct, each sentence they write, each paragraph they draft. They know that direct, powerful writing says precisely what the writer means to say—no more, no less, no ambiguity, no blurry meanings, no wasted words, no flabby prose. They know that this kind of writing is the result of many decisions mindfully made, many questions thoughtfully asked. *What am I trying to say? Is this what I mean? Is it* precisely *what I mean? Is this the* very best *way to say what I mean?*

Writers who care about the quality of their work constantly question themselves as they write, edit and revise. Then, word by word, they create clear, forceful prose. You can, too.

Choosing Words

As we gather our thoughts to begin writing, we are immediately confronted with the most fundamental choice: the individual word. The words we choose must communicate precisely what we mean with a minimum of fuss and a maximum of power. This is particularly true with verbs, the engines of the sentence. Choosing the *correct* verb is a matter of grammar; choosing the *right* verb is a matter of conciseness and clarity. Consider the following word choice problems, remembering that every choice, no matter how minor, no matter how seemingly mechanical, affects the clarity of your prose.

"Verbizing" Nouns

The new boss is committed to <u>monetizing</u> the business model by <u>componentizing</u> operations and <u>incentivizing</u> employees.

The suffix *-ize* is on the loose, "verbizing" and "uglyizing" our language. Some people think you can tack *-ize* onto any noun and create a verb. Most of those makeshift verbs are unnecessary. *Fractionalize*, for example, means nothing more than *split*. Other words with longer linguistic histories, such as *utilize* and *signalize*, serve no distinct purpose. *Utilize* has come to mean nothing more than *use*. *Signalize* means signal. Many of these *-ize* words are not only useless but also grating to the ear and uncomfortably bureaucratic.

Of course, yesterday's awkward jargon is today's respectable word. *Pasteurize* must have raised the hackles of nineteenth-century grammarians, but few would be upset about it today. It is difficult to say how many of the newly created, tongue-twisting *-ize* verbs will become permanent additions to our language. (The fewer the better, we hope.) While we are all awaiting the verdict, we can subject an awkward-sounding *-ize* verb to three tests.

1. Is it listed in the dictionary as an acceptable (not informal, colloquial or slang) word?

2. Does it have a unique meaning?

3. Does it have a sound that is, at the very least, not displeasing?

If the word passes the three tests, use it. If it fails, find another word. Do not "jargonize" and "awkwardize" the language. It may be all right to *pasteurize* milk, but it is not yet acceptable to *chocolatize* it.

Vague Words

When we speak, thinking as we talk, sometimes searching for words or fumbling with thoughts, we often insert placeholder phrases such as *a type of, a kind of* or *in terms of.* You might hear yourself say something like: "It was the type of thing I was kind of proud of, I mean in terms of personal accomplishments." You are thinking out loud, speaking before you know what you want to say. Writing is not like that. Writing is thoughtful and premeditated. Think before you write, then edit, edit, edit.

Years of writing term papers and hearing dense and sluggish bureaucratic language—passed along not only by dense and sluggish bureaucrats but also by journalists and, sad to say, textbook authors—have cemented (*cementized?*) in our minds such filler words as *aspect, element, factor, situation, character* and *condition.*

> **The aspect of the situation that will be a factor will depend on the character of the elements we must contend with.**

This is what you say (or write) when you don't know what you're talking about. The result is the opposite not only of clear writing, but of *any* communication. Should these words crop up in your prose, weed them out mercilessly.

Euphemisms and "Fancy Words"

The vet doesn't tell you "We're going to have to kill your dog." The vet says, "We're going to have to put Fido to sleep." Putting an animal "to sleep" is a euphemism, an expression designed to be less offensive or disturbing than the word or phrase it replaces. The term used for radiation leaked from an improperly operating nuclear power plant—a mightily disturbing event—is the lovely phrase "sunshine units." Euphemisms like this, sometimes called *doublespeak,* can be a way of shielding the bearer of negative information from taking responsibility for the information.

For example, when the Internal Revenue Service finally stopped pursuing a taxpayer who had, in fact, done nothing wrong, the agency sent this note:

The audit issue was reconsidered and determined not to have existed.

Audit issue is a euphemism for a fierce, three-year battle between the taxpayer and the agency. *Reconsidered,* in this case, means the IRS finally figured out it was wrong. Note how skillfully this eerie sentence substitutes clear expression—*we made a mistake*—with euphemism. The sentence is carefully constructed to obscure an admission of error. Note also that the sentence is in passive voice, another way of masking responsibility.

Euphemisms are all around us. A company, deeply in debt, might announce to its stockholders that it is "currently experiencing a budgetary shortfall." Another, found guilty of dumping toxic waste in a river, might admit that its "environmental compliance statistics showed a downturn." The military wins the dubious prize for creating both the most and the most chilling euphemisms. *Enhanced interrogation techniques* is the military's term for what is widely considered torture. *Entry into a nonpermissive environment* is the military's way of evading the word *invasion. Friendly fire* softens the terrible tragedy of the action it describes: gunfire against troops by their own troops. *Collateral damage* is a euphemism for killing civilians.

Let's say it's snowing outside with a wind chill factor of 10 degrees below zero, and you look out the window and see a man running down the street clad only in boxers. What would you most likely say? What would clearly, precisely and directly express the moment? "Look at that guy! He must be nuts!" A master of euphemism would see the same thing and quietly comment that the man was "somewhat inappropriately attired given the climatic conditions." Writers can't stop others from manufacturing euphemisms, but they can refuse to transmit them.

A related clarity problem is "fancy words." We don't mean three-dollar words like *prestidigitation* or *ovolactovegetarianism*. We mean silly, inflated words that take the place of good, plain, ordinary, serviceable words: *disambiguate* for *clarify,* to cite one particularly egregious example. Beware of more common inflated words like *facility* for *building, infrastructure* for *roads and bridges, domicile* for *home.* Stay clear of these pretensions. If others use them, your responsibility as a public communicator is to not pass them on.

Jargon

Poker players talk about a "bellybuster"—an inside straight draw. Computer geeks refer to problems caused by the incompetence of users as PEBKACs, which stands for Problem Exists Between Keyboard and Chair. Cops say, "The perp is exiting the vehicle" instead of "The criminal is getting out of the car." This is jargon, the specialized language of a group of people engaged in an activity, trade or occupation.

Jargon is shorthand communication, a kind of code. It works well within the group because everyone knows and understands it. Sometimes jargon migrates and becomes part of accepted and understood vocabulary. *Spam,* meaning unsolicited e-mail (not the yummy canned meat-like product) is a good example. But jargon is often confusing to others. A secret language, it can act to insulate the group and exclude nonmembers from the conversation. Because media writers have a responsibility to communicate clearly and simply to wider audiences, we should be jargon slayers, not jargon purveyors.

Here is a researcher deep in the throes of jargon:

Within this regional population, total caloric intake from all sources regardless of nutritional value as measured by standard methods is insufficient to balance overall metabolic output, including both resting and active components. (Translation: These people don't have enough food.)

Jargon can be used to obscure ideas or make ordinary ideas sound more important. It can also be used to hide meaning or desensitize people to issues. For a writer to perpetuate such jargon signals a failure to communicate. Using jargon does not make you sound impressive. On the contrary, you impress (and help) your audience by lucidly explaining difficult material, not repeating words and phrases you do not understand.

Redundancy and Wordiness

In the world of writing, less is often more: the economical phrase, the lean sentence, the stark image. Such writing grabs readers and stays with them. On the other hand, clutter—words that serve no purpose—interfere with clear and memorable communication.

Make your words count. Ignorance of the real meanings of words, attempts at false erudition, repetition of other people's jargon, murky thinking and sheer sloppiness can all result in prose that is wordy or redundant. Consider these all-too-common examples of redundancy:

mutual cooperation
(*Cooperation* means "acting for mutual benefit." *Mutual* is redundant.)

end result
(The *result*, by definition, is the consequence.)

advance warning
(A warning does, by definition, tell you in advance.)

incumbent officeholder
(The definition of *incumbent* is "officeholder.")

consensus of opinion
(*Consensus* means "collective opinion.")

repeat again
(*Repeat* includes *again* in its definition.)

refer back
(*Refer* includes *back* in its definition.)

completely destroyed
(Destruction is complete.)

Also note *added bonus, anonymous stranger* (as opposed to all those familiar strangers), *ATM machine* (what do you think the *M* stands for?), *armed gunman*.

A number of wordy, sluggish expressions have crept into writing. Here are some of the more common ones to avoid.

Instead of	Use
as of now	now
at the present time	now
at this point in time	now
despite the fact that	although
due to the fact that	because
on account of	because
seeing as how	because
during the course of	during

Just *One* Word

Flabby prose is the enemy of clarity and conciseness. Sometimes that flabbiness is easy to detect—verbose sentences, unintelligible jargon— but sometimes it is more subtle. It might come in the form of a single unnecessary word. Should you care about a single unnecessary word? You bet. Here are two you will want to eschew.

Avoiding *Up*

She was selected to <u>head up</u> the commission.

The candidate must <u>face up</u> to the issues.

The storm <u>slowed up</u> [down] traffic all morning.

None of these verbs needs the preposition *up*. *Up* doesn't add meaning to these verbs; it takes away crispness. This may seem like a minor point, but it is at this basic level that good writing begins.

She was selected to <u>head</u> the commission.

The candidate must <u>face</u> the issues.

The storm <u>slowed</u> traffic all morning.

Beware of *free up* (free), *wake up* (awake), *stand up* (stand) and *shake up* (shake). In these instances, *up* is more than unnecessary; it is sloppy.

Of course, some verbs need *up* to complete their meaning. *Make* does not mean the same thing as *make up*. *Break* is not synonymous with *break up*. *Up* is necessary to the meaning of *pick up*. In these cases, *up* is not clutter, but neither is it strong, precise writing.

The editor accused the reporter of <u>making up</u> sources.
(weak)

The editor accused the reporter of <u>fabricating</u> sources.
(stronger)

The investigation <u>broke up</u> the crime syndicate.
(weak)

The investigation <u>shattered</u> the crime syndicate.
(stronger)

The market for serious fiction is <u>picking up</u>.
(weak)

The market for serious fiction is <u>improving</u>.
(stronger)

That

That performs several grammatical functions.
It is an adjective:

<u>That</u> book changed my life.
(*That* describes book.)

It is a demonstrative pronoun:

> **<u>That</u> will change your life.**
> (*That* takes the place of a noun.)

It is a relative pronoun:

> **This is a book <u>that</u> will change your life.**
> (*That* introduces a relative clause.)

It is a conjunction:

> **The author said <u>that</u> writing the book changed her life.**
> (*That* links two independent clauses.)

The troublesome uses of *that* are as a conjunction and as a relative pronoun. Simply put, writers overuse the word. *That* is often unnecessary in a sentence. Its inclusion can rob the sentence of its grace and rhythm. If a word does not add meaning, get rid of it. Consider these sentences, all of which would be crisper without *that*:

> **The author said <u>that</u> writing the book changed her life.**
>
> **The researchers admitted <u>that</u> they falsified data.**
>
> **Government sources say <u>that</u> the study is flawed.**

Often all you need do is remove the useless *that*; however, some sentences demand revision. Conciseness is the issue:

> **This is a book that will change your life.**
> (wordy)
>
> **This book will change your life.**
> (improved)
>
> **Police recovered the laptop that was stolen.**
> (wordy)
>
> **Police recovered the stolen laptop.**
> (improved)
>
> **The Web site that he designed won first prize.**
> (wordy)
>
> **His Web site won first prize.**
> (improved)

That is sometimes used legitimately to link sentence parts. To discover whether *that* is necessary to a sentence, ask yourself two questions:

1. Can *that* be eliminated with no change in the meaning of the sentence?

2. Can the clause introduced by *that* be expressed more succinctly?

If you answer yes to either question, edit or rewrite.

Putting Words Together

Clear, concise, coherent writing depends on more than careful word choice. Proper placement of words is imperative. Misplacement mistakes can easily harm the clarity of your prose.

Misplaced Words

In a sentence, a modifier needs to point directly and clearly to what it modifies. This means placing the modifier next to or as close as possible to what it is modifying. Adverbs such as *only, nearly, almost, just, scarcely, even, hardly* and *merely* create the biggest potential difficulty because their placement can drastically change the meaning of the sentence. Note how placement changes meaning in the following examples:

> **<u>Only</u> he can help you.**
> (No one else can help you.)

> **He can <u>only</u> help you.**
> (He can't do anything more than help you.)

> **He can help <u>only</u> you.**
> (He can't help anyone else.)

Notice how the placement of *almost* in the next two sentences changes the meaning:

> **Negotiations <u>almost</u> broke down on every clause in the contract.**
> (Negotiations did not quite break down.)

> **Negotiations broke down on <u>almost</u> every clause in the contract.**
> (Just about every clause caused problems during negotiations.)

When we speak, we often have a devil-may-care attitude toward the placement of adverbs. But, because placement most surely changes meaning, stick to the old rule: Place the adverb (or other word) next to or as close as possible to the word you intend it to modify.

Misplaced Phrases and Clauses

Like individual words, phrases and clauses should be placed next to or near what they modify. Sometimes the effect of a misplaced phrase is (unintentionally) hilarious, as in this gem from a Danielle Steel novel:

> **She wore a dress the same color as her eyes her father brought her from San Francisco.**

Amusement aside, placement affects meaning, as this examples illustrates:

> **The proposal <u>that the student council is debating</u> will alter the university's free speech policy.**

> **The proposal will alter the university's free speech policy <u>that the student council is debating</u>.**

In the first sentence, the student council's *proposal* is being debated. In the second example, the university's *policy* is being debated.

Dangling Modifiers

A modifier "dangles" when what it is supposed to modify is not part of the sentence. For example:

> **To learn the craft of writing, discipline is needed.**

The phrase *to learn the craft of writing* does not modify anything in the sentence. The only word it could modify is *discipline,* but that makes no sense. The sentence needs to be revised:

> **To learn the craft of writing, you must be disciplined.**

Now the phrase correctly modifies *you*. Not only that, the revised sentence is in the active voice. The dangling-modifier sentence was in the passive voice. Here is another dangling modifier:

> **After traveling for more than three years, home looked good to him.**

Clearly, *home* did not do the traveling; *he* did. Coherence is at stake here. The sentence needs to be rewritten so the introductory phrase clearly modifies the correct word:

> **After traveling for more than three years, he was happy to be home.**

Split Constructions

Just as modifiers need to rest closely to what they modify, so other parts of the sentence must be placed carefully to maintain clarity and coherence of thought.

Split verbs often lead to incoherence. In most cases, it is best to keep auxiliary verbs next to the main verb and to avoid splitting infinitives. Consider what happens to sentence unity and graceful expression when you separate auxiliary verbs from the main verb:

> She **has** for the entire spring semester **subsisted** on Red Bull and brown rice.
> *(auxiliary and main verb split)*

> For the entire spring semester, she **has subsisted** on Red Bull and brown rice.
> *(improved)*

The more words you place between the verb parts, the less coherent the sentence becomes. Occasionally, however, it is acceptable—even preferable—to split a multipart verb. Almost always the verb is split by a single word, an adverb:

> Junk food **has** always **been** an issue in the school cafeteria.

Placing *always* between the verb parts does not hinder coherence. In fact, it adds emphasis.

Infinitives (*to* forms of the verb) should also, in most cases, remain intact. Split infinitives contribute to awkwardness and interfere with coherent expression. A sentence should read smoothly and make sense:

> The parent group promised **to** within the next month **explore** the feasibility of a school-community vegetable garden.
> *(split infinitive)*

> The parent group promised **to explore** the feasibility of a school-community vegetable garden within the next month.
> *(improved)*

To aid sentence clarity and help readers or listeners understand quickly what you are trying to say, keep the subject and the verb as close to each other as possible. Look what happens to coherence when subject and verb are interrupted by lengthy explanatory material:

> The school **board**, after months of rancorous public debate
> (subj.)

resulting in the cancellation of all vending machine contracts, <u>endorsed</u> the garden proposal.
(verb)

The sentence forces readers or listeners to wade through 16 words between the subject *(board)* and its verb *(endorsed)*. But readers may have neither the time nor the inclination to slog through such constructions, and listeners can easily lose the thread of meaning. Be kind to your audience. Keep subject and verb close:

After months of rancorous public debate resulting in the cancellation of all vending machine contracts, the <u>board endorsed</u> the garden proposal.

Consider one more common splitting problem: a verb and its complements. The simplest construction to understand is subject–verb–object. It answers the basic question *Who did what to whom?* Just as splitting the subject *(who)* from the verb *(did what)* interferes with clarity and coherence, so too does splitting the verb *(did what)* from its complement *(to whom)*. Keep the verb and its complements (object, adverb, descriptive phrase) as close together as possible. You will promote sentence unity, readability and coherence. Consider this example:

Consumer advocates <u>protested</u> yesterday morning in front of three
(verb)

local toy stores <u>what they say is the marketing of violence to</u>
(complement)

<u>children</u> <u>through the sale of toy guns</u>.

This sentence is clumsy. To avoid losing coherent thought—and your audience—rewrite:

Consumer advocates protested today what they say is the marketing of violence to children through the sale of toy guns. Marching [picketing, assembling, gathering] in front of three local toy stores, they . . .

Making Sense

Every good grammatical decision you make contributes to clarity, conciseness and coherence. Choosing strong, precise words is the first step. Placing these words correctly is the next. Focusing on the architecture of sentences is the third level.

Parallel Structure

Parallel structure aligns related ideas and presents them through the repetition of grammatical structure. It is vital to both clarity and unity, and helps create rhythm and grace in a sentence. To create parallel structure using single words, use a series of words that are the same part of speech. For example:

The scheme was complicated, clever and illegal.

The related ideas are the characterizations of the scheme. The grammatical pattern is the repetition of single adjectives.

To create parallel structure using phrases or clauses, replicate the grammatical pattern:

Exercise can <u>clear the mind</u>, <u>energize the body</u> and <u>lift the spirits</u>.
(repeats phrases)

Because we have the resources, because we know what's right and because we have no other choice, we should rid our air and water of toxic chemicals.
(repeats clauses)

Parallel structure binds ideas and enhances the audience's understanding of each idea by creating a lucid, easily recognizable pattern. If you begin a sentence by establishing a particular grammatical pattern and then break it, you create confusion and disharmony.

Parallel structure is commonly used to introduce complementary, contrasting or sequential ideas. The relationship between the ideas can be implicit (as in the examples offered thus far) or it can be made apparent by using signal words:

- Complementary relationship: *both/and, not only/but also*

  <u>Both</u> the addition of attic insulation <u>and</u> the installation of triple-paned windows will dramatically lower energy costs.
  (complementary relationship, parallel structure)

- Contrasting relationship: *either/or, neither/nor*

  <u>Either</u> we solve the problem <u>or</u> we suffer the consequences.
  (contrasting relationship, parallel structure)

- Sequential relationship: *first/second/third*

  <u>First</u>, define the problem; <u>second</u>, gather the information; <u>third</u>, brainstorm the alternatives.
  (sequential relationship, parallel structure)

Whether you make the relationship explicit by using signal words or implicit by letting the ideas speak for themselves, parallel structure is vital to clarity and coherence.

Sentence Fragments

As you remember from Chapter 4, a *fragment* is a group of words that lacks a subject, a predicate, a complete thought or any combination of the three. Grammatically, a fragment cannot stand alone. When readers see a group of words beginning with a capital letter and ending with a period, they expect a complete sentence. If instead you offer them a fragment, you confuse them. Unintentional fragments hinder both coherence and clarity.

> **Bloggers are revolutionizing international reporting. <u>Although there are credibility issues</u>. Traditional media are citing blogs as sources.**

This fragment (underlined) is confusing. Maybe the writer meant:

> **Although there are credibility issues, bloggers are revolutionizing international reporting.**

But it may be that the writer meant:

> **Although there are credibility issues, traditional media are using blogs as sources.**

Fragments leave your audience hanging, forcing them to guess your intended meaning. Offer clear, complete thoughts. Fragments used knowingly, sparingly and stylistically are another story. See Chapter 10 for a more in-depth discussion.

Run-On Sentences

A *run-on sentence* is composed of two, three or any number of whole, complete sentences joined together ungrammatically. Chapter 4 discussed the run-on as a grammatical problem. Here we want to emphasize it as an obstacle to concise and coherent writing.

The two most common run-on sentences are those inappropriately linked with *and* and those incorrectly spliced with commas. Both can confuse and frustrate a reader:

> **The public schools must deal with a shrinking budget and class sizes will increase.**
> *(run-on)*

When you use *and* to link two independent clauses as above, you are saying that the two thoughts reinforce or directly complement each other or follow one another sequentially. If this isn't the case, as in the preceding example, you have created not just a run-on but also a less-than-coherent sentence. If the thoughts in the clauses are not related in a definable, explicit way, rewrite the run-on as two separate sentences. If the thoughts are related, use a connecting word to signal the correct relationship:

> **Because the public schools must deal with a shrinking budget, class sizes will increase.**
> *(improved)*

Note that the run-on was corrected by subordinating one thought (clause) to another to clarify and make explicit the relationship between the two clauses.

Commas alone cannot link independent clauses. Independent clauses are sentences all on their own. To link them grammatically, you have a number of choices. Consider this run on:

> **The legislature mandated cutbacks throughout the public school system, class sizes increased dramatically, elective classes decreased significantly, teachers were instructed to take three furlough days.**

Here's one grammatical fix:

> **The legislature mandated cutbacks throughout the public school system, including increased class size, decreased elective classes and three furlough days for teachers.**

Or, depending on intended meaning, you could subordinate one independent clause to the others.

> **<u>Soon after</u> the legislature mandated cutbacks throughout the public school system, class size increased dramatically, elective classes decreased significantly, and teachers were asked to take three furlough days.**

Clarity, Conciseness, Coherence

Writers write to be understood. Whether they are writing to inform, amuse, uplift, persuade or cajole, their thoughts must be clear and their sentences comprehensible. Clarity, conciseness and coherence begin with individual word choice. From that point, every grammatical decision either enhances or detracts from this triple goal. Imprecision, clutter, misplaced phrases and murky construction have no place in good writing. The goal is lean, powerful communication.

Chapter 10

Style

Is this style?

What is the size of a pumpernickel . . . and crouches like a thunder-cloud above its bellymates, turgid with nourishment? What has the industry of an insect, the regenerative powers of a starfish, yet is turned to a mass of fatty globules by a double martini? It is . . . the liver, doted upon by the French, assaulted by the Irish, disdained by the Americans and chopped up with egg, onion and chicken fat by the Jews.

Is this style?

Patti's dating a man. His name is Cecil Waite, a logger and hunting guide. She met him getting gas. He had a turkey in his truck that he had just shot. She told him, "Wow, you've got a nice turkey there!" Flattery like that works magic in Vermont.

The answer is yes, and yes again. Yes, the first elegantly written paragraph, an excerpt from one of the many elegantly written essays penned by surgeon and author Richard Selzer, is a fine example of writing with style. And yes, the spartan paragraph (note the absence of any adjective except *nice* in the quote), an excerpt from a New York Times feature story by N. R. Kleinfeld, is a fine example of writing with style.

So is this ad copy written to promote travel in the Hudson River Valley (and yes, we both acknowledge and forgive the purposeful fragments):

> Red apples, white wines, blue herons, purple mountains, pink lilies, green acres. And then there's the scenic route.

And this lively snippet from an environmental blog:

> Greenwashing. We all know those ads—earnest, heartfelt, evocative, replete with images of virgin forests and cerulean skies—that proclaim how environmentally caring and sensitive a company is. Take Exxon Mobil, for example, or our friends at Dow Chemical. While mega corporations craft eco-images, everything from lipstick to linoleum, messenger bags to mayonnaise are being recast as "green" products. And don't forget SUVs.

Style comes from the Latin word *stylus*, "a pointed instrument used for writing." Few of us use pointed instruments to write anymore (unless the tips of acrylic nails tapping on a keyboard count), but style could still be defined, metaphorically if not literally, as "a pointed instrument used for writing."

What is Style?

Style is the writer's unique vision—and the lively, original expression of that vision—that transforms text from interesting to irresistible, from momentarily of note to distinctly unforgettable. Style is first and foremost the reflection of the writer's way of seeing and thinking, and so decisions about style begin with the kind of story a writer decides to pursue, and how the writer approaches and thinks about the material. Style has much to do with the depth, breath, originality and quirkiness of the writer's research. And, of course, style is evident in the writing. Is there talent involved? You bet. But style is also the product of purposeful choices, the culmination of many small things done well, the result of sheer hard work. Style has an important place in all writing, from a lengthy feature piece to the one-sentence captions under a multimedia slide show, from the script for a documentary to the tweet you want everyone to read.

Novice writers, and some experienced ones as well, often don't have the right idea about style.

- They believe if they write clean, clutterless prose, their writing will lack style.

- They believe style is like a garnish or a spicy condiment added after the fact to bring zest to bland writing.

- They believe style is always flashy.

- They fear that style, because it is hard to define ("I don't know what it is, but I know it when I see it"), is therefore mysterious and unattainable.

They are wrong.

Style emerges from—and cannot exist without—crisp, clean language use. First come the fundamentals: strong verbs, grammatical consistency, well-constructed sentences. Then comes style. Novelist John Updike looks at style by comparing the process of writing to the process of becoming a musician. Musicians begin by learning to identify and play individual notes. They learn how to read music. They practice scales. They play simple compositions. Only after mastering these fundamentals can they begin to develop their own manner of musical expression, their own style. Writers, too, must master the basics before they can find their own voice.

Style, then, has little to do with ostentatious language. Window dressing (a gaggle of adjectives, for example), verbal ornamentation (big words or purple prose) and fancy tricks do not generally contribute to compelling writing. In fact, verbal flashiness can obscure coherent thought. There is nothing flashy about this sentence:

This year Americans will consume 35 million cows, 115 million pigs and nine billion birds.

In choosing to express meat as animals—cows instead of beef, pigs instead of pork—the writer takes us by surprise and makes us think about our consumption in a different way. These simple word choices create a powerful sentence that does more than communicate information.

The final misconception, that style is mysterious and unattainable, is the hardest to discount. Because it is unique to the individual writer, style does seem to defy definition. But that doesn't mean it's mysterious. It means it's personal, idiosyncratic and distinctive. Far from being enigmatic, style is the sum of a series of good, solid decisions—many of them as basic as word choice or sentence construction—that a writer is aware enough, smart enough and experienced enough to make time after time.

As we've said, style begins with a unique vision—and this cannot be taught. What can be taught (or at least learned) is how to give expression to that vision. The process is rooted in correctness and clarity, and then purposefully, creatively, energetically moves to something more: stylish, graceful, compelling writing. This is not an easy task. It is, after all, a writer's life work, the evolution of craft. Style doesn't just happen. It is thoughtfully, patiently learned.

Let's demystify style by examining some of its key components: liveliness, originality, rhythm and sound, and imagery.

Liveliness

Lively writing is not excitable, overwrought, exclamation-point-studded prose, but rather clutterless composition that moves along at a good clip, involving readers or listeners and carrying them briskly from paragraph to paragraph. Like all components of style, liveliness depends not only on the way you use the language but also on what you have to say.

Style and substance go hand in hand. Your skills as an observer, interviewer and information gatherer net the raw material. Your skill as a writer transforms that material into vibrant prose. Here's how to make your writing lively.

Choose Verbs Carefully

Strong, precise verbs give energy to a sentence; weak, vague or over-modified verbs sap a sentence of its power. Instead of tacking on adverbs to clarify the meaning of a verb, spend time searching for the one right word.

Instead of	Use
talk incessantly	jabber, chatter, blab
look into deeply	delve, probe, plumb
walk slowly	amble, trudge, saunter
eat quickly	gobble, wolf

Consider the abundance of simple, colorful verbs in this introduction to an article on our obsession with hair. Note rhythm and rhyme as you read.

We twirl, curl, cut and pluck it. We shave, brush, tint and wax it. We wash, braid and pomade it. We spend more than $2 billion a year pampering it and have more of it per square inch than a chimpanzee.

Use Intensifiers Sparingly

The adverbs *very, really, truly, completely, extremely, positively, absolutely, awfully* and *so* that *so very* often (see what we mean?) sprinkle our casual conversation often add nothing but clutter to written work. They show sloppiness of thought and generally add a too-colloquial tone to writing. Instead of intensifying a weak word, search for a strong, precise one.

Instead of	Use
very angry	irate
extremely tired	exhausted
really happy	elated
awfully hot	scorching

When you've found a strong word, leave it alone. Don't rob it of its impact by unnecessarily intensifying it:

~~really~~ famished

~~extremely~~ sweltering

~~truly~~ extravagant

Avoid Redundancies

Understand the meanings of words before you use them. *More equal, more parallel* and *most unique* are redundant expressions you can easily avoid if you pay attention to the meanings of *equal, parallel* and *unique.* Remember that we discussed redundancies in Chapter 9. Why not go back and take a second look?

Edit to Remove Wordiness

Nothing destroys the vitality of prose faster, or as completely, as does verbosity, clutter, "purple prose" or bureaucratese. Each word, each phrase, each clause, each sentence should survive your rigorous editing process because it adds meaning, substance or color to the piece. Making every word count is the challenge. You may want to review what "Vague Words," "Euphemisms and 'Fancy Words,'" and "Jargon" in Chapter 9.

Use Active Voice

As you know from Chapter 4, active voice contributes to clear, vigorous sentence construction. In an active-voice sentence, the actor performs the action. In a passive-voice sentence, the actor has the action performed upon it. Passive-voice construction almost always weakens the verb and adds unnecessary words. It often sounds stilted and formal.

Use Present Tense

Present tense often allows the reader or listener to experience the story as it unfolds. When you use present tense as an element of style, you create a scene with urgency and immediacy. Consider this account, written in present tense, from a longer piece about a women's basketball team:

> Down near the basket, Karen is guarding Courtney, a five-foot-two freshman walk-on. Courtney has the ball. Karen is trying hard to get into the rhythm of this fast-paced drill. Courtney is little and quick, but Karen is quick, too. Or she used to be. Okay, she thinks to herself, let's do it. Let's move.
>
> She lunges at Courtney, looking to steal the ball. At the same time, Courtney moves toward Karen. Karen's right hand connects with Courtney's shoulder. The fingers jam back. Karen hears a pop. For a moment, the sound makes her so nauseous that she doesn't feel the pain. Then she feels the pain. She freezes in place, feet planted on the floor, white-faced, disoriented. She grabs her hand. It is her shooting hand.

Of course, the scene took place in the past. The writer is recounting it for the audience much later. But the present tense makes us feel as if we are there watching. The scene is alive. Not all stories can or should be told in present tense. Often past or future tenses are essential for historical accuracy. But the technique of narrowing the gap between audience and story by using present tense has many applications. Scene setting is certainly one of them.

Another is *attribution*. Using present tense to attribute quotations or present dialog in a story—*says* instead of *said*, for example—shows the immediacy and current relevance of the comments. If a person said something yesterday, he or she would be likely to say the same thing today (unless, of course, we're talking about politicians or disgraced sports heroes). Present tense attribution, like present tense in general, subtly quickens the pace of the story.

No single element ensures lively writing. But if you use strong, precise language, rid your prose of clutter, stick with the active voice and use the present tense when appropriate, your writing will be crisper, snappier and more inviting.

Originality

Originality of style cannot be separated from originality of substance. If, as a thinker, observer, interviewer and cultural forager, you gather fresh material and come to novel insights, the written work you produce can be distinctive and original. When magazine writer Mary Roach visited Florida to write about, of all things, Tupperware, she began her story this way:

> The Tupperware World Headquarters in Orlando, Florida, is a collection of long, low modular buildings, the sort of shapes you could easily stack one on top of another for just-right storage in your pantry, fridge or freezer, if that's the sort of person you were.

The playful tone and the unique visual image create an unusually enticing first sentence. This is what originality is all about: a novel vision translated into simple but imaginative language. This is style.

Or consider this wonderful sentence in the middle of a National Public Radio story about the emergency room of an animal hospital:

> In the examination room to the right of Dr. Cabe, a rust-colored dog is lying very still on the mirror steel table, its four legs splaying out at odd angles over the counter, as the couple who owns him hold one another, their faces colorless and almost round from crying.

The writing here is spare; the description is precise, controlled and original. The writer could have described the faces of the dog owners as "pale and swollen from crying." But this is a familiar image, too familiar to touch the reader deeply. Faces "colorless and almost round from crying"—that's fresh and poignant.

Avoid Clichés

A *cliché,* by definition, lacks originality. It is a trite or overused expression or idea. It's the image or the phrase that springs immediately to mind. We've heard it before; we've read it before. We know it *like the back of our hand.* It's as *comfortable as an old shoe.* Get it? A cliché is someone else's idea, and the more it is used, the less power it has. As poet and author Donald Hall writes, "When we put words together . . . we begin to show our original selves, or we show a dull copy of someone else's original." Note the following cliché-ridden remark from an economist offering the year's forecast. Unfortunately for the economist, the remark was quoted extensively in the national media.

> Let's remember we climbed up the hill pretty darned quickly. We've had the rug pulled out from under us, but we've picked ourselves up, and maybe we can see the light at the end of the tunnel.

If the *light at the end of the tunnel* serves only to illuminate a cliché, it's not worth the trip, is it? The challenge is to use your imaginative and linguistic powers to create original expressions.

Because we can't resist, here's a shining example of a (ludicrously inappropriate) cliché.

> Just as a beautiful face has been said to launch a thousand ships, a delicious, high-quality ham can launch a multitude of convenient, great-tasting meals.

The "face that launched a thousand ships" cliché would be bad enough. But likening Helen of Troy to pork butt—*that* is transcendentally bad. We promise we didn't make this up. The sentence actually began a story (enticingly titled "Take Ham to New Heights") in an honest-to-goodness magazine.

On the other hand, you can play with clichés and make them work for you by tweaking them just enough, as in this clever headline:

> Chocolate Gets Hot But Holds Its Temper

The writer knows and acknowledges that *hot-tempered* is a cliché. But there's a linguistic trick going on here based on a play on the word *temper*, which is both a noun meaning "angry disposition" and a verb referring to the process of melting and reforming chocolate. If you knew that— and a decent percentage of readers of the Dining section of the New York Times, where this headline appeared, would—you would delight in this stylistic tidbit.

Play with Figures of Speech

Consider this clever and appropriate simile in a story about home make-over shows on TV:

Since "Trading Spaces" had its premiere on TLC . . . copycats and variations on the idea have been multiplying like wire hangers in a walk-in closet.

Or how about this metaphor in the middle of a quirky feature about a man who collects antique toasters and opened a toaster museum:

Ten years ago, Norcross' toaster obsession was unshaped dough on the breadboard of his life.

Here is a movie reviewer describing the main character (Jeff Bridges) in the movie "Crazy Heart":

He smokes and drinks as if trying to settle a long-ago bet between his liver and his lungs about which he would destroy first.

These writers are having fun. What grabs us when we read these sentences, what makes us smile, is the unique vision, the odd, surprising or wonderfully apt comparisons.

Similes are verbal comparisons that use *like* or *as* to announce themselves. Original similes have power, impact, even humor. Run-of-the-mill comparisons or clichés contribute nothing: *as black as night, as cool as a cucumber, hair like spun gold.* These comparisons lack verve and originality. Where is the imaginative stretch in *as black as night?* Night *is* black. What's the interesting comparison here? There is none.

Whereas similes are explicit comparisons using *like* or *as, metaphors* express a more direct comparison. Instead of stating that item A is "like" item B (a simile), a metaphor states that item A *is* item B. In the example above, the toaster collector's obsession was not *like* unshaped dough, it *was* unshaped dough.

When you attribute human characteristics, feelings, or behaviors to nonhuman or inanimate objects, you are using a device called *personification.* As you walk down the aisle of your food market, a package of double chocolate chunk cookies "beckons" to you. Cookies, of course, don't beckon. You've attributed a human quality to a bakery item. You've personified the package of cookies. Following, author Susan Orlean has fun introducing Biff, who is a boxer (of the canine persuasion), in a New Yorker feature article:

Biff is perfect. He's friendly, good-looking, rich, famous and in excellent physical condition. He almost never drools. He's not afraid of commitment. He wants children—actually, he already has children and wants a lot more. He works hard and is the consummate professional, but he also knows how to have fun.

If you are thinking to yourself, "Figures of speech are fine for poets and novelists, but I'm a journalist," think again. As the examples in this section show, media writers can and do use literary devices as part of original, stylish writing. As information consumers become increasingly inundated with media messages, it becomes even more important to craft your message in original and memorable ways, like using similes, metaphors, analogies and personification.

Play with Words

When we first saw Bella and her pretty dead guy, Edward, in *Twilight*, the series hadn't been saga-fied yet.

Saga-fied isn't a word, of course. It's the result of a writer having fun with a word. Here's the tagline for an AT&T ad that takes on Verizon. The word play is simple and effective.

When you compare, there's no comparison.

Note the bit of linguistic fun the writer has in the next sentence:

For millions of vegetarians, *beef* is a four-letter word.

Here the word play turns on the accepted meaning of *four-letter word* as a curse word.

There's nothing fancy about what these writers have done. You will note no pyrotechnics. Word play need not be complicated or devastatingly witty to be effective. It need only be original, memorable and, of course, appropriate to the tone of the message.

Rhythm and Sound

Words march to a beat. Long sentences move gently, liltingly, picking up momentum as they flow. Short sentences create a staccato beat. Repetition of words or phrases can add accent and meter. Sentence construction communicates. Words may have power, but words set in rhythmic sentences have clout. Let's examine six components of rhythmic sentence construction: repetition, parallelism, sentence length, fragments and run-ons, and the sounds of words.

Use Repetition

Purposeful repetition of words or phrases can add rhythm and grace to sentences. But, like all stylistic devices, it should be used sparingly. Too much repetition leads to boredom and clunkiness.

In the following magazine essay, note the repetition of *I don't mean:*

> I love the rain. I don't mean I grudgingly appreciate its ecological necessity. I don't mean I've learned to tolerate it. I don't mean I wait it out, flipping through the calendar to see how many more pages until the sun might break through. I mean I love it.

Repetition performs three stylistic functions here: It quickens the pace of the story by establishing a rhythm that pulls the reader from sentence to sentence; it creates smooth transitions; it sets up a mystery (What *does* the author mean?) that presumably the reader will want to read more about.

In tapping out a meter, repetition creates emphasis. The word or phrase you repeat assumes prominence and becomes a focal point. In the following passage, repetition of the word *gray* makes the point rhythmically and emphatically. Note, too, how the purposeful absence of commas in the second sentence helps the meter:

> At 5:30 on a December morning in Oregon you have to dig deep just to make it out of bed. About the best you can hope for this time of year is a slate gray dawn that lightens to a dove gray morning that slips into a pearl gray afternoon.

Repetition can be a powerful, dramatic and compelling technique. Perhaps that's why it is so often used in passionate, memorable speeches like Martin Luther King's "I Have a Dream" incantation.

Create Power with Parallelism

Parallelism is actually a kind of repetition, the repetition of grammatical patterns used to convey parallel or similar ideas. Parallelism is thus simultaneously a component of agreement (Chapter 7), coherence (Chapter 9) and style. Parallelism has the potential to create rhythm, emphasis, and drama as it clearly presents ideas or action. Consider the pleasant parallelism in both of these sentences, part of the opening paragraph of a column on food:

> [Americans] optimistically purchase Emeril's cookware, download Daniel's recipes and watch cooking shows. Yet they eat breakfast in their cars, lunch at their desks and chicken from a bucket.

Parallelism in the first sentence results from the verb/object construction (purchase cookware, download recipes, watch shows). The parallelism in the second sentence is a little more sophisticated because the writer, having established a pattern (breakfast, lunch) stays with the parallel structure but surprises you with the content.

Here's a combination of parallel structure and word play that makes for lively, rhythmic writing in a magazine column by Lisa Kogan:

> I've done a lot of things for men. I have worked for men and worked out for men. I have cooked for men, cleaned for men, dressed for men, and undressed for men. . . . I have tried meditation, medication, tennis, chess, golf, poker, laser tag and escargot for men.

Vary Sentence Length

Short sentences are naturally punchy, emphatic and dramatic; long sentences are naturally lilting, rolling and restful. Sentence length communicates just as surely as do the words within the sentence. Consider this excerpt from a blog about mothers and their teen daughters (www.myteenagewerewolf.com). Note the increasingly clipped sentences and their power to deliver a punch.

> The WORST thing about being the mother of a teenage daughter is the daily drama. It gives you whiplash, a migraine. The emotional turbulence shakes you to the core. The stormy waters make you seasick. Her mercury rises and falls. You sweat and freeze. You question her sanity. You question your sanity. You curse.

On the other hand, consider this 52-word sentence about the creative work of an advertising copywriter who is the subject of an Esquire profile:

> He did some memorable commercials in the "McDonald's and You" series, including one marathon spot to launch the campaign, which

ran on for as long as a travelogue and had grandparents and riverboats and airplanes and little kids in it, and made you proud, as well as hungry, to be an American.

Note how the sentence construction mirrors the idea the writer is communicating: the marathon length of the McDonald's commercial with its overabundance of kitschy images. The sentence is playful and seemingly endless (much like a commercial). It has rhythm. You can almost dance to it.

Take care with sentence length. If you construct a series of sentences of similar lengths, you run the risk of creating a plodding, deadening rhythm. If the sentences are all short, your prose may sound truncated and choppy, like a page from a children's book: "See the ball. The ball is green. Throw the ball." If the sentences are all long, the audience's attention may wander. Varying sentence length helps maintain interest while giving you the opportunity to use rhythm for drama and emphasis. For example, consider this passage from a profile of the author's mother. Note the length of the first three sentences followed by the long, almost rambling fourth.

> She taught herself to be a gourmet cook. She learned boeuf bourguignon and coq au vin from Julia Child. She perfected scampi. She created a garlic-studded pork loin I still dream about and occasionally spent all day pounding veal into paper-thin scaloppini which she wrapped around chopped proscuitto into individual rolls sewn closed with needle and thread before being braised in Marsala.

The long sentence at the end changes the rhythm of the passage. It also communicates: The sentence goes on and on, mirroring the day-long production of the entrée.

Here's another example of using sentence length to communicate. Note the relatively long sentences followed unexpectedly by a short, clipped sentence at the end.

> Duane Coop is standing 20 feet away from his practice target—a three-foot-diameter log with a painted red bull's-eye—throwing a two-and-a-half-pound, 32-inch double-bladed ax. The ax makes long, slow, end-over-end revolutions as it sails toward the target. Sprawled under the target, the family cat suns himself, listening without interest to the crack the six-inch blade makes as it slices into the log. The cat figures Duane won't miss. The cat's right.

Consider Fragments and Run-Ons

A fragment (an unfinished piece of a sentence) and a run-on (two or more complete sentences spliced together incorrectly) are grammatical errors. But certain grammatical rules can be bent by knowledgeable writers who are striving to achieve special effects. The rules against fragments and run-ons can occasionally be broken when you have a specific purpose in mind, when your audience (and editor) will stand for it and when the material warrants it. Of course, some forms, like blogs, lend themselves to a more conversational style that naturally includes fragments and run-ons. Advertising copywriters seem to be particularly fragment-happy. They can overdo it, creating choppy, confusing messages. On the other hand, they can use fragments effectively, as in this Toyota ad:

All science. No fiction.

Or this Hyundai ad:

It gives. You take. What a beautiful relationship.

The first two sentences are simple, grammatical subject-verb sentences. *What a beautiful relationship* is a fragment. It's punchy, funny and appropriate to the subject and medium. It works.

Fragments can create excitement, set a quick pace and grab attention. Like short sentences—but even more so—they have a brisk, staccato beat. They can be dramatic and emphatic. Here's an excerpt from a version of Chapter 2 of this book, published as a column in the online magazine Etude (http://etude.uoregon.edu)

What does grammar have to do with text messaging?
Nothing.
And therefore, everything.

These fragments are used purposefully to grab the reader's attention and to create a bit of drama.

Unlike the staccato beat of fragments, run-ons can communicate a breathless, sing-song rhythm. Depending on the words and ideas, a run-on can quicken the pace with a giddy rush of words or slacken the pace with a languid, rolling motion. Consider this run-on sentence from a Washington Post story about a Marine drill sergeant:

He is seething, he is rabid, he is wound up as tight as a golf ball with more adrenalin surging through his hypothalamus than a cornered slum rat, he is everything that these Marine recruits with their heads shaved to dirty nubs have ever feared or even hoped a drill instructor might be.

That sentence rushes forth, as full of adrenalin as the drill sergeant.

Do remember that breaking grammatical rules is serious business, and that there's an important distinction between breaking a rule purposefully and breaking a rule because you don't know the rule. Before you use fragments or run-ons, ask yourself these questions.

- Is the device appropriate to both the subject I am writing about and the medium I am writing for?

- Is this device the best way to achieve the effect for which I am striving?

- Does it work?

Don't use fragments or run-ons unless you can answer yes to all three questions. Even then, use these techniques sparingly. Like all stylistic devices, they lose both meaning and impact when overused.

Listen to the Sounds of Words

"A sentence is not interesting merely in conveying a meaning of words; it must do something more," wrote poet Robert Frost, who knew what he was talking about. "It must convey a meaning by sound." Broadcast journalists and speechwriters learn to write for the ear, but online and print writers often pay little attention to the sounds of the words they choose. That's unfortunate because most readers *hear* the word in their minds as they read. Print and online writers should be writing for the "inner ear" of their readers. Words chosen and arranged for their sound, as well as their meaning, add style and verve to prose.

Our language is full of words that sound like what they mean. Onomatopoeic words like *crack, buzz, snap, bang* and *chirp* imitate the sounds they define. They are crisp, colorful and doubly descriptive. Note how the "liveliness quotient" increases when you choose a word for its sound:

Instead of	Use
run	dash, dart, bolt, sprint
complain	grumble, squawk, growl
fracture	smash, shatter, snap
talk (a lot)	jabber, yammer, chatter

Some words are not actually onomatopoeic, but their sounds add to their meaning. Words beginning with the *s* sound, for example, often communicate (by sound and meaning) a kind of unpleasantness: *sneer, smirk* and *snigger* are stronger, nastier words than *mock, deride* or *look askance. Entanglements* can be *complications, problems* or *puzzles,* or they can be *snarls* or *snags.* A dog can *dribble* or *drool,* or it can (even more unpleasantly) *slobber* or *slaver.* The meanings are the same; sound adds the extra dimension.

Words beginning with the percussive *k* sound often communicate harshness or force. Politicians can have *power,* but when they have *clout* you know they're powerful. *Claws* seem more menacing than *talons. Carcass* or *corpse* is a harsher way of saying *dead body.* An ungraceful person is more *awkward* if described as a *clod.* In Chapter 9, we stressed the importance of choosing precise, accurate words. Here we are saying the writer striving for style ought to go one step further. Sound communicates. Look at both the meanings of words and their sounds.

Imagery

As writers, we are the eyes and ears of our audience. If we do our job well, we should be able to accurately re-create an event, a scene, a person, a moment in time for our audience. If we try harder, if we write with style, we can re-create in such vivid detail that our audience feels it has experienced what we write about. Including descriptive detail, showing rather than telling and using quotations and anecdotes are all stylistic techniques that can bring the subject close to the audience.

Use Descriptive Detail

Remember the buildings at Tupperware headquarters that looked like plastic containers? This is descriptive detail. Descriptive detail does not mean a truckload of adjectives. It means a word, a phrase, a sentence or the makings of an entire scene that focus on illuminating particulars. Consider this description of a woman of another era:

> She had style: the silk kerchief tied at the throat, the high heels she wore even to go food shopping, the straight skirts with kick pleats, the single eyebrow raised, a trick she perfected as a teenager after long hours in front of the mirror. She had beautiful eyebrows, high and arched, never plucked too thin. She had beautiful eyes, too, a clear, pale blue, with dark lashes that needed no mascara.

The details, carefully observed, bring the reader closer.

Descriptive detail can capture an action, help re-create an event or paint a scene. The writing need not be fancy. Plain, crisp language is your best ally, as in this description of a house:

> Pancho's new house was on the outskirts of town on a half-acre of scorched dirt stubbled with desert weed and brush, an old wooden barn in back, a big, misshapen tamarisk tree in front. It was a squat, ugly, flat-roofed building made of chunks of rock set in concrete troweled over chicken wire. The rock was the color of dried blood.

Show, Don't Tell

When you *tell* the audience something, you stand between the audience and the subject to offer judgments:

Leah was a busy girl.

This "descriptive" sentence fails to describe. It summarizes the writer's conclusions instead of presenting details, images, and concrete examples that would help readers draw their own conclusions. It *tells* rather than *shows*. Contrast it with this:

Leah rushed from basketball practice to a clarinet lesson to her a capella singing group, after which she studied her lines for the play, did two hours of French homework and cleaned her room.

Now *that's* busy. The details—not the writer's judgment—lead the reader to the conclusion.

Use Quotations

Lively, involving writing almost always includes people. The Wall Street Journal discovered this decades ago and pioneered a style for writing about complex economic issues. It was deceptively simple: The stories all began with people whom the reader got to know through description, quotation and anecdote. A complicated analytical piece on student loans would begin with one student and his story. Those who may have had little initial interest in reading a story about the economics of student loans would suddenly find themselves involved in the compelling personal story of a single student. Now hooked, they read on.

One way to bring people to the forefront of a story is to let them talk, to quote them. A *quotation* is a verbatim statement—the words between the quotation marks are the actual words spoken by the person being quoted. During the information-gathering process, media writers may listen to speeches, attend meetings and conferences, interview by e-mail, telephone or in person or stand in the background and listen to conversation. All the while they are scribbling notes or taping or both. When it comes to writing, they can be faced with pages and pages of quotations. How do they decide which to use and which to discard?

The first and most important consideration is *content*. Quoted material, like everything else the writer decides to include, should add to the audience's understanding of the message. The next consideration is *style*. Well-chosen quotations can be powerful elements in a story. They can:

- Bring the audience in direct contact with the person

- Capture and communicate a person's uniqueness

- Contribute to showing rather than telling

- Bring personality and passion to issues (even "dull" ones)

- Make a person—and a story—come alive

A well-chosen quotation clearly and vividly communicates something about the person. It is brief enough to hold the audience's interest. It expresses an idea that you, the writer, could not have said better. The last criterion is important. Sometimes people are long-winded; sometimes they go off on tangents. If you quote them (unless you are trying to show their long-windedness), you risk boring or confusing your audience. If the material is important enough to include, paraphrase it in your own words. Save quotations for strong, lively material.

But it's not just a quotation that can capture a person's uniqueness and enliven a story, it is how what was said was said—the *context*. The audience must be placed next to the person, must see and hear the person as he or she speaks. Consider the way quotations in context make this locker-room scene come alive:

> The heat and the anger redden Jody's face as she stalks off the court and down to the locker room. She doesn't wait for the team to find seats on the long wooden bench before she starts in on them.
> "You're making them look like goddamn all-Americans out there!" she screams. "You're dragging up and down the court with your tongues hanging out." She makes her voice whiny without lowering the decibel level. *"It's too hot and you're too tired. I am just not*

interested in hearing that, ladies. You should never have let them back into the game. Never. Now go back out there and *play*."

Here's another example. Note how the writer incorporates the contextual material as she goes along. Description and quotation work hand in hand as the writer introduces the subject of this newspaper profile, then 90-year-old Alice Roosevelt Longworth:

> "I still," she muses, rapping her bony fingers against her graying head, "more or less have my, what they call, marbles," and she pulls her flowered shawl around her a little closer, throws her head back and laughs gleefully.

This quotation does everything a good quotation should. The reader can *hear* the subject talking.

Use Anecdotes

An anecdote is a short account of an incident, a "mini story" with a beginning, middle and end. An anecdote illustrates a key point in the story, captures the essence of a character or highlights an important theme, offering detail and insight not possible any other way. It *shows* something the writer could have *told*, but in the telling would have weakened. Anecdotes can require a major expenditure of words, and media writers are often strapped for space or time. That's why it is vital to choose wisely, selecting that one moment that reveals, unmasks or captures some important truth about the subject. Consider this anecdote from the book "Dancing with Rose: Finding Life in the Land of Alzheimer's."

> It's lunch break, but Lena is not eating. "You ought to eat something," I tell her. I am not really thinking about nutrition. I am thinking that if her mouth is full she will stop talking.
> "I got something out of the machine," she says. That means, at best, a bag of Doritos. I ask how, if she doesn't eat lunch, she keeps up her strength for working. She's forty-five but looks a hard sixty.
> She shrugs. She smokes and watches me eat the salad I brought from home. "I bought fresh vegetables once," she says. I nod encouragingly. She takes another drag. "Yeah, they stayed in the refrigerator until they rotted."

This anecdote illuminates Lena's character as it touches on the unhappy truth that caregivers often don't take care of themselves. Could the writer have just written that? Sure. But the telling is flat and colorless; the showing brings it to life. Well-told anecdotes are the product of superior observation and interviewing skills as well as sophisticated writing skills. They are tough to do but very much worth the effort. Like descriptive detail, quotations and other "show, don't tell" techniques, anecdotes add zest to your writing.

Writing with Style

"Rich, ornate prose is hard to digest, generally unwholesome and sometimes nauseating," writes E. B. White in the classic "Elements of Style." Lively, original, writing, on the other hand, is a delicately seasoned dish one can savor.

Writers spend their lives learning how to create irresistible prose. They read voraciously. They play with different ideas. They sweat the details. They make mistakes. They try again. They make more mistakes. But if they love their craft, and they love the language—and they have the patience and perseverance it takes—they *(you!)* can learn to write compelling, memorable prose.

Chapter 11

Appropriate and Sensitive Language

South Carolina Republican Congressman Joe Wilson yells "You lie!" at Barack Obama during the president's health care speech before a joint session of Congress. (The incident resulted in a formal rebuke by the House of Representatives.)

Guests on the *Jerry* "Springer Show," the epitome of trash talk TV, jump out of their seats, curse savagely and pummel each other on camera. (Most likely, these "interactions" are staged.)

Radio shock jock Don Imus refers to the Rutgers women's basketball team as "nappy-headed hos" on his morning radio show. (CBS fires him four days later.)

At a time when this kind of glaring incivility reigns in our culture, what is there to say about a media writer's responsibility to respectful linguistic behavior?

A lot.

It is the responsibility of those of us who write for a living, those of us who write about the society in which we live, to contribute to, uphold and foster civil discourse. We do this by our ethical actions, by our sensitivity to both our sources and our audience and by our careful, accurate, thoughtful and appropriate use of language.

Sticks and Stones

Language can be empathetic (*I know just how you feel.*) or antagonistic (*Get out of my face!*). It can be nurturing (*I care about you.*) or threatening (*I'm going to kill you*). And as anyone who has ever been called—take your pick—stupid, ugly, cheap, geeky, skanky, lazy, idiotic, dim-witted or any of thousands of other words we can't and won't print here, language can also be hurtful. (It's astonishing, and instructive, to note that virtually all of the current insults hurled by high schoolers at other high schoolers are unprintable. It almost makes one yearn for the days when a solid insult was calling someone a "scurrilous knave," those days being the 1500s.)

Whoever said "Sticks and stones may break my bones, but names will never hurt me" apparently didn't get called many bad names—or had thicker skin than most of us. In fact, language *can* hurt. Words can sting. Language matters, words matter, in important, specific and very human ways. As writers, it is our job, our collective responsibility (there's that word again), to use language not just correctly, crisply and creatively—but sensitively as well.

Few journalists other than shock jocks (if they can be considered journalists) would consider using direct insults in writing. But using language embedded in stereotypes can be just as insulting (and hurtful): the helpless female, the brutish male, the cranky oldster, the terrorist Arab, the mobster Italian, the miserly Jew. Stereotypes are never kind. They demean not only the group being stereotyped but also all of us who strive to live in a civilized society.

What can writers do about this? We can do our part. Words by themselves do not cause nor can they solve the problems associated with insulting, unfair, discriminatory or hurtful treatment of others. But if we writers consciously or unconsciously use language that insults or that reinforces stereotypes, we support a world of prejudice and inequity. On the other hand, if we treat people fairly and sensitively—and individually—in our writing, we help create the kind of world in which most of us would like to live.

Unfortunately, this simple, reasonable concept of eschewing stereotypes and treating people fairly with words has itself become an object of insult and ridicule. Mocked as "political correctness" by some, it has been exaggerated to the point of silliness. As Principal Skinner announced on an episode of "The Simpsons:" "And in a gutless act of political correctness, Pizza Day will now be known as Italian-American Sauced Bread Day."

"Gee," political correctness critics smirk, "should we start calling short people *height disadvantaged*? How about people who can't carry a tune? Let's call them *tonally challenged*." It's certainly true that any reasonable concept can be taken to a ridiculous extreme, as these examples show. The point is that sensitive use of the language is a reasonable concept, not an ideological stance.

Language should help us appreciate and write about differences among people as it promotes fairness and tolerance. Choosing and using nondiscriminatory language is simple once you attune your sensitivities. Let's consider how to avoid several hurtful -*isms* in writing: sexism, heterosexism, racism, ageism, and, for lack of a better term, "able-bodiedism."

Sexism

Sexist language insults, stereotypes or excludes women. It treats men as the norm and women—although they make up 52 percent of the population—as the exception, the "other." Sexist language treats women as subordinate to men, thus contributing to both the perception and the reality of lingering, well-entrenched inequalities between the sexes. Inclusive, nonsexist, nondiscriminatory language, on the other hand, reflects the many positive changes that have happened and continue to happen in our society.

Man Does Not Include Woman

We understand the word *man* to mean a male human being (as in "The man wore a suit and tie"). But we use the same word to mean both male and female human beings (as in "Peace on earth, goodwill to *men*" or "All *men* are created equal"). How can one word simultaneously support two different meanings? How can one word be both gender-exclusive (male only) and gender-inclusive (male and female)? It's like saying: "Sometimes when I write the word *apple*, I mean apple. But other times when I write the word *apple*, I mean apple and orange. I leave it to you to figure out which is the operative meaning." It's confusing.

When elementary school girls and boys were asked to draw pictures to accompany a hypothetical history textbook with supposedly gender-inclusive chapter titles like "Colonial Man" and "Democratic Man"—*man* here was supposed to be synonymous with *people*—they weren't confused at all: All the boys and just about all the girls drew pictures of men—male human beings, that is. We may talk about the generic, or gender-inclusive *man*, but in fact *man* is generally understood as male only.

If you mean "male only," then, of course, use *man*. If you mean both men and women, our language has a wide variety of inclusive words. General references should always be inclusive.

Instead of	Use
man, men	person, people
mankind	people
founding fathers	founders, forebears
gentlemen's agreement	informal agreement
manpower	work force
to man (verb)	to staff, operate

Note that many words with *man* in them have nothing to do with gender. The root *man*, from Latin and then French, means "hand," giving us words like *man*ual, *man*ufacturing, and *man*ipulate.

The Myth of the Generic *He*

Just as *man* cannot mean both men only and men and women both, *he* cannot refer to a male person at certain times and both genders at other times. When you use *he,* you communicate maleness, whether that is your intention or whether that is the reality. For example:

A doctor must care first about <u>his</u> patients.

A child will gain confidence if <u>he</u> is allowed to make <u>his</u> own decisions.

Are all doctors men? Are all children male? Use of *he* or *him* presumes and communicates gender exclusivity. The rule is simple: Never use *he* or *him* unless you are referring to a male. If you mean to be gender-inclusive, you have three choices.

1. When you must use a pronoun to refer to a noun of undetermined or inclusive gender (*doctor, child*), recast the sentence with plurals. *They* and *them* are gender-inclusive:

    <u>Doctors</u> must care first about <u>their</u> patients.

    <u>Children</u> will gain confidence if <u>they</u> are allowed to make their <u>own</u> decisions.

2. If sentence structure or meaning would be impaired by the plural, use *he or she, his or her,* or *him or her.* This construction can be a bit awkward—but not as awkward as excluding more than half the human race:

    A doctor must care first about <u>his or her</u> patients.

3. Consider whether the pronoun is actually needed. Perhaps the sentence can be rewritten:

A child will gain confidence if allowed to make independent decisions.

The words *everyone* and *everybody* can present problems here. Their meaning is clearly plural, as in *many people* (presumably both male and female). But grammatically, these words take the singular, as in *Everyone is invited to the party*. Because they take the singular but imply the plural, look what can happen:

Everyone should remain in *his* seat.

To be grammatically correct, the sentence needs a singular pronoun. But a singular pronoun—*he* is almost always chosen, not *she*—communicates gender exclusivity. What to do? First, what not to do: Do not break a grammatical rule to create gender inclusivity. Do not write:

Everyone should remain in *their* seat.

You could write:

Everyone should remain in *his or her* seat,

but there's a clunkiness factor at work here. Better to find another way to say *everybody*, as in:

People should remain in their seats.

All concert-goers should remain in their seats.

From Exclusive to Inclusive Job Titles

A few hundred feet from a group of workers cutting roadside brush, you see (in most areas of our country) the sign "Crew at Work." Not so long ago you would have seen "Men at Work." Our language responds to societal change. Jobs that used to be male only and that carried male-only designations are now filled by both men and women. It is important to use the inclusive job designations. Here are some common ones.

Instead of	Use
mailman	mail carrier
policeman/policemen	police officer, police force
fireman	firefighter
newsman	reporter, journalist

businessman	businessperson, business executive, entrepreneur
salesman	sales clerk, sales representative
foreman	supervisor
congressman	senator, representative
chairman	head, presiding officer, chair
spokesman	representative, leader, spokesperson

Consistent Treatment of the Sexes

The consistency rule is simply stated and easily followed: When you write about men and women, treat them the same. If you refer to a man by last name only, do so for a woman. If you include such details as marital status, age and physical appearance when writing about a woman, make sure you would do the same if the subject were a man.

Let's say Mr. X is your city's newly elected mayor. Would you consider writing the following?

With his flashing brown eyes and warm, gracious smile, Mr. X, grandfather of four, took over city hall yesterday.

It sounds ludicrous, doesn't it? But because of deeply entrenched sexism that allows women to be judged by different criteria than men, a female mayor might very well be written about in this way. How about a sports story in which the new female coach is described as a "curly-headed blonde"? Just imagine using a similar physical description for a male coach. It is laughable. If it would be inappropriate (not to mention irrelevant) to offer this information about a man, it is equally so to offer it about a woman.

Contrary to the cliché, consistency is *not* the hobgoblin of small minds. It is a tool for nonsexist writing. Concern yourself particularly with consistency in the following five areas.

1. **Titles, names and references.** *Ms.,* which signals that the person named is female, but unlike *Miss* or *Mrs.* does not give information about her marital status, is the courtesy title for women. It parallels *Mr.,* which signals maleness without marital status. When you use one, use the other. If you use titles like *Pres., Sen.* or *Rev.* to refer to a man, refer to a woman in the same way.

   Many media outlets are doing away with Ms./Mr. courtesy titles, especially on second reference. In that case, refer to both men and women by last names only, except when you are writing about a couple who share the same last name. Full names or first names (used equally for both halves of the couple) will provide clarity. Some writers like the informality of referring to people by their first names. If the story warrants such a tone, and it would be appropriate to both the medium and the audience, go right ahead—but be consistent. Do not write "Mr. Garrett and his co-worker, Thea."

2. **Marital status and children.** Sometimes a person's marital or parental status is an appropriate and relevant piece of information that should be included in a story. Too often, though, women are defined by marital and parental status and men are not. Test yourself: If you would include the information for a man, do so for a woman. Consider this example:

   Economist David Evans has just launched his own consulting firm. Evans, a trim green-eyed father of three and husband of hospital administrator Claire Rosenfeld, invested more than $1 million of his own money.

   It appears—doesn't it?—that Evans's marital and parental status has nothing to do with this particular bit of news. It is unlikely a writer would think of including it. But if the story was instead about Rosenfeld, it is far more likely her husband and children would be mentioned. Question that. Then avoid doing it.

3. **Physical appearance.** Physical appearance may be completely appropriate to a story. Everyone wants to know how tall the new basketball center is (male or female). The overweight diet doctor, the business executive who wears Birkenstocks—these are all appropriate descriptions that add to readers' understanding. But too often women's clothes, bodies and mannerisms are described regardless of their relevance to the story. Women are not objects to be inspected and evaluated; they are, like men, subjects to be written about.

4. **Adding gender.** Most nouns in the English language are gender-inclusive: *writer, author, artist, scientist, doctor*. Treat them as such. Just as you do not need to insert *male* or *man* in front of these nouns when referring to a man in these positions, you should not insert *female* or *woman* when referring to a woman. You would probably never consider writing "*male* author Stephen King." Why then do we see such constructions as "*woman* poet"? Too frequently, writers add female gender to nouns that are actually gender-inclusive. The implied message: Only men are authors, artists, poets, writers and so

on. A woman is the rare exception. Of course, if women—or men—
are the exception, it's worth noting in some more sophisticated way.

5. **Equal treatment in word pairs.** When you pair men and women,
    make sure you choose equal words to refer to both sexes. Adult
    males and females are men and women; children are boys and girls.
    Man and *wife* is not an equal word pair. *Husband* and *wife* is.

Heterosexism

Discriminatory or stereotypical language exists for any group whose
physical appearance, behavior or beliefs vary from those in the main-
stream. Gays, lesbians, bisexuals and transgendered folks have had a
particularly difficult time swimming against that tide, and our language
proves the point. We have dozens of words that insult and demean gay
men and lesbians (*fag, fairy, dyke, butch*) and many more meant to tease
and torment any woman who exhibits traditionally male behavior and
any man who does not. Consider the simple ways writers can rid their
language of bias and bigotry. Doing so has nothing to do with endorsing
or approving of a "lifestyle" and everything to do with treating people as
distinct human beings.

Not Everyone Is Heterosexual

Just as sexism in language assumes maleness, heterosexism assumes
wholesale heterosexuality. But everyone is not heterosexual. Because
homosexuality has carried such a stigma in our society, until recently few
gay men and lesbians have gone public with their sexual orientations.

If you don't immediately assume the heterosexuality of those you
write about, you can avoid awkwardness (for example, asking an interview subject why he or she never married) and surprise (upon learning,
for example, that a "feminine-looking" woman is a lesbian).

A Person Is Not His or Her Sexual Orientation

Although a person's sexual orientation may be vital to the story—a profile
of a gay activist, a church and its homosexual parishioners—many times it
is not. If you would not consider writing "The company is owned by heterosexual entrepreneur Mical Lewis" (and, of course, you wouldn't), then
why include information about homosexual orientation if, for example,

Lewis was gay? Even worse is such wording as "an admitted homosexual" (as if the person were admitting to a heinous offense) or a "practicing homosexual" (do we ask heterosexuals if they "practice," too?).

Beware of Stereotypes and Exceptions

Homosexuals cannot be stereotyped any more than can heterosexuals. They are all ages, all races and ethnicities, all religions. They live in different parts of the country and are employed in all occupations. Some are single; others live with lifelong partners. Some have children; others do not.

It is important to understand this diversity for two reasons. First, it will help you avoid thinking of (and describing) a gay person as a "type." Second, and probably more important, it will help you guard against making a point of characteristics that don't conform to the "type," calling special attention to such "oddities" as the lesbian with long hair or the gay man with children. The assumption behind these observations is that all lesbians look a certain way, that all gay men live a certain kind of life. Do all heterosexuals look and act alike?

Racism

Those Americans of African, Asian, Native American or Hispanic descent—that is, those who look noticeably different than Americans of European descent—are the most obvious victims of racist attitudes, behavior and speech. (Members of these groups collectively make up about one-third of the U.S. population.) Racism can affect every part of their lives, from where they live to the medical services they receive, from the quality of their education to their self-esteem and self-image. Racism is a problem of enormous proportion in the United States and worldwide. Americans of various European ancestries labor under the burden of ethnic stereotypes as well: the stingy Scot, the dumb Pole, the drunken Irish. There are more than enough negative and hurtful slurs to go around.

It is unlikely that you would demonstrate overt racism in your writing. But it *is* likely that your judgment would be affected by the long-standing and pervasive stereotypes that exist in our society. Regardless of your own personal goodwill, you assuredly harbor some prejudices; you undoubtedly "see" people through the filter of stereotype. Here is how to make sure your language is prejudice-free.

Don't Identify People by Race

Do not identify a person's race or ethnicity unless it is a relevant or an interesting part of the story. If someone is the first of his or her racial or ethnic group to achieve a certain goal, that fact may be newsworthy (although those "first who" stories can quickly become trite). But if you would not normally identify a person as being white in a story, do not use racial identity at all. Relatively few situations require the inclusion of race.

Don't Reinforce Stereotypes by "Exceptions"

Language can reinforce racism by treating people as exceptions to stereotypes, which is just as demeaning as using the stereotype itself. For example, making it a point to call an Italian-American "respectable and law-abiding" implies that most are not, thus reinforcing the Mafia stereotype. Writing that a Mexican-American is "hardworking and even-tempered" implies that Mexican-Americans in general are indolent and volatile. The negative stereotype is embedded in the positive attributes.

Avoid Using "Non-Whites"

Eurocentrism—using white, European culture as the norm—is evident when you refer to people as "non-whites." Why describe people by what they aren't? Would you call a 25-year-old a "non-teen"? Would you call a brunette a "non-blonde"? Of course not. Be particularly careful when using the word *minority* as well. In a growing number of U.S. cities, in the state of California, and in the world in general, whites are the minority.

Be Sensitive to Group Names

Be aware of what members of various racial and ethnic groups call themselves and want to be referred to publicly. These names change with the times. Early in the twentieth century, black Americans were called "coloreds" and pressed hard to be called the more respectable term *Negro*. In the 1960s, *black* and *Afro-American* were the terms of choice. Today many people prefer *African-American,* a term consistent with how we refer to other Americans of international heritage (*Asian-Americans,* for example). Indians are generally referred to as *American Indians,* as *Native Americans,* or as members of particular tribes or confederations.

Those descended from Spanish-speaking cultures might be referred to as *Chicano(a), Latino(a), Hispanic* or, more specifically, by country of origin *(Cuban-American, Mexican-American)*.

Given that the word *minorities* may be factually inaccurate and that *non-whites* is Eurocentric, the search continues for a more sensitive aggregate term. *People of color,* although sometimes used, sounds oddly formal and also can be somewhat less than accurate, as olive-skinned whites of Mediterranean ancestry can be more "colorful" than some people of color. Rather than lump together a variety of racial and ethnic groups and hunt for a single descriptor, it seems preferable to simply list the groups themselves.

Ageism

Codger, fogy, fossil. geezer, duffer, coot. Hag, nag, bag, crone. Senile citizens. Our language is not kind to older people.

Older people are feeble, frail, forgetful, crabby, creaky, constipated and curmudgeonly. These are the stereotypes, and they are not only insulting, they are largely inaccurate. The vast majority of older people live healthy, productive and independent lives. The active, alert, involved older person is the rule, not the exception.

At the turn of the twentieth century, one in 16 Americans was 60 or older. At the turn of the twenty-first, that ratio was one in six. Within the next decade, it will be one in five. That's more than 86 million people. It is past time for writers to learn how to deal accurately and sensitively with older people.

Few writers would actually use any of the offensive terms listed at the beginning of this section, but many might find the stereotypes pervading their writing in more subtle ways. Generally, ageist language reinforces damaging stereotypes by expressing great surprise over those who do not conform to them.

She is still vigorous at 70.

His mind is still sharp at 75.

The implication is that most 70-year-olds lack vigor and that most 75-year-olds are senile. If you refuse to accept the inaccurate stereotypes, you will avoid making insulting statements about "exceptions."

Although our society (and its language and images) is unkind to older people of both genders, more women than men may be victimized by ageist language. The stigma of aging is greater for women, who, throughout their lives, have traditionally been evaluated more by what they look like than by who they are. A gray-haired or balding man of 65 might be thought of and described as "distinguished" or "at the height of his powers." (Note the Louis Vuitton ads featuring a ruggedly handsome eighty-year-old Sean Connery.) A gray-haired woman of 65 is rarely thought of or described in such complimentary terms—nor is she featured advertising any products other than those meant to mitigate certain medical conditions.

Ageism exists on both ends of the life span. Teenagers are irresponsible, inarticulate, hormone-driven slackers—or so goes the stereotype. That accounts for the ageist singling out of "responsible" and "thoughtful" teens, as if they were the surprising exception rather than, in fact, the rule.

To write sensitively and accurately about people in any age group, question your assumptions and reject stereotypes. Write about people as individuals, not as representatives of, or exceptions to, their age group.

"Able-Bodiedism"

No, that is not a word, and we are not suggesting that it should be! *Able-bodiedism* is a term we've coined here to stand for language discrimination against people with disabilities. In the United States, Americans with disabilities constitute the third-largest minority (after persons of Hispanic origin and African-Americans). A few years ago, the U.S. Census Bureau estimated that there were 37 million disabled adults and children. Some have physical or mental disabilities that limit their activities and impair their performance; some do not. A disability does not necessarily "disable" or make one a "disabled person." Some disabilities simply don't affect one's work. (Is the writer in a wheelchair a disabled writer? Was Beethoven a disabled musician?) Other disabilities, in fact, create new abilities.

When writing about people with physical or mental limitations, ask them how they want to be referred to. Also keep in mind this vital rule: People are not their handicaps. People *have* handicaps (limits, impairments, different abilities). Never write:

Arthur Thomas, an epileptic . . .

The handicapped children . . .

Assuming it's relevant, write instead:

Arthur Thomas, who has epilepsy . . .

The children, who all have disabilities . . .

The *-isms* Golden Rule

All this advice boils down to one rule: Write about others as you would want them to write about you. You see yourself as an individual who may be male or female, old or young, fat or thin, black, brown, red or white. Consider the stereotypes for each one of these categories. Are you the stereotype or are you a distinct individual? You are, of course, an individual. See—and write about—others with the same regard for and sensitivity to their individuality. This is not a matter of being politically correct. It is a matter of being human.

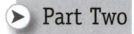

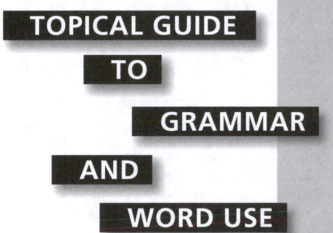

Part Two

TOPICAL GUIDE

TO

GRAMMAR

AND

WORD USE

Consider this section a quick "pit stop" in the often long and pressure-packed race against time and errors. You'll find speedy answers to grammatical questions and explanations of terminology here in Part 2. These brief alphabetical listings are not meant to take the place of the longer discussions in the main text.

Guides like these have personalities. Some are scolding and authoritarian. Others are so permissive that they give little sense of direction. Still others are eccentric and seem to reflect the personal preferences of the author rather than the logic of word use.

We hope the personality of this guide is that of a mentor, an older and (a little) wiser writer who respects and loves the language and encourages others to do the same.

AB–AD

-able/-ible endings These suffixes (endings to root words) can be frustrating. Why do we have *acceptable* on one hand and *impossible* on the other? It's hard to come up with a reasonable answer! But it may help to remember that *-able* endings are more common and that in most cases the *-able* suffix is attached to a complete root word (change + *able* = changeable). See Appendix A for more about spelling.

acronym Like a peak formed by a seismic shift, an acronym is a word created by using the beginning letter or letters of a group of words, such as PAC (**P**olitical **A**ction **C**ommittee) and SONAR (**SO**und **NA**vigation and **R**anging).

Inventive and economical, yes? Acronyms do not use periods between letters unlike abbreviations that cannot be pronounced as a single word, such as A.C.L.U., the American Civil Liberties Union.

active voice/passive voice Voice refers to the form of a verb. When the subject of the sentence performs the action of the verb ("She wrote the story"), the verb (wrote) is in the active voice. If the subject receives the action ("The story was written by her"), the verb (was written) is in the passive voice. The active voice is always stronger and more direct than the passive voice. You might want passive voice when you need to stress the receiver of the action rather than the performer or when the performer is unknown. See pp. 35–42.

adapt/adopt These two verbs are distinct in their differences. *Adapt* refers to a "change to fit a situation" both in physical and conceptual ways:

> **Bryce and Jackie <u>adapted</u> their Tony-winning script to Hollywood's commercial needs.**

> **The anthropologist had to <u>adapt</u> to the customs of the tribal villagers to live among them.**

Adopt, however, denotes the action of "taking on," as in

> **The commissioners <u>adopted</u> a wait-and-see attitude on**
>   ("took on")
> **a $45-million budget.**

It also denotes "taking in," as in

> **The family <u>adopted</u> a black Labrador.**
>   ("took in")

adjective This part of speech is a "finishing touch" for a noun or a pronoun. As a modifier, the adjective describes, limits and adds important detail. The writer's biggest challenge with adjectives is choosing the right ones—in meaning, nuance and tone—for the job. Adjectives are the hue and chroma of our writing. The spectrum they can provide is almost limitless. Remember: Participial phrases are always adjectives. (Check our entry on dangling modifiers.)

adverb Adverbs generally answer how, why and when. Strong adverbs work in tandem with descriptive verbs to create powerful imagery. In expressing matters of degree, time, place and manner, however, adverbs can modify not only verbs but also adjectives and other adverbs. Like the adjective, the adverb must be chosen carefully and applied precisely. Remember that not all adverbs end in *-ly.* (That would be much too simple!)

adverse/averse Although these adjectives sound alike, they have distinct meanings. *Adverse* means "unfavorable or hostile":

> **Investment bankers were surprised by the sudden onset of <u>adverse</u> economic conditions.**

If you want to describe someone's reluctance or opposition, you should use *averse:*

> **I am not <u>averse</u> to approving your vacation request.**

advice/advise Don't mix these up! *Advice* is a noun denoting an "opinion," while *advise* is a verb that means "to counsel" or "to recommend."

He wondered about his friend's <u>advice</u> to break up with his
  (noun: "suggestion")
girlfriend.

The lawyer <u>advised</u> a quick response to the threatened lawsuit.
  (verb: "to suggest")

affect/effect This pair, one of our "hot buttons," is also one of the most common usage errors. It's true that the words sound alike, but they are most often different parts of speech. *Affect* is almost always a verb that means "to influence" or "to pretend to have." *Effect* is almost always a noun that means "result" or "impact." For example:

The new program will <u>affect</u> millions of previously uninsured
  (verb: "to influence")
adults.

The defendant <u>affected</u> a carefree manner.
  (verb: "to pretend to have")

Voters are questioning the <u>effect</u> of term limits.
  (noun: "impact")

But just to make life interesting, *effect* is occasionally used as a verb in formal writing to mean "to bring about," and *affect* can be a noun in very narrow usage to denote certain behavior in psychology:

Top management <u>effected</u> some personnel changes.
  (verb: "to bring about")

Michael's flat <u>affect</u> concerned his psychologist.
  (noun: "psychological state")

-aholic endings Here is proof that language indeed lives. Through slang usage, *-aholic* tacked onto a word has come to mean "one obsessed with," as in *workaholic* and *chocaholic*. Presumably these new words owe their existence to *alcoholic*. But instead of taking the accepted suffix *-ic* meaning "of or pertaining to," from the root word *alcohol*, the creators of these new words stole (and misspelled) another syllable and a half. That this linguistic configuration makes no sense bothers only purists. The rest of us enjoy new words with effective and distinct meanings.

aid/aide Don't be fooled: Aides ("assistants") give aid ("help, assistance") to their bosses. *Aid* also can be a verb, but *aide* can be only a noun. So, constructions such as "the president's aide" and "giving aid and comfort to the enemy" are correct.

all/any/most/some These pronouns can take singular or plural verbs, depending on the meaning. If the word carries the meaning of "general amount or quantity," it is singular:

> **All** of the contraband was seized at the port.

> **Some** of his testimony was stricken from the record.

If you can read "individual and number" into the sentence, the plural verb should be used:

> **All** of the children are safe.

> Have **any** viewers called to complain?

See p. 81 and the entry for *none*.

all ready/already By the end of this section, you should be all ready to avoid confusion between the adjective phrase *all ready* and the adverb *already*. You are "completely prepared" to do something when *all* modifies *ready*. But you've learned something "by now" or "by this time" when you know the meaning of the adverb *already*.
So:

> Tom was **all ready** to board the flight when his pager beeped.

> Tom was **already** on the plane when his pager beeped.

allude/elude These meanings shouldn't elude you. If you are making an indirect reference to something, you allude to it. If you want to mention it directly, you refer to it.

> The candidate **alluded** to his opponent's prison record.

Elude is your choice if you mean "to escape or to avoid detection."

> The fugitive **eluded** the search party for two weeks.

a lot Yes, the word *lot* can mean "a parcel of land." But the usual confusion with this casual phrase meaning "many" or "much" is its appearance as one word. It is not correct to write *alot*. Always use the phrase as two words.

> I have seen **a lot** of bad grammar errors in my time.

altar/alter The noun *altar* is defined as "a table-like structure used in religious ceremonies." *Alter* (the verb) means "to change or modify." So:

> The congregation voted to **alter** the angle of the **altar** in their church.

among/between *Among* generally relates to more than two persons or things, and *between* applies to only two. But it's not that simple. A truer guide is this: If there is a definite relation involved, *between* is preferred, no matter what the number:

> **Between you and me, this business will never succeed.**

> **Negotiations have broken down between the government mediator, autoworkers and management.**

Among is properly used when there is no explicit relationship stated and when distribution is stressed:

> **The reward was divided among five families.**

antecedents Often hiding in a sentence like a serpent in tall grass, an antecedent is the noun to which a pronoun refers. A clear connection between the antecedent and the pronoun is necessary for the sentence to make sense and read well. But sometimes the antecedent of a pronoun is unclear, and writers may have problems with agreement between the antecedent and the verb. In the following sentences, proper antecedents are underlined:

> **Sarah is one of those people who never require more than four hours of sleep.**

Why is the antecedent *people* instead of *one*? Because the sentence tells us that there is more than one person who can get by on that amount of sleep, the dependent clause needs a plural verb.

> **Geronimo Jackson is the only one of the finalists who isn't nervous.**

In this sentence, only one finalist isn't nervous, hence the singular verb.

> **Zane's theory is intriguing, but not many of his colleagues agree with it.**

The pronoun *it* properly refers to the antecedent *theory*. The intriguing theory, not Zane, is the focus.

a number of/the number of The intended number of these phrases depends on the article. If the article is *a*, the meaning is plural:

> **A number of students are going on the field trip.**

If the article is *the*, the meaning is more indefinite (or is seen as a unit) and therefore is singular:

> **The number of swine flu cases is increasing.**

Here is an easy-to-remember tip about subject-verb agreement: If the phrase or word denotes a general amount or quantity, the verb is singular; if the phrase or word denotes a more definable number of individuals, the verb is plural. See p. 78.

anxious/eager Why are so many people eager to use *anxious* improperly? Are they anxious about writing too slowly? Read this carefully: *Anxious* implies fear and worry:

> **Engineers are <u>anxious</u> about bridge safety in the county.**

If you are stimulated and excited at the prospect of doing something, you are eager to do it:

> **The new coach is <u>eager</u> to meet her team.**

You can be anxious *about* something; you cannot be anxious *to do* that thing!

anybody/anyone and **any body/any one** As compound words, *anybody* and *anyone* are indefinite pronouns that refer to no one in particular. As two separate words, they become adjective-noun combinations that are more pointed—one (person or thing) of a defined group.

> **<u>Anybody</u> can learn to swim with an attentive instructor.**
> (possible for all who are interested)
>
> **<u>Any one</u> (of the players) could be substituted in the soccer game.**
> (any player on the team)

It's common for *any one* to be followed by *of.* If you can insert a noun after an implied *of,* then the adjective-noun combination is a must.

appositive This is a word, phrase or clause that renames or adds information about the word that precedes it. Words in apposition have a side-by-side relationship. They are important to identify because they have some bearing on punctuation and case decisions. For example, a restrictive appositive is one that is essential to the meaning of a sentence and thus requires no commas:

> **My friend <u>John</u> helped write headlines while his friend <u>Susan</u>**
>   (appos.)   (appos.)
>
> **did the design.**

A comma would not be correct after *friend* because John and Susan are essential to the meaning of the subject.)

A nonrestrictive appositive still has a side-by-side relationship, but its meaning is not essential to the sentence. It must be set off by commas:

> **Mullins, <u>a proven clutch player</u>, has a secure place on the roster.**
> (appos.)

as if/like These are not interchangeable. *As if* acts as a conjunction and introduces a clause:

> **It looks <u>as if</u> it will rain.**

Like, a preposition, takes a simple object and cannot introduce a clause:

> **It looks <u>like</u> rain.**

Some grammarians say that *like* may evolve into a conjunction. (We're not holding our breath.)

as/than Because *as* and *than* can be both prepositions and conjunctions, case selection may be tricky. If these words are used as conjunctions, it is most likely to make comparisons. If so, the nominative case of the pronoun is needed:

> **There's no one more handsome <u>than</u> he.**

In the example above, *than he is handsome* is understood as the second clause.

However, *as* and *than* can also be prepositions:

> **Why did you pick Beth rather <u>than</u> her?**

Obviously, no comparison is being made here. The pronoun following the preposition must be in the objective case.

as well as This phrase, which connects a subordinate thought to the main one, can cause agreement problems between subject and verb. Remember that the main subject—not any word or phrase parenthetical to it—controls the number and the person of the verb:

> **The house, <u>as well as</u> its contents, was destroyed in the early-morning fire.**

Similar parenthetical phrases are *together with, in addition to* and *along with.* You'll find it easier to isolate the true subject of the sentence if you set off these phrases with commas. See p. 77.

bad/badly Don't feel bad if you use these words badly! *Bad* is an adjective. In linking-verb constructions in which you want to describe the subject, *bad* is the correct choice:

> **Teachers feel <u>bad</u> about the budget defeat.**
>   (l.v.) (adj.)

This sentence describes the mayor's state of being, not his physical ability to feel. When you describe some quality of the verb instead of the subject, you use the adverb *badly*:

> **The prime minister took her defeat <u>badly.</u>**

Here, *badly* describes the verb *took,* not the noun *prime minister.)*

because of/due to You should always use *because of* when matching cause to effect. It is used when the writer can ask why in a sentence:

> **The stock market crashed <u>because of</u> panic selling.**

Due to should be used only in a linking verb construction. *Due* is an adjective; its preposition *to* relates to the condition of a subject:

> **The increase in the cost of burritos is <u>due to</u> soaring prices of jack cheese.**

Note that you can't ask why in this construction, but you can in the next, which is why *because of,* not *due to,* is correct:

> **<u>Because of</u> the budget crunch this year, no new positions will be created.**

beside/besides *Beside* means "next to" or "at the side of." *Besides* means "in addition to":

> **The nervous guard stood <u>beside</u> the visiting dignitary.**
>   (next to)

> **<u>Besides</u> Jake and me, only Jill knew of the escape plan.**
> (in addition to)

Remember that simple objects of prepositions always take the objective case.

bi-/semi- *Bi-* means "two," and *semi-* means "half." *Bimonthly* means "every two months"; *semimonthly* means "twice a month." If you are referring to something that happens twice a year, use *semiannual* rather than *biannual,* even though the dictionary recognizes both. That will avoid confusion with *biennial* (something that happens every two years). Note that words containing the prefixes *bi-* and *semi-* are hyphenated only when the root word (the word the prefix attaches to) begins with an *i* or is capitalized.

both/few/many/several These indefinite pronouns always take a plural verb. See p. 80.

brand names/trademarks   These are business-created words that have not fallen into generic usage. Do you really want to refer to a specific product, or do you just want to mention the process? If you want to mention the process or the generic name, avoid brand name reference. Do not write, for example:

> **The spy <u>xeroxed</u> all the documents.**

For one thing Xerox, a registered trade name, isn't a verb; the spy can photocopy the documents, but he or she can't xerox, canonize or savinize them. Other examples are Scotch tape (a brand of cellophane tape), Coke (one of many cola beverages), Mace (a brand of tear gas), Jell-o (a gelatin dessert) and Kleenex (a brand of facial tissue). All brand names and trademarks should be capitalized.

bureaucratese/jargon Jargon has changed our language—but not for the better. These words and phrases, used by government workers, scientists, doctors, computer programmers and a host of other professionals, usually do more to obscure than elucidate. For example, you no longer measure the effect of deficit spending on a budget; you "ascertain how the program will impact fiscal planning." You no longer evaluate things; you "effect a needs assessment." A heart attack becomes an "M.I." (myocardial infarction). When these professionals talk to one another, their language may be both efficient and precise. But when journalists write for broader audiences, this specialized language does not work. See p. 128.

but   *But* is most frequently a conjunction, connecting words and phrases of equal rank and implying a contrast between those elements. It almost always requires a comma between the clauses it separates:

> **The commissioners approved the budget, <u>but</u> they vetoed a room tax provision.**

But also can be a preposition meaning "except":

Everybody <u>but</u> me went to the party.

Note that the objective case is required for the pronoun.

Can *but* be used to begin a sentence, like the conjunctive adverb *however*? But of course—if you don't overdo it.

CA–CE

can/may Please preserve the distinction between these words. *Can* denotes ability, and *may* denotes possibility and permission. If your sentence is in the form of a question, *may* is almost always your choice:

<u>May</u> I go to the exhibit?
(Permission, not ability, is the question.)

Do you think I <u>can</u> win this election?
(Do I have the ability to win?)

Some stylebook authorities have thrown in the towel on the interchangeability of *can* and *may,* but we're not willing to give up the fight. However, remember that *may* can also express a possibility.

I <u>may</u> buy that new boat we've been talking about.

case *Who* or *whom? Us* or *we?* Understanding case helps us make these grammatical choices. The three cases are nominative, objective and possessive. Certain pronouns change their form to accommodate a change in case. Nouns change only in their possessive case. See pp. 84–93.

capital/capitol The distinction is simple: The capital is the city in which a state government is headquartered, as in Salem, Oregon. The Salem building where government meets and legislates is called the capitol.

censor/censure These words have different meanings, pronunciations and spellings, so what's the confusion? Perhaps it's because the meanings are interrelated. You can censor materials by screening, changing or forbidding them.

The general <u>censored</u> all dispatches from the battle lines.

You generally can censure only people—by condemning them or expressing disapproval of their actions.

The senators <u>censured</u> their colleague because he <u>censored</u> a staff report.

These words can also be nouns. So, you can have an "official government censor" as well as a "resolution of censure."

chair/chairperson The term *chairman* incorrectly assumes maleness of that position. It is one of many such terms in our language (others are *policeman* and *businessman*). For years, authoritative dictionaries have defined *chair* as "a person who presides over a meeting" and "an office or position of authority." A person—man or woman—can chair a meeting or be a program chair. It assumes nothing but the position itself. *Chairperson* seems a bit more awkward to us, but it may be what an organization chooses to call its leader. The person's official title should be used. See Chapter 11.

cite/site/sight These homophones have nothing in common except their pronunciation. You make reference to a person or thing when you *cite*, a piece of land when you are on *site*, or a visual spectacle when you *sight*.

Cite is always a verb:

> The tribunal <u>cited</u> the leader as one of the world's worst
> dictators.

Site is always a noun, though there is evidence that some writers probably influenced by architects, are trying to use it as a verb:

> The <u>site</u> of the 1964 World's Fair used to be a garbage dump.

But you can *sight* (verb) or have *sight* (noun):

> She <u>sighted</u> the island from the ship after thinking that none was
> (verb: saw)

> in <u>sight.</u>
> (noun: a view)

clause This is a group of words that contains both a subject and a verb. An independent clause (otherwise known as a sentence) expresses a complete thought and can stand alone. A dependent clause has a subject and a verb, but the meaning is incomplete, and the clause cannot stand alone. See p. 26.

clutter This is the excess baggage that obscures clarity in writing. Mercilessly prune from your prose flabby words, redundant phrases or just plain long-winded expressions.

collective nouns They look singular (*jury, herd, committee*) but obviously imply plurality. Or they can look plural (*athletics, politics*) but imply singularity. What's a writer to do? Here's the answer: If the noun is considered as a whole, the verb and associated pronouns are singular:

> **The committee <u>is</u> meeting today.**

> **Politics <u>is</u> a dirty business.**

If the unit is broken up or considered individually, the plural verb is required:

> **The herd of cattle <u>have</u> scattered.**

> **The senator's politics <u>are</u> changeable.**

See p. 81.

collision This is a violent contact between moving bodies. An accident between a moving car and a stationary telephone pole is not a collision; it is a crash. But an oil tanker might collide with a frigate on the high seas. In a more figurative sense, ideas, opinions and, yes, words can collide.

colon This punctuation mark (:) introduces thoughts, quotations, examples or a series. Capitalize matter following a colon only if it can stand alone as a sentence:

> **Her parting words inspired them for years<u>:</u> "<u>Y</u>ou must think outside the box."**

> **Besides cartooning, Charles Schulz had one great passion<u>:</u> <u>h</u>ockey.**

comma splice Also known as a *comma fault,* this is a mistake by the careless writer who joins two independent clauses without either a coordinating conjunction or a semicolon:

> **A 10-vehicle pileup blocked the interstate <u>highway, state</u> officials estimate it won't reopen for two days.**

The example above lacks the conjunction *but* or a semicolon between clauses.

> **He enjoys reviewing <u>movies, however,</u> he says he can't waste his time on "trash like this."**

In this sentence, the presence of the conjunctive adverb *however* requires a semicolon between clauses—that is, between *movies* and *however.*

In short sentences, the comma splice has received the blessing of most grammarians. "You'll like her, she's a Leo" can survive without a conjunction or a semicolon. An accomplished writer who does not want the harsh stop of a semicolon to slow the meter of a sentence might employ the comma splice as a stylistic tool. But, like the sentence fragment, the comma splice should be used sparingly—and only by writers who know what they're doing.

comparative/superlative   refers to the "degrees" of certain adjectives and adverbs. Let's take the word *soft* and examine its degrees as an adjective *(soft)* and adverb *(softly)*:

soft (adj.)	softer	softest
	(comparative)	*(superlative)*
softly (adv.)	more softly	most softly
	(comparative)	*(superlative)*

Obviously, when you establish a comparative degree for an adjective, it is redundant to attach an adverb to it as well, as in *more softer*.

compared to/compared with   These are about as interchangeable as American and European voltage. When you liken one thing to another, you *compare* it *to*:

> **The mayor's behavior can be <u>compared to</u> that of a 3-year-old in the throes of a tantrum.**

When you place items side by side to examine their similarities and differences, use *compared with*:

> **<u>Compared with</u> housing prices in the year 2000, real estate costs today seem like an incredible bargain.**

As you can see, the use of *compared to* is both figurative and metaphorical. *Compared with*, on the other hand, is statistical rather than creative.

complement/compliment   Both can be nouns or verbs. *Complement* means "that which completes something, supplements it or brings it to perfection." *Compliment* means "an expression of praise or admiration." So, a necklace might complement a blouse, but you would compliment the wearer on her good taste in necklaces.

compose/comprise   *Compose* is not as direct as *comprise*. Something is *composed of* other things (made up of); however, one thing *comprises* (takes in, includes) other things. The following are correct usages:

His salad dressing was <u>composed of</u> olive oil, balsamic vinegar and puree of turnip.

Adams' new symphony <u>comprised</u> five dramatic movements.

As you can see from the last example, the whole (symphony) comprises the parts (movements). A whole is never comprised of the parts. That would be the same as saying (nonsensically) that "the whole is included of its parts." But *comprise* is not a word we would use more than occasionally. Sometimes it just doesn't sound right.

compound modifiers These are two adjectives or an adverb joined to an adjective to modify a noun. Often a hyphen is needed to join these modifiers to make the meaning clear:

<u>well-intentioned</u> offer

<u>hard-driving</u> perfectionist

Modifiers do not require a hyphen if they are preceded by *very* or an *-ly* adverb. These adverbs obviously modify what follows, and there is no mistaking their connection:

<u>very energetic</u> teacher

<u>highly motivated</u> student

Don't string together too many modifiers in the name of description and economy. You'll simply get clutter.

conjunction The conjunction links words, phrases and clauses; if used properly, it provides both logic and rhythm to a sentence. Note how the conjunction *and* provides parallelism or equality to a clause:

The border guard quickly stamped the passport <u>and</u> cheerfully directed the tourist to the nearest town.

But (what a great conjunction—it provides a contrast or shows a lack of unity) note how the conjunction *and* is used improperly when it links obviously unequal or unrelated elements in a sentence:

She refuses to work overtime, <u>and</u> she is a great crossword puzzle solver.

Also see **as if/like** on p. 180.

conjunctive adverb Words like *however, therefore* and *nevertheless* may look like conjunctions, but they are really adverbs. Why is this distinction important? It's because conjunctive adverbs need a semicolon—not a comma (as conjunctions do)—to link sentence parts. For example:

> **The book is a best seller; <u>however,</u> I find it pretentious and poorly written.**

See pp. 67, 107.

continual/continuous *Continual* means "repeated or intermittent." *Continuous* means "unbroken":

> **Must I suffer these <u>continual</u> interruptions?**

> **The parched hiker imagined a <u>continuous</u> line of canteens stretched across the barren horizon.**

contraction An usually successful and sensible merging of words for economy and informality. Examples: *It's* (it is), *who's* (who is), *doesn't* (does not). We use the apostrophe to span the missing letter or letters, as with this gem: *it'd* (it would or it had). Now don't let this "smooshing" get out of hand!

convince/persuade If you think these words are identical in meaning, we're just going to have to *persuade* you that they're not. We'll do that until you're *convinced*! To begin with, people do not convince others of anything; that action is persuasion:

> **The House speaker <u>persuaded</u> the representative to change her vote.**

To be convinced is to be secure in a decision or a principle. It is an adjective, not a verb:

> **I'm not <u>convinced</u> that I should change my vote.**

If a person attempts to persuade another and is successful, the first person is considered persuasive. Obviously the argument has been convincing. The process is to persuade; the hoped-for result is to be convinced. Got that now? Convinced? Or do you need to be persuaded?

council/counsel The difference between *counsel* (a verb or noun, depending on use in a sentence) and *council* (always a noun) is "one to many." When you seek *counsel*, you generally pursue advice from one person, such as an attorney or school teacher. But when you look to a *council*, you attend the meetings or hear the deliberations of a body of elected or appointed officials. Three examples:

> **The teacher <u>counseled</u> her students to carefully review the**
>   (verb)
> **sample exam.**

> **I have always appreciated his thoughtful <u>counsel</u>.**
>   (noun)

DA

> **The city <u>council</u> will meet tonight.**
>   (noun)

damage/destroy The distinction here is one of degree. There can be various levels of damage (slight, widespread), but destruction is the highest degree of damage. Therefore, it is redundant to say that "the building was completely destroyed in the fire." Anything less than destruction is simply some level of damage, as in

> **Fire <u>damaged</u> the offices of Planned Parenthood last night.**

Destruction needs no intensification:

> **The tornado <u>destroyed</u> 20 homes and severely <u>damaged</u>**
> **30 others.**

dangling modifiers A modifier "dangles" when it does not directly modify anything in the sentence. For example:

> **Facing indictment for insider trading, the board demanded his resignation.**

The participial phrase *facing indictment for insider trading* has nothing to modify. The first referent we see is *the board*. But that can't logically be the referent. Poor sentence construction has buried the true referent—the person who is facing indictment. The sentence needs to be rewritten:

> **<u>Facing indictment</u> for insider trading, <u>Stewart</u> was asked to resign.**

Yes, this is in the passive voice, but the recipient of the action, Stewart, is more important than its initiator, the board.

    Dangling modifiers most often occur at the beginnings of sentences. Although they tend to be verbals (participial phrases, gerund phrases and infinitive phrases), appositives, clauses and simple adjectives can dangle as well. The test is whether the person or thing being modified by the word, phrase or clause is in the sentence. See p. 133.

dash An enticing piece of punctuation because of its informality, direct-ness and drama, the dash (—) is often used excessively and incorrectly. Media writers should consider routinely using commas, colons and parentheses and save dashes for special occasions. The two main uses of the dash in media writing are as follows:

1. To create drama and emphasis at the end of a sentence:

    The film was beautifully photographed, superbly acted and expertly directed—but a box office flop.

2. To clearly set off a long clause or phrase that adds information to the main clause:

    The closing ceremonies of the Olympics—a dazzling spectacle of international patriotism—sent the network's ratings through the roof.

DA–DE

data **and other foreign plurals** Many English words have their roots in Latin; some are derived from Greek. Some of these words conform to singular-plural rules unlike our own. *Data, media* and *alumni* are com-mon Latin plurals. Magazines are one *medium*; radio and TV are broad-cast *media*. The word *alumni* presents its own complications: A group of men and women who have graduated from a school are *alumni*; one male graduate is an *alumnus*; one female grad is an *alumna*. And to be perfectly correct, a group of female grads would be *alumnae*. The Greek words *criteria* and *phenomena* are plural. Their singulars are *criterion* and *phenomenon*.

  Data can be a confusing word. It's plural, but it is most often consid-ered a unit—a collective noun—and should take a singular verb:

Your data is invalid.
(unit)

If the sense of *data* is individual items, however, use a plural verb:

The data were collected from seven tracking sites.
(individual items)

dependent clause Although it contains both a subject and verb, a depen-dent clause does not express a complete thought and cannot stand alone as a sentence. Dependent clauses rely on main clauses for their completion:

Although the movie had a star-studded cast
(dep. clause)

Although the movie had a star-studded cast, <u>it failed miserably at the box office.</u>
(dep. clause linked to indep. clause)

Recognizing dependent clauses will help you (1) avoid fragments (treating dependent clauses as if they were complete sentences) and (2) vary sentence structure. Place the dependent clause in front, in the middle or at the end of the main clause to vary sentence structure. See p. 26.

See p. 26.

different from/different than For those who take comfort from edicts, here's one: Use *different from* and you will never be wrong. Unless you're interested in delving into the nether regions of structural linguistics or semantic compatibility, consider using *different than* only when it introduces a condensed clause (a clause that omits certain words without loss of clarity).

DI

Open-meeting laws are <u>different</u> in Illinois <u>than</u> [they are] in Oregon.
(condensed clause)

In general, however, play it safe with *different from*. So the previous example would read:

Open-meeting laws in Oregon are different from those in Illinois.

differ from/differ with Politicians who *differ from* (are unlike) others may not necessarily *differ with* (disagree with) each other. Although these phrases express contrast, they are not interchangeable. When you mean two items are dissimilar, use *differ from*. When you mean items are in conflict, use *differ with*:

The competing proposals did not significantly <u>differ from</u> one another.

City councilors <u>differed with</u> the zoning committee's recommendations.

discreet/discrete Both of these words are adjectives, and both are pronounced the same. But they do have discrete meanings! *Discreet* means "prudent or careful," especially about keeping confidences, as in this sentence:

The diplomat is known to be <u>discreet</u> in all matters.

Discrete means "distinct or separate," as in this sentence:

> **The two words have <u>discrete</u> meanings.**

disinterested/uninterested A *disinterested* (impartial) observer may be *uninterested* (lack interest) in the situation, but the words are not synonymous.

drug A drug is any substance used as medicine in the treatment of a disease. Headline writers have made this word synonymous with narcotics, a particular group of sense-dulling, usually addictive drugs. All narcotics are drugs; all drugs are not narcotics.

DI–EI

each/either/neither When used as subjects, these pronouns always take singular verbs:

> **<u>Each</u> <u>is</u> responsible for his or her own equipment.**

> **<u>Neither</u> of the defendants <u>was</u> found guilty.**

When these words are used as adjectives, the nouns they modify always take a singular verb:

> **<u>Either</u> answer <u>is</u> correct.**

> **<u>Neither</u> choice <u>is</u> a good one.**

either . . . or/neither . . . nor Called *correlative conjunctions,* these word pairs (including *both . . . and, not so . . . as,* and *not only . . . but also*) connect similar grammatical elements in parallel form:

> **You can <u>either</u> pay the fine <u>or</u> go to jail immediately.**

Correlative conjunctions can pose agreement problems. When a compound subject is linked by a correlative conjunction, the subject closest to the verb determines the number of the verb:

> **<u>Neither</u> the researcher <u>nor</u> her <u>assistants</u> <u>were</u> available for comment.**

When the subject closest to the verb is singular, you must use a singular verb. Such a construction is grammatical but sometimes graceless:

> **<u>Neither</u> the assistants <u>nor</u> the <u>researcher</u> <u>was</u> available for comment.**

Avoid awkwardness by placing the plural subject next to the verb.

elicit/illicit These two words may sound alike, but the similarity stops there. *Elicit,* a verb, means "to bring out or draw forth." *Illicit,* an adjective, means "illegal or unlawful."

His **illicit** behavior **elicited** strong community reaction.

eminent/imminent These are both adjectives, but they describe very different qualities. *Eminent* means "distinguished or prominent":

The **eminent** scientist Linus Pauling won two Nobel Prizes.

Imminent means "about to occur" or "impending":

The company faces **imminent** bankruptcy.

Note that there is one *m* in *eminent* and two in *imminent.* Don't ask us why!

energize/enervate Here is a perfect example of words that have similar pronunciations but opposite meanings. To *energize* is to invigorate or give energy to. *Enervate,* on the other hand, means "to weaken or deplete." So:

Terri's optimism **energizes** everyone.

Simon's cynicism **enervates** even the most cheerful optimist.

enormity/enormousness These words are not synonymous, though recent usage (even by a U.S. president) would indicate otherwise. Although the pair starts with similar pronunciations, the differences are clear. *Enormity* means "wickedness." *Enormousness* refers to size.

The **enormity** of the September 11 attacks is still difficult to comprehend.

The **enormousness** of the budget deficit has staggered even the most cynical politicians.

Perhaps some writers find *enormousness* a bit graceless and odd-sounding. Fine. They should use *magnitude* rather than improperly suggesting horror or wickedness.

everyone/everybody These collective pronouns are troublesome because they "feel" plural even though they are actually singular.

Everyone should remain in his or her seat.

It is common to see and hear the incorrect plural: *Everyone should remain in* their *seats.* Don't make that mistake! Also, in keeping this construction in the singular, remember fairness and accuracy. If all people included in *everyone* are male, then it is fine to write: *Everyone should remain in* his *seat.* If the group is mixed, gender inclusivity needs to be reflected in the pronoun choice. If you think *his or her* is awkward, you can always rewrite, as in:

All <u>theater-goers</u> should remain in <u>their</u> seats.

exclamation point Indicating strong emotion or surprise, the exclamation point (!) is rarely used in journalistic writing. Its use is almost always limited to direct quotations. Remember to place the exclamation point inside the quotation marks:

"I love this game<u>!</u>" the contestant told the host.

Note that a comma is not required after the exclamation point.

farther/further Use *farther* to express physical distance; use *further* when referring to degree, time or quantity:

The planning commission wants to extend the boundaries <u>farther</u> south.

The planning commission will discuss the boundary issue <u>further.</u>

Any questions? We'd be happy to discuss this further.

fewer/less This is a much-abused pair, but the distinctions are clear: When you refer to a number of individual items, *fewer* is your choice; when you refer to a bulk, amount, sum, period of time or concept, use *less*:

<u>Fewer</u> doctors result in <u>less</u> medical care.

At Data Corporation <u>fewer</u> than 10 employees make <u>less</u> than $50,000 per year.

In the latter example, we are not talking about individual dollars but rather a sum (amount) of money.

flaunt/flout Whether you flaunt or flout, you are overtly acting up with these verbs. Care to "outrageously or pretentiously display"? You *flaunt.* But when you "scorn rules and laws," you *flout.*

She seems to enjoy <u>flaunting</u> her new-found wealth.

The farmer <u>flouted</u> the law that banned domestic livestock within city limits.

fragments An unfinished piece of a sentence, a fragment may be a single word, a phrase or a dependent clause. It may lack a subject, a predicate, a complete thought or any combination of the three. Therefore, a fragment is not a complete sentence; it cannot stand alone. Example:

Waiting for the commissioners to make up their minds.
(Where's the verb?)

Fragments can be rewritten to include subject, predicate and complete thought; incorporated into complete sentences; or attached to main clauses. However, here's the loophole: Fragments, when used purposefully by skillful writers, can be an effective technique. With their clipped, punchy beat, fragments can create excitement and grab reader attention. But this stylistic device must be appropriate to both subject and medium and should be used sparingly.

gender-specific references (he/she) Language reflects culture and beliefs. When a society changes, we believe language ought to keep pace. We are speaking not of faddish words or slang expressions but of the way language treats people. The language in the following sentences is no longer an accurate reflection of our society:

A nurse ought to be attentive to her patients.

A state legislator has a responsibility to his constituents.

In these sentences we see outdated gender stereotypes—nurses are all female, legislators are all male. Because the singular neuter pronoun *(it, its)* cannot refer to a person, we have two grammatical options if we want to avoid gender stereotyping:

1. Use both the masculine and the feminine pronoun when referencing a noun that could refer to either sex:

   A <u>nurse</u> ought to be attentive to <u>his or her</u> patients.

2. Change the neuter noun to the plural and use plural neuter pronouns *(they, them, their)*:

   State <u>legislators</u> have a responsibility to <u>their</u> constituents.

In your effort to treat both sexes fairly in language, don't fall prey to easy (and incorrect) solutions that accept errors in agreement:

Everybody deserves to make it on their own.

This may be well-intentioned, but it is grammatically incorrect. Two solutions are obvious:

Everybody deserves to make it on his or her own.

All people deserve to make it on their own.

GO–HI

good/well If you understand the role of linking verbs and adverbs, you will know when to use the adjective *good* and the adverb *well*. A linking verb establishes a relationship between the subject and a modifier. When the subject of the sentence is linked to positive or desirable traits, then use the modifier good:

The outlook for an improved economy is good.

When the verb reflects an action properly, skillfully, or sufficiently, use the adverb *well:*

The old dog performed his new tricks well.
                                                (performed how?)

So, stick to *good* for relating to subjects and *well* for characterizing verbs. Another example:

The doctors said she was doing well after the surgery.
                                                (doing how?)

hanged/hung The verb *hang* is conjugated differently depending on the object of the hanging. The conjugation *hang, hung, hung* refers to objects:

The portrait hung in the museum foyer.

The conjugation *hang, hanged, hanged* refers to people (executions or suicides):

He hanged himself in his prison cell.

historic/historical These adjectives both deal with history, but their difference is significant. When something is historic, it has particular importance to history, as in

The Rev. Martin Luther King's "I have a dream" address in 1963 is considered an <u>historic</u> speech.

Historical is a more general reference, connected to anything that is related to history, as in

I enjoy reading <u>historical</u> novels.

homophones, homonyms and homographs If you're looking for more reasons to love the English language—or lose patience with it—look no further. Homophones are words that sound the same but are spelled differently and have unrelated meanings, like *fair* and *fare, alter* and *altar,* and *whose* and *who's.* Homonyms are words that sound the same, and are spelled the same, but—oddly—have completely different meanings, as in *stable* (horse stall) and *stable* (unwavering). As if this were not enough, homographs are spelled the same but—maddeningly—are pronounced differently (and have different meanings), as in *bow* (in archery) and *bow* (of a ship). Please see Appendix B.

HO–HY

hopefully Possibly the single most abused word in our language, *hopefully* means "with hope." It describes how a subject feels (hopeful). Therefore, this sentence would be correct:

She opened the mailbox <u>hopefully</u>, looking for the check.

Hopefully—regardless of what you may hear or read—does not mean "it is hoped that." Therefore, the following sentence is incorrect:

<u>Hopefully</u>, the check will arrive.

The check is not "hopeful." *Hopefully* does not describe anything in the preceding sentence. It is, in fact, a dangling modifier.

hyphen Whereas the dash creates a dramatic break in a sentence, the workhorse hyphen creates a typographical bridge that links words for several purposes.

1. It joins compound modifiers unless one of the modifiers is *very* or an *-ly* adverb:

   a <u>well-known</u> actor
   (hyphen needed)

   the <u>newly appointed</u> ambassador
   (*-ly* adverb, no hyphen needed)

2. It links certain prefixes to the words that follow. One basic guide-line: If the prefix ends in a vowel and the next word begins with the same vowel, hyphenate (except *cooperate* and *coordinate*). It's best to check a dictionary or stylebook on this rule because exceptions abound. Some examples:

the <u>pre-election</u> suspense

but:

a <u>precursor</u> of the election results

3. It links words when a preposition is omitted:

IC–IF

score of <u>10-1</u>
(preposition *to* omitted)

closed <u>June-August</u>
(preposition *through* omitted)

See p. 116.

-ics words   Words ending with the suffix *-ics* (*athletics, politics, graph-ics, acoustics, economics*) can create problems with agreement. Although their final *s* makes these words look plural, they can be either singular or plural, depending on context. If the word refers to a science, art or general field of study, it is treated as singular and takes a singular verb. If the word refers to the act, practices or activities of the field, it takes a plural verb:

<u>Politics is</u> an impossible career.
(the field of politics, singular)

His <u>politics seem</u> to change every year.
(the practice of politics, plural)

Some *-ics* words do not carry both meanings. *Hysterics,* for example, always takes the plural because it always refers to acts and practices.

if I were   The subjunctive mood of verbs expresses a nonexistent, hypo-thetical or improbable condition. That mood calls for what itself seems grammatically incorrect—a plural verb with a singular subject. But this sentence is grammatically correct:

<u>If I were</u> the world's richest person, all medical care would be free.

If you want to express a condition that is possible, however, it would be correct to say:

If I was plant supervisor, our productivity would increase.

if/whether These conjunctions are not interchangeable. *If* means "in the event that," "granting that" or "on the condition that." It is often used to introduce a subjunctive clause (expressing a hypothetical or improbable condition):

If Smith wins, the Democrats will have a majority.
(in the event that)

If the volcano were to erupt again, thousands of lives could be lost.
(hypothetical condition)

Whether means "if it is so that," "if it happens that," or "in case." It is generally used to introduce a possibility:

He wondered whether he should attend the briefing.
(if it is so that)

Whether he wins or loses, this will be his last campaign.
(introduces possibilities)

impact This noun means a "collision" or a "violent or forceful striking together." Often writers use *impact* when they really mean something much less forceful, such as "effect" or "influence."

When her car hit the guardrail, the impact threw her from the vehicle.
(correct)

We can't predict what impact this report will have on future negotiations.
(misuse—better to use *effect* or *influence*)

Unfortunately, *impact* has also fallen prey to those who toss it around as a verb ("The televised debates impacted the election") or an adjective ("federally impacted areas"). The only thing that can be impacted is a tooth, and that's unpleasant enough!

imply/infer These verbs are not interchangeable. *Imply* means "to suggest or hint." *Infer* means "to deduce or conclude from facts or evidence."

When she implied that Smith was unethical, her supervisor inferred that she had an ax to grind.

IF–IM

indefinite pronouns Because indefinite pronouns *(anyone, everyone, few, some* and so on) don't always specify a number, they can cause agreement problems. Here are a few rules to follow.

- When used as subjects, *each, either, anyone, everyone, much, no one, nothing* and *someone* always take a singular verb.

- Acting as subjects, *both, few, many* and *several* always take a plural verb.

- Pronouns such as *any, none* and *some* take singular verbs when they refer to a unit or general quantity. If they refer to amount or individuals, they take a plural verb:

Some of the shipment <u>was</u> delayed
(general quantity)

because <u>some</u> of the workers <u>were</u> on strike.
(individuals)

See pp. 78, 81.

independent clause An independent clause contains a subject, a verb and a complete thought. This is an independent clause:

Students complained to the professor.

This is not:

that she didn't give them enough time to finish the exam.
(this is a dependent, or subordinate, clause)

All together, we have what is called a complex sentence:

Students complained to the professor that she didn't give them enough time to finish the exam.

See pp. 26–29.

-ing endings A common suffix, *-ing* is added to a verb to create the present progressive form ("She is running for office.") or a verbal ("Running for office requires tenacity."). It can also be added to a noun, creating a verbal (a gerund) that gives the noun a sense of action. For example, *parenting* is the action of being a parent. Although "inging" a noun may occasionally create new words with distinct meanings, it can also be unnecessarily trendy.

Consider this example:

The boss believes in <u>gifting</u> her staff during the holidays.

This is an ugly, awkward construction. Use new *-ing* words sparingly and only when they capture a unique meaning without damaging the rhythm and sound of the language. See also the **-ize** entry.

in/into These prepositions are not interchangeable. *In* denotes location or position. *Into* indicates motion.

The photographer was already <u>in</u> the gallery when the star
(location, position)

witness was ushered <u>into</u> the courtroom.
(movement)

Regardless of current slang, *into* should never be used as a substitute for "involved with" or "interested in." This colloquial use is not only sloppy but also weak and ambiguous:

For the past year, she's been <u>into</u> swimming.
(ambiguous slang)

She's been swimming a mile a day for the past year.
(improved)

initiate/instigate At our own instigation, we have initiated an investigation of this troublesome pair. When you mean that someone began or originated a contest, for example, it is not correct to write this:

He <u>instigated</u> the first tofu sculpture contest.

Instead, he *initiated* (began) it. This would be a proper use of *instigate*:

She <u>instigated</u> the city's first recall campaign.

In this case she did not begin the movement—she pressed for it.

insure/ensure/assure Be assured: These words are different! If you limit the meaning of *insure* to activities of insurance companies, you'll always be correct.

Tom wants to <u>insure</u> his house for earthquake and flood damage.

Ensure means (in a noninsurance sense) "to guarantee" or "to provide something":

Are you certain you can <u>ensure</u> our safety on this trip?

What about *assure?* Used correctly, this verb speaks directly to a person, to give him or her confidence in a promise:

She <u>assured</u> them that the check was in the mail.

invoke/evoke   Probably because both words contain *-voke* from the Latin root *vocare* (to call), these very different words are often used interchangeably. *Invoke* means "to appeal to or call forth earnestly." *Evoke* means "to produce or elicit" (a reaction, a response) or "to reawaken" (memories, for example):

When the speaker <u>invoked</u> God, he <u>evoked</u> a strong reaction from the audience of atheists.

irregardless   Strike this silly word from your vocabulary! *Regardless,* which means "without regard for" or "unmindful of" is what you're after. The *-less* suffix creates the negative meaning. If you add the *ir-* prefix, you create a double negative.

its/it's   This is a scandalous pair! Once and for all: *Its* is the possessive form of the neuter pronoun *it.* Do not confuse this with *it's,* which is a contraction for *it is* or *it has:*

The council has not reviewed <u>its</u> budget options.
                    (neuter possessive)

"<u>It's</u> simply a matter of time," he said.
(contraction of *it is*)

By the way, please use *it* or *its*—not *she* or *her*—when referring to nations or ships:

The cruise ship SS All You Can Eat sails for <u>its</u> home port tomorrow.

-ize words   An occasionally useful suffix, *-ize* has been employed since the time of the ancient Greeks to change nouns into verbs (*final/finalize, burglar/burglarize*). But the "-ization" of words has now reached epidemic proportions. We've been alarmed at the growing use of "incentivize," for example. Writers interested in the clarity, precision and beauty of language need to take precautions. Tacking *-ize* onto nouns often creates useless, awkward and stodgy words. Will it get worse? Will we soon read something like this?

IN–IZ

The agency may <u>permanentize</u> its position by <u>routinizing</u> its appointment procedures.

Before you use an *-ize* word, check your dictionary. Make sure the word has a unique meaning, and pay attention to its sound.

lay/lie *Lay,* a transitive verb form, always takes a direct object; *lie,* an intransitive verb, never takes a direct object:

Please <u>lay</u> the briefcase on the table.
    (dir. obj.)

The Seychelles <u>lie</u> in the Indian Ocean.
    (prep. phrase)

Be careful not to confuse *lie* and *lay* in the past tense. The past tense of *lie* is *lay:*

He finally <u>lay</u> down for a long winter's nap.

lend/loan In spoken language, the distinction between these two is almost nonexistent. But rather than worry about the differing niceties observed by various editors, play it safe: Use *lend* as a verb and *loan* as a noun. The one exception currently favored by most experts is *loan* as a verb in financial contexts:

The bank <u>loaned</u> the troubled firm $45 million.

This would be an appropriate use of *lend:*

Please don't <u>lend</u> him your car again!

less than/under If you mean "a lesser quantity or amount," use *less than:*

The project estimate is <u>less than</u> $100 million.

If you mean "physically beneath," use *under:*

The troll hid his treasure <u>under</u> the bridge.

linking verbs A linking verb connects a subject to an equivalent or related word in the sentence. That word—a predicate noun, a predicate pronoun or a predicate adjective—refers to the subject by either restating it or describing it. The principal linking verbs are *be, seem, become, appear, feel* and *look.*

LA–LI

She <u>is</u> a well-known designer.
(*Designer,* a predicate noun—also called a *predicate nominative*—restates the subject *she.*)

It <u>is</u> he.
(*He,* a predicate pronoun, restates the subject *it* and stays in the nominative case.)

He <u>feels</u> bad.
(*Bad,* a predicate adjective, describes the subject *he.*)

Note that *badly,* an adverb, cannot be used in this construction. See the entry for **bad/badly.**

literal/figurative Considering these two words have opposite meanings, it's amazing that writers will substitute one for another. *Literal* means "word for word" or "upholding the exact meaning of a word":

This is a <u>literal</u> translation of the Celtic myth.

Figurative, on the other hand, means "not literal; metaphorical, based on figures of speech":

<u>Figuratively</u> speaking, she's on top of the world.

loath/loathe An errant vowel is all that stands between you and the adjective *loath* when you intend the verb *loathe. Loath* means "unwilling" or "disinclined."

I am <u>loath</u> to wake up before 10 a.m.
(The linking verb *am* joins the subject *I* with its adjective *loath.*)

But *loathe* is a verb that means "to dislike greatly."

Sandra <u>loathes</u> these early morning press conferences.

loose/lose *Loose* is an adjective denoting "unrestrained, unfixed or unbound," as in "loose shoes." *Lose,* a verb, means "fail to keep."

<u>Loose</u> lips are a plastic surgeon's dream.

Don't <u>lose</u> your sense of humor!

mantel/mantle It's easy to understand how these words are confused, given the closeness of their spellings. Try this: If you place a covering (a *mantle*) over your fireplace overhang or shelf *(mantel)*, you should understand the difference. A mantle can also be more figurative, as in

A lush <u>mantle</u> of dandelion wisps graced the front yard.

may/might Time to split proverbial hairs! Both of these verbs indicate possibility, as in "I may go to Sara's party tonight," but some usage experts contend that *may* indicates a stronger possibility than *might*. So what to do? Our advice is to stick with *may* unless the possibilities for action are extremely remote:

I <u>might</u> as well be talking to the wall.

median/average (mean) A median is the middle value in a distribution of items, the point at which half of the items are above and half are below. An average is the sum of a group of items divided by the number of items in the group. *Mean* is statisticians' talk for *average*. Statistically, *average* and *mean* are virtually synonymous.

Number of years spent on death row by prisoners of state X:

Prisoner A 18	Prisoner D 10	Prisoner G 6
Prisoner B 14	Prisoner E 7	Prisoner H 6
Prisoner C 10	Prisoner F 6	Prisoner I 4

The median years spent on death row is 7; that is, half of the prisoners spent more than 7 years in jail, half spent 7 or less. The average (or mean) number of years spent on death row is 9; it is the sum of all the years (81) divided by the number of prisoners (9).

modifiers These are words that enhance (modify) nouns, adjectives and verbs. Used properly, they provide description, as in

She is a <u>fabulously</u> <u>successful</u> entrepeneur.
        (adverb)   (adjective) (noun)

and

The turtle dove cooed <u>sweetly.</u>
        (verb) (adverb)

Adjectives modify nouns; adverbs modify verbs and adjectives. See pp. 64–68 and **dangling modifiers.**

more than/over Like *less than* and *under*, these words are not interchangeable. Use *over* when you are referring to a spatial relationship. For figures and amounts, the correct phrase is *more than:*

> **More than 100 jets flew bombing and support missions <u>over</u> the desert.**

none This indefinite pronoun often causes agreement problems. Use a singular verb when *none* clearly suggests "no one or not one." When *none* clearly indicates "no two, no amount or no number," use the plural. Don't be fooled by a plural prepositional phrase—*none* is the subject:

> **<u>None</u> of the suspected rioters was arrested.**
> (not one rioter)

> **<u>None</u> of the taxes were paid.**
> (no taxes-no amount)

See pp. 81–82.

numerals Many organizations have specific style rules concerning numerals and a host of other issues. Check first; a stylebook may hold the answer. In the absence of other guidelines, however, follow these rules:

1. Spell out whole numbers below 10: *three, seven.*

2. Use figures for 10 and above: *14,305.*

3. Spell out fractions less than one: *two-thirds, three-quarters.*

4. Spell out *first* through *ninth* when these words indicate a sequence:
   She was <u>first</u> in line.
   The <u>Ninth</u> Amendment came under scrutiny.
   Use figures for 10th and above.

5. Spell out numerals at the beginning of a sentence. The only exception is a calendar-year date.

There are also many guidelines for ages, percentages, fractions, election returns, monetary units, dimensions, temperatures and other specific cases. *The Associated Press Stylebook* is a good, comprehensive reference; *The MLA Handbook* and *The Chicago Manual of Style* are also widely used.

occur/take place *Occur* refers to "all accidental or unscheduled events"; *take place* refers to "a planned event":

> **The downtown bombings <u>occurred</u> within 15 minutes of each other.**

> **Graduation ceremonies will <u>take place</u> at 2 p.m.**

off of Be wary of prepositions that enjoy one another's company. They often practice grammatical "featherbedding"—having two do the job of one. *Off of* is one of those redundant, bulky constructions. *Off,* all by its lonesome, suffices.

> **<u>Get off</u> [of] my back!**

> **Electricians <u>walked off</u> [of] the job early this morning.**

one of the/the only one of the Having a verb agree in number with its subject is not difficult when you identify the proper subject. When the subject is a pronoun (*who* or *that,* for example) and refers to a noun elsewhere in the sentence, the task is more challenging. Subject-verb agreement then depends on determining the correct antecedent. These guidelines should help.

1. In *one of the* constructions, the relative pronoun refers to the object of the preposition of the main clause, not the subject:

> **Easter is <u>one of the</u> best ballplayers   who   have played the**
> (subj.)   (obj. of prep.) (pron.) (verb)
> **game in the last 50 years.**

If you examine this sentence, you will see that Easter is not the only ball-player who has played the game in 50 years. We are talking about many players who have played the game in that period.

2. In *the only one of the* constructions, the relative pronoun refers to the subject of the main clause:

> **Thompson is <u>the only one of</u> the commissioners who**
> (subj.)   (pron.)

> **opposes the tax levy.**
> (verb)

There are no other candidates who oppose the levy. The antecedent clearly is *Thompson.*

ordnance/ordinance It's hard to imagine confusing this pair, but it happens. *Ordnance* is weaponry; it explodes, among other things. An *ordinance* (a law or regulation enacted by an elected body) can be politically explosive, but, well, you get the idea. (When you have a chance, take a look at the definition of *ordonnance*. Interesting word!)

parallel structure Placing like ideas in consistent grammatical patterns creates parallel structure. This consistency among elements gives order to writing and helps make the message clear. Parallelism also creates balance, symmetry and sometimes rhythm in a sentence. Common errors in parallelism include mixing elements in a series, mixing verbals and switching voice. See p. 94–96.

paraphrase This is a form of editing—when it is a correct and concise summary of a direct quotation that may be too long or semantically awkward to use. Accuracy is the key here. In this example, the writer took a three-sentence direct quotation and put the essential information in one simple sentence:

OR–PA

> **According to Mayor Johnson, the proposed zoning change will hamper the city's plan to develop more low-income housing.**

Paraphrasing can create the wrong context or even change meaning, so the writer must be sure that the content of the paraphrase matches the essence of the quotation.

parentheses Parentheses should provide additional information within a sentence when this type of "aside" flows well within that sentence. Be careful not to overdo it, however. When you do use them, here is a simple rule concerning punctuation: Put the period inside the parentheses only if the parenthetical material is a complete sentence and can stand independently of the preceding sentence:

> **Tom is not the accountant who was indicted in the dot-com scandal. (It was his partner Sam, who goes to trial next month.)**

If the parenthetical material is essential to the main sentence, the period goes outside, ending the entire sentence:

> **The mourners chanted, "Vaya con Dios" ("Go with God").**

See pp. 120–121.

passive voice This is a generally ineffective and occasionally deceptive construction in which the subject of the sentence is actually the recipient of the verb's action. It adds words but diminishes clarity. Note the difference in directness and conciseness between these two examples:

> **The accounting scandal dubbed "Restatementgate" by journalists and commentators will be investigated by the Senate subcommittee.**
> (passive, in two constructions)

> **The Senate subcommittee will investigate the "Restatementgate" accounting scandal.**
> (active)

However, there are some suitable uses for passive voice. See pp. 40–41.

people/persons Some editors contend that a group of human beings should be referred to as *people*, but individuals should be called *persons*. So, what is the scale of acceptable use for *persons?* Three? Six? We suggest you save yourself the headache—there are more pressing decisions in life. So if you are referring to one individual, you are referring to a person:

> **She's a wonderful <u>person,</u> don't you think?**

If you are referring to more than one, use *people:*

> **Twelve <u>people</u> were arrested this morning in the jaywalking sting operation.**

possessives Chapter 8 discusses the formation of possessives. This point, however, deserves emphasis: Possessives of personal pronouns are not the same as subject-verb contractions. Remember that the personal pronoun possessives *(my, mine, our, ours, your, yours, his, her, hers, its, their, theirs)* do not require an apostrophe. See the entry for **its/it's.**

poor/pore/pour *Poor* means "lacking," whether it's health or wealth. But you *pour* a glass of juice in the morning before you *pore*, or "study attentively," over "When Words Collide."

precede/proceed These two verbs differentiate between looking back and moving forward. *Precede* means "to come or exist before."

> **The 9.0 magnitude earthquake <u>preceded</u> the tsunami.**

Proceed means "to go forward" or "carry on an action" (especially after an interruption).

Despite audience protests, the conductor <u>proceeded</u> with the performance.

predicate The simple predicate of a sentence is the verb. The complete predicate includes the verb plus all its complements and modifiers.

I <u>read</u> "When Words Collide."
(simple pred.)

I <u>read</u> "When Words Collide" with great enthusiasm.
(complete pred.)

predicate adjective/predicate nominative A predicate adjective and a predicate nominative follow a linking verb. The predicate adjective modifies the subject, and the predicate nominative defines or restates the subject in different terms. Remember that a predicate nominative can be either a noun or a pronoun.

The movie's <u>plot</u> seems <u>weak.</u>
       (subject)   (predicate adjective)

Her <u>dogs</u> are delightful <u>charmers.</u>
  (subject)   (predicate nominative)

preposition This hard-working part of speech links phrases and neatly ties a sentence into a coherent package:

The burglar was hiding <u>behind</u> the freezer.

In the example above, the preposition *behind* begins the prepositional phrase. Although a preposition can occasionally introduce a clause, it almost always precedes a phrase. When that phrase contains a pronoun, that pronoun must stay in the objective case:

Don't lay the blame on <u>us</u> reporters for this spate of bad news.

Avoid burdening a sentence with an unnecessary series of prepositions:

Dr. Flagranto followed his victim <u>through</u> the French doors <u>next to</u> the solarium, <u>with</u> the evil intent <u>of</u> murder <u>on</u> his mind.

Let prepositions enhance a sentence—don't let them drain the power of the verb!

preventive/preventative Why use *preventative?* It has two more let-ters and still means "preventive." Practice preventive language arts—avoid overweight, unnecessary words.

principal/principle As a noun, *principal* refers to "someone who is first in rank or authority," such as the principal of a school. As an adjec-tive, *principal* still means "first in rank or authority," such as the "prin-cipal reason for the levy's defeat." *Principle,* however, is only a noun. It means "a truth, doctrine or rule of conduct," such as "an uncompromis-ing principle of honesty."

prone/supine You're lying in the street, facedown. You're in a *prone position.* On your back? Now you're in a *supine* position. Facedown or on your back seems clearer to us—and easier to remember.

pronoun It means, literally, "in place of a noun." Pronouns change their form in the possessive (for example, *their* for *they*), which is why pronoun possessives don't need apostrophes. (And that's why the subject-verb contraction *it's* is not a pronoun!) Careless writers often posi-tion their pronouns indiscriminately, causing problems with antecedent identification:

> <u>Pentagon briefers</u> **tried to explain the field reports to the** <u>journalists</u>**, but it was apparent that** <u>they</u> **were hopelessly confused.**

See the problem? Be sure that antecedents are clearly identified. See pp. 83–84.

proved/proven *Proved* is a verb. *Proven* is an adjective. This is a simple distinction, but some writers persist in using *proven* as part of a verb. Some dictionaries even list *proven* as an alternate verb form. We suggest you keep it simple. Examples:

> **The district attorney** <u>has proved</u> **the defendant's guilt beyond a reasonable doubt.**

In the above example, *proved* is used with helping verb *has* to create past perfect tense. In the example that follows, *proven* modifies the noun *track record.*

> **The district attorney has a** <u>proven</u> **track record for convictions.**

PR

quotation marks Here is a brief recap about the use of other punctuation with quotation marks:

1. Periods and commas always go inside the quotation marks. Question marks and exclamation points go inside if they are part of the quoted material.

2. The most common error in quotation mark punctuation is in placement of the question mark. Two examples show its correct placement:

    The senator asked the company president: "Can you honestly tell me that your baby food formula has never caused the death of a child in a Third World country?"

The question mark belongs inside because it is part of a quoted question.

What did you think of "Avatar"?

The entire sentence is a question; the movie title is not. See Chapter 8.

quotation/quote *Quotation* is a noun. *Quote* is supposed to be a verb. However, *quote* is often used as a noun. ("Get me some good quotes for this piece. It's dying of boredom.") In general, remember to quote only the effective quotations!

real/really We're really serious about these differences—they are real. Remember: *Real* is an adjective, and thus it can only be used to modify a noun. *Really* is an adverb; it can only modify adjectives. So, just to be clear: It would be *really* bad writing to say that you write *real* well. Got it?

reek/wreak They're both verbs, they sound similar, but their differences are real—really! *Reek* means to "emit or give off," as with an odor.

The crack house <u>reeked</u> of noxious chemicals.

Wreak means "to cause or inflict."

The typhoon <u>wreaked</u> havoc on the New Guinea coast.

rebut/refute It's easier to rebut a statement than to refute it. When you rebut a statement, you contradict it or deny it. But that doesn't mean you have conclusively proved the truth of your position. When you refute a statement, you have proved that you are correct. Use *refute* in your news writing only if there is consensus that the denial has been successful.

reluctant/reticent Don't be shy about enforcing this distinction. People who are *reluctant* to do something are not necessarily *reticent*. A *reluctant* person is unwilling to do something:

> **The banker is <u>reluctant</u> to approve the company's loan.**

If a person is unwilling to speak readily or is uncommonly reserved, we generally describe that individual as *reticent*:

> **The professor has instituted a class for <u>reticent</u> speakers.**

renown/renowned *Renown*, a noun, means "fame or eminence"; *renowned*, an adjective, means "famous or celebrated":

> **She is a psychotherapist of great <u>renown.</u>**
> (noun—obj. of prep.)

> **Nobel laureate Linus Pauling was <u>renowned</u> for his**
> (pred. adj.)
> **groundbreaking work in chemistry.**

restrictive/nonrestrictive A restrictive clause is clause that is essential to the meaning of a sentence. Understanding this helps you in at least two ways:

1. The restrictive clause does not need to be set off by commas.

2. In a choice between *that* and *which, that* is always the correct pronoun subject or object for the restrictive clause.

    > **The city bond issue <u>that</u> voters approved last week may be challenged in court.**

A nonrestrictive clause, however, is not essential to the full meaning of a sentence. You must set off the clause with commas and use *which* instead of *that*:

> **The Gifford Pinchot fire, <u>which</u> already has destroyed 800 acres of old-growth timber, may be brought under control by this weekend.**

See also the entry for **that/which/who** and pp. 100–101.

run-on sentence Like the tedious infomercial, it doesn't know when to stop. Note how two complete sentences collide when an improperly placed comma can't stop the run-on:

> **Picket lines went up for a fourth straight <u>day, nurses</u> vowed to continue to honor them until contract talks resume.**

Use a semicolon instead of a comma or insert the conjunction *and* after the comma to correct this fault. See also the entry for **comma splice**.

semicolon This punctuation mark helps you avoid the run-on sentence. When two independent clauses are in one sentence and are not separated by a conjunction such as *or, but* or *and,* they must be separated by a semicolon:

> **This is not your ordinary, barn-twirling <u>tornado; it</u> is the perfect storm.**

When two independent clauses are joined by a conjunctive adverb such as *however, nevertheless* or *therefore,* a semicolon also is needed before that adverb:

> **I cannot support this committee's recommendation<u>; however,</u> I plan to abstain rather than cast a negative vote.**

sentence A sentence is one or more properly punctuated independent clauses that present a complete thought. Sorry to say, writers do awful things to sentences: They make one run into another, they clutter them with unnecessary punctuation, and sometimes they neglect to put a verb in one but still call it a sentence:

> <u>**Such as this fragment.**</u>

A good sentence is an enlightenment, a forceful directive, an amusing bit of play. But it is always well-contained; its thought is always complete. See Chapter 4.

set/sit Normally the verb *set* requires an object:

> **Have you <u>set</u> the <u>agenda</u> for the annual meeting?**
>   (verb) (dir. object)

Sit, however, never takes an object:

> **Please <u>sit</u> down for a few minutes.**

since/because They are not synonymous. *Since* is properly used when it denotes a period of time, whether continuous or broken:

> **It's been years <u>since</u> I've seen a good movie.**

Because gives a reason or cause:

> **His parents refused to co-sign the loan <u>because</u> of his wild spending habits.**

In most circumstances, a comma is not needed before *because*.

split constructions The split infinitive is a frequent complaint of grammarians. However, the chief reason for objecting to the split infinitive—loss of clarity—is also the reason for avoiding unnecessary splits of a subject and a verb and of a verb and its complement. Example:

> **The Secretary of Defense has agreed <u>to</u> before the start of the next Congressional session <u>reveal</u> the nature of troop buildups in the Gulf region.**

In this sentence, insertion of two prepositional phrases between the two parts of the infinitive is both awkward and sloppy.

SI–TH

stanch/staunch *Stanch*, a verb, means to "stop or extinguish," as in

> **Paramedics struggled to <u>stanch</u> the man's arterial bleeding.**

Staunch, however, is an adjective that means "steadfast or true," as in

> **McMillan is a <u>staunch</u> supporter of United Way.**

Note that some dictionaries cite *staunch* as an older variation of *stanch*. Let's underscore *older*—don't use older or secondary citations. They are there for historical context.

than/then *Then*—an adverb denoting time—is often confused with *than*. If you are comparing something, use *than*:

> **No one is more aware of America's breakfast habits <u>than</u> our fast-food franchise executives.**

Then, on the other hand, carries the sense of "soon afterward":

> **Let's visit our favorite café and have caramel lattes; <u>then</u> we can head to the gym to suffer at the hands of our aerobics instructor.**

Note that *then* cannot connect these two independent clauses on its own. A semicolon is needed.

When *than* is used to introduce an implied clause of comparison, the pronoun that may follow is most likely in the nominative case:

Tom is a lot smarter <u>than I</u> [am smart].

But some sentences won't permit this implied arrangement:

There is not a more dedicated volunteer <u>than her.</u>

"Than she is a volunteer" would not make sense here.

that/which/who As the entry for restrictive/nonrestrictive clauses says, *that* is used to restrict meaning and *which* is used to elaborate on it. These pronouns are used only in their particular types of clauses, but *who* can be used in both types when it refers to people or to things endowed by the writer with human qualities:

Recipes <u>that</u> require soy products are easy to follow.
(Restrictive—comma not needed)

Construction bonds, <u>which</u> can be a dependable tax shelter, carry different interest rates according to the credit standing of the local government.
(Nonrestrictive—gives explanation, and a comma is required.)

The demonstrators <u>who</u> interrupted the senator's speech were arrested.
(Restrictive—in this case, *who* is preferred over *that* because we are talking about real people, not inanimate objects or concepts. In this construction, a comma is not required.)

Newland, <u>who</u> is running for the state Senate seat from Medford, charged this morning that the governor's office has been "grossly mismanaged."
(Nonrestrictive—explanatory material follows *who*. Note the inclusion of commas.)

their/there/they're Here's a vexing trio. Although they sound alike, they are (they're!) quite different. *Their* is the possessive form of the pronoun *they:*

<u>Their</u> Web site is truly innovative.

In the example above, the possessive pronoun *their* modifies the nouns *Web site.*

When it begins a sentence, *there* is called an expletive. It is sometimes called a false subject because it doesn't help determine the number of the verb:

There are many reasons to deny your petition.

In the above example, note that the noun *reasons,* not *there,* controls the number of the verb.

They're is a contraction of *they* and *are,* used only informally when you want to combine subject and verb:

"They're ready for you, Mr. President," the aide announced.

there are/there is Beginning a sentence with the expletive *there is* or *there are* is generally an indirect and ineffective way to communicate. It adds clutter rather than meaning. When you have to use these constructions, however, be aware that *there* is not the subject of the sentence and does not control the number of the verb. In these sentences, the subject usually follows the verb and controls its number:

There are many ways to fend off bankruptcy.
      (verb)   (subj.)

Generally speaking, only the first part of a compound subject following the verb in these sentences is used to determine the number of the verb:

There is too much waste and inefficiency in this company.
      (verb)   (subj.)   (subj.)

tortuous/torturous The origin of these adjectives is the same, "to twist," but their usage is different. *Tortuous* connotes "twists and turns" and "complexity":

The tortuous road led to the fire lookout atop the mountain.
      ("twisted")

The council took fifteen hours to decipher the tortuous
                                         ("convoluted")
budget plan.

Torturous is used in the context of its verb *torture,* "to inflict pain as a means of punishment."

The late diagnosis of cancer led to four torturous rounds of chemotherapy.

toward/towards Dictionaries call *towards* "archaic and rare." Save it for an antique convention.

try and/try to Avoid *try and.* It adds nothing but awkwardness. *Try to* does the job:

> **Rescuers said they would <u>try to</u> reach the stranded climbers by late afternoon.**

unique Why is this adjective regularly adorned with superficial and redundant words, as in *most unique* or *very unique*? *Unique* means, simply, "the only one of its kind." Don't succumb to embarrassing overstatement.

up It is anything but upbeat when it is coupled with a verb. Phrases such as *face up, slow up* and *head up* are clutter:

> **He must <u>face up</u> to his new challenges.**

So—down with *up!* See p. 130.

verb and verbals The verb is the heart of a sentence. It provides action and voice; it drives all the other sentence parts. When chosen correctly, it is in command. Verbals, however, are not verbs. They are nouns, adjectives or adverbs. Can we be any more direct than that? See pp. 54–55.

TO–WH

very Be wary of *very* when you are tempted to give an adjective more punch. Don't overlook better, more precise adjectives and contribute to clutter. *Very* is but one example of an overused intensifier. Others are *really, completely, extremely* and *totally*. Rather than describe someone as very sad, you could choose among these words: *depressed, melancholy, sorrowful* or *doleful*. See p. 143.

waiver/waver A waiver (noun) is a document that relinquishes a right, while to waver (verb) is to waffle on a commitment, or to move/react unsteadily.

> **The dean approved a <u>waiver</u> for all application fees.**

> **He never <u>wavered</u> on his commitment to the company.**

who's/whose If you want to combine subject and verb, use *who's*:

> <u>Who's</u> **making dinner tonight?**
> (Who is making dinner tonight?)

If you need the possessive pronoun, use *whose*:

Whose turn is it to make tofu burritos tonight?

who/whom Sloppy speech has done its best to eliminate *whom* from this handsome pair of pronouns, but the case for their proper use remains strong. The use of *whom* is not elitist; it is merely correct. *Whom* always is used as an object in a sentence. *Who* is always the subject. So:

Who will win the scholarship award?

Easy call. *Who* is the subject of the sentence.

Whom did you call first with your exciting news?

Yes, this takes a little more work to analyze, but the subject is *you* and the direct object is *whom*. You can quickly rearrange the sentence to understand this relationship:

You did call whom first with your exciting news.
(subj.)   (dir. obj.)

your/you're The same distinctions made in the entries for *their/there/ they're* and *who's/whose* apply here. If you want to use the possessive form of the personal pronoun *you*, use *your*:

Your Facebook page is impressive.
(*Your* modifies *Facebook page.*)

If you want to compress (contract) the subject-verb *you are*, use *you're*.

You're going to be a great grammarian!

WH–YO

Spelling

It's true. Spelling correctly isn't easy. But it's not impossible.

We believe that if you focus on proper pronunciation, careful reading of words and their definitions, and a targeted look at some common exceptions to spelling rules, you can be an effective speller.

However, our advice is similar to that given to the New York City tourist who asked, "How do I get to Carnegie Hall?"

The time-honored answer? **Practice, practice, practice.**

So, here is a list of words that are most commonly misspelled by students and professionals alike. Note the letters in boldface type for each word; they will alert you to the problem areas for each word. For example, look how we list *definitely*: the emphasis on **i** shows that the common misspellings for this word are *definately* and *defanitely*.

Remember: When in doubt, look it up. And remember, too: The "first" or primary spelling in the dictionary entry controls—"other" or "secondary" spellings won't work.

Be sure to add your own troublesome words to this list. Here we go.

accepta**ble**	ac**qu**it	**athle**te
acces**sible**	admis**sible**	atten**dance**
accident**ally**	advis**er**	author**ize**
acco**mm**odate	all**ege**	ball**oon**
acc**u**mulate	ann**i**hilate	bank**r**uptcy
ach**ie**ve	arg**u**ment	basic**ally**
acknow**ledg**ment	assa**ss**in	bel**ie**ve

benefited

bookkeeper

broccoli

business

caffeine

calendar

canceled

cemetery

changeable

cigarette

commitment

comparable

conceive

condemn

congratulations

conscious

consensus

consistent

contempt

coolly

counselor

courageous

criticize

curiosity

definite

definitely

desirable

desperate

deterrent

dilemma

disastrous

dumbfound

ecstasy

eighth

embarrass

endeavor

environment

equipped

exaggerate

excitable

excusable

exhilarate

existence

extremely

fierce

fiery

financier

forcible

foreign

forfeit

fulfill

gauge

government

grammar

harassment

hemorrhage

hierarchy

hygiene

incredible

indispensable

innocuous

inoculate

insistence

irascible

irresistible

jeopardy

judgment

knowledgeable

legitimate

leisure

liaison

likable

likelihood

loneliness

maintenance

manageable

millionaire

mischievous

missile

misspell

necessary

niece	protein	super**sede**
notic**eable**	questio**nnaire**	supervis**or**
oc**cas**ion	re**cede**	su**rpr**ise
occur**rence**	reco**mm**end	ta**riff**
omitted	refe**rr**ed	temp**era**ment
op**ti**mistic	relev**ant**	tomat**oes**
para**llel**	remem**br**ance	usable
pastime	repetitious	va**cill**ate
perc**ei**ve	resist**ant**	va**cuu**m
permiss**ible**	r**hy**thm	vilify
persist**ent**	seizure	vi**llain**
potat**oes**	separate	vis**ible**
pre**cede**	sheriff	weird
predecess**or**	sizable	wield
prejudice	ski**ll**ful	wi**ll**ful
priv**ilege**	sover**eign**	with**h**old
proc**eed**	succeed	woo**ll**y
prof**ited**	superintend**ent**	**y**ield

This is a manag**eable** list, yes?

Remember: The more you use these words—the more you write them—the easier your spelling task becomes. There's a lot to be said for repetition! We repeat: There's a lot to be said for r-e-p-e-t-i-t-i-o-n!

Appendix B

Homonyms, Homophones, Spell-Checks, Oh My!

In the previous appendix, we offered a list of difficult spellings. Now let's focus on another great (or is that *grate?*) challenge to everyone who is far too (or is that *two?*) dependent on spell-checkers. You can call them homonyms or homophones, but understand that word groups such as these—words that have similar pronunciations but different meanings and spellings—threaten the precision and credibility of your writing.

This grouping should remind you of the importance of understanding the definitions and proper contexts for words. Believe us, spell-checks won't help you here—did you hear that?

Here is our priority list of more than 200 pairs—or trios—or even quartets! Believe us, there are many more to consider. However, these should make the point: Know the meaning of a word, no matter how it is pronounced.

accept	except
aid	aide
ail	ale
aisle	isle
all	awl
allowed	aloud
altar	alter
ascent	assent
assistance	assistants
aural	oral
away	aweigh
bail	bale
bare	bear

base	bass		
bazaar	bizarre		
beach	beech		
beat	beet		
berry	bury		
billed	build		
berth	birth		
bite	byte		
bloc	block		
boar	bore		
board	bored		
boarder	border		
bolder	boulder		
bough	bow		
boy	buoy		
bread	bred		
brake	break		
brewed	brood		
brews	bruise		
bridal	bridle		
brows	browse		
buy	by	bye	
cache	cash		
cannon	canon		
canvas	canvass		
carat	carrot	caret	karat
cast	caste		
cede	seed		
cell	sell		
cellar	seller		
censer	censor	sensor	
cent	scent	sent	
cereal	serial		
chance	chants		
chic	sheik		
chilly	chili		
choral	coral		
chord	cord		
chute	shoot		
cite	sight	site	

clause	claws	
coarse	course	
colonel	kernel	
complement	compliment	
core	corps	
correspondence	correspondents	
council	counsel	
creak	creek	
cue	queue	
currant	current	
cymbal	symbol	
days	daze	
dear	deer	
desert	dessert	
dew	do	due
disburse	disperse	
discreet	discrete	
dual	duel	
earn	urn	
elicit	illicit	
ewe	yew	you
faint	feint	
fair	fare	
faze	phase	
feat	feet	
find	fined	
fir	fur	
flair	flare	
flea	flee	
flew	flu	flue
flour	flower	
for	four	fore
foreword	forward	
forth	fourth	
foul	fowl	
gait	gate	
gene	jean	

gnu	knew	new
gorilla	guerilla	
grate	great	
groan	grown	
hair	hare	
hall	haul	
halve	have	
hangar	hanger	
heal	heel	he'll
hear	here	
heard	her	
higher	hire	
him	hymn	
hoard	horde	
hoarse	horse	
hole	whole	
holy	wholly	
hold	holed	
hour	our	
idle	idol	
in	inn	
incite	insight	
instance	instants	
its	it's	
knead	kneed	need
knight	night	
knot	not	
know	no	
knows	nose	
lay	lei	
leach	leech	
lead	led	
leak	leek	
lean	lien	
leased	least	
lessen	lesson	
levee	levy	

lie	lye	
links	lynx	
load	lode	
loan	lone	
locks	lox	
loot	lute	
made	maid	
mail	male	
main	mane	
maize	maze	
mall	maul	
manner	manor	
mantel	mantle	
marry	merry	
marshal	martial	
meat	meet	mete
medal	metal	mettle
might	mite	
mince	mints	
miner	minor	
missed	mist	
moose	mousse	
morn	mourn	
muscle	mussel	
naval	navel	
none	nun	
oar	or	ore
oh	owe	
one	won	
overdo	overdue	
overseas	oversees	
pail	pale	
pain	pane	
pair	pare	pear
palate	palette	pallet
passed	past	
patience	patients	

pause	paws	
peace	piece	
peak	peek	pique
peal	peel	
pedal	peddle	petal
peer	pier	
plain	plane	
pleas	please	
pole	poll	
poor	pore	pour
pray	prey	
presence	presents	
prince	prints	
principal	principle	
profit	prophet	
rack	wrack	
rain	reign	rein
raise	rays	raze
rap	wrap	
rapped	rapt	wrapped
read	red	
read	reed	
real	reel	
reek	wreak	
rest	wrest	
review	revue	
right	write	
ring	wring	
road	rode	rowed
roe	row	
role	roll	
rote	wrote	
rung	wrung	
rye	wry	
sail	sale	
scene	seen	
sea	see	
seam	seem	
seas	sees	seize

serf	surf	
sew	so	sow
shear	sheer	
shone	shown	
slay	sleigh	
soar	sore	
sole	soul	
some	sum	
stair	stare	
stake	steak	
stationary	stationery	
steal	steel	
straight	strait	
suite	sweet	
tail	tale	
taught	taut	
team	teem	
tear	tier	
tern	turn	
their	there	they're
theirs	there's	
threw	through	
thrown	throne	
tic	tick	
tide	tied	
to	too	two
toe	tow	
told	tolled	
vain	vane	vein
vale	veil	
vary	very	
vial	vile	
vice	vise	
waist	waste	
wait	weight	
waive	wave	
waiver	waver	
ware	wear	where

way	weigh	whey
weak	week	
weather	whether	
we've	weave	
wet	whet	
which	witch	
while	wile	
whine	wine	
who's	whose	
wood	would	
yore	your	you're

Irregular (Make That Troublesome) Verb Forms

Let's give it up for the quiet but hard-working dictionary! It is true that it gives you a proper spelling and a rank-ordered set of definitions, but when it comes to verbs, the dictionary entry begins with an important trio: the verb's present tense, its past tense and the formation of its past participle.

Why is this important?

Well, many verbs end in *-ed* in the past tense, as do their past participles, as in

I appear. (present tense)

I appeared. (past tense)

I have appeared. (past perfect tense)

However, as you look at this list of almost 100 groups of verbs, you'll see that the English language has a great number of what are called "irregular" constructions. For example, the present tense of the verb *leave* would not change to

He <u>leaved</u> the past behind.

As the list that follows shows, the past tense of *leave* is *left*.

We hope this list is helpful, but please remember: Keep your dictionary nearby. Look it up, and be sure.

Present Tense	Past Tense	Past Participle (have/had)
arise	arose	arisen
awake	awoke	awaken
be	was, were	been
become	became	become
begin	began	begun
bleed	bled	bled
blow	blew	blown
break	broke	broken
bring	brought	brought
build	built	built
burst	burst	burst
buy	bought	bought
catch	caught	caught
choose	chose	chosen
come	came	come
cut	cut	cut
deal	dealt	dealt
dig	dug	dug
do	did	done
draw	drew	drawn
drink	drank	drunk
drive	drove	driven
eat	ate	eaten
fall	fell	fallen
feed	fed	fed
feel	felt	felt
fight	fought	fought
find	found	found
flee	fled	fled
fly	flew	flown
forbid	forbade	forbidden
forget	forgot	forgotten
forgive	forgave	forgiven
freeze	froze	frozen
get	got	gotten
give	gave	given
go	went	gone
grow	grew	grown
hang (to execute)	hanged	hanged
hang (to suspend)	hung	hung

Present Tense	Past Tense	Past Participle (have/had)
have	had	had
hear	heard	heard
hide	hid	hidden
hold	held	held
hurt	hurt	hurt
keep	kept	kept
know	knew	known
lay	laid	laid
lead	led	led
leave	left	left
lend	lent	lent
let	let	let
lie	lay	lain
light	lit	lit
lose	lost	lost
make	made	made
meet	met	met
pay	paid	paid
quit	quit	quit
read	read	read
ride	rode	ridden
ring	rang	rung
run	ran	run
say	said	said
see	saw	seen
seek	sought	sought
sell	sold	sold
send	sent	sent
shake	shook	shaken
shine	shone	shone
sing	sang	sung
sit	sat	sat
sleep	slept	slept
speak	spoke	spoken
spend	spent	spent
spring	sprang	sprung
stand	stood	stood
steal	stole	stolen
stink	stank	stunk
swim	swam	swum

Present Tense	Past Tense	Past Participle (have/had)
swing	swung	swung
take	took	taken
teach	taught	taught
tear	tore	torn
tell	told	told
think	thought	thought
throw	threw	thrown
understand	understood	understood
wake	woke	woken
wear	wore	worn
weave	wove	woven
win	won	won
wind	wound	wound
write	wrote	written

Index

EXERCISE 1 • GRAMMAR CHECKUP:
100 IMPORTANT QUESTIONS

The following questions reflect the range of material discussed in "When Words Collide," 8th edition. They also represent a "snapshot" of the grammatical competencies you need to master as you develop your writing skills. Before you attempt the other 35 exercises in this book, complete this review and then carefully note the answers provided. Your performance on this checkup will be an important benchmark for the work that is ahead.

Part 1. A Warmup

These first 10 questions probe your understanding of basic grammar. Select the correct answer from the choices offered.

_____ 1.   What is *sent* in the following sentence?
            The company sent a team of investigators to the accident scene.
            A. It is the only verb in the sentence.
            B. It is the key word to making the sentence a complete one.
            C. It is the "action" word in the sentence.
            D. It is a verb in the past tense.
            E. All of the above are correct.

_____ 2.   What is the subject of the sentence in question 1?
            A. team
            B. company
            C. investigators
            D. accident
            E. scene

_____ 3.   How many verbs are in the following sentence?
              Sarah wants to attend a university that has a strong
              program in international relations.
              A. none
              B. one
              C. two
              D. three
              E. four

_____ 4.   What is the past tense of the verb *throw?*
              A. thrown
              B. has thrown
              C. had thrown
              D. threw
              E. through

_____ 5.   What's the error in the following sentence?
              The number of bank failures has startled the government
              and its chief advisers.
              A. The verb does not agree with its subject in number.
              B. *Government* is misspelled.
              C. *Its* should be *it's.*
              D. A comma is needed before *and.*
              E. The sentence is correct as written.

_____ 6.   Which of the following underlined items is *not* an adjective?
              A. the <u>smartest</u> student
              B. a <u>really</u> bright student
              C. the <u>tallest</u> building on the block
              D. a <u>principled</u> decision
              E. a truly <u>charming</u> individual

_____ 7.   What's the difference between a homonym and a
              homophone?
              A. There is no difference—they're synonymous.
              B. Both refer to words that have the same pronunciation,
                  but homophones have different spellings and different
                  meanings.
              C. Both refer to words that have the same meaning and
                  the same spelling.

      D. Words that are homonyms may have several different
         pronunciations.

      E. *Homonym* is used instead of *homophone* in Great
         Britain and Australia.

_____ 8. Which of the words below means "to cause to feel
resentment"?

      A. peek

      B. peak

      C. pique

      D. piek

      E. None of the above matches that definition.

_____ 9. What verb below correctly completes this sentence?
If the number of airline flights _____, ticket prices will
soar.

      A. drops

      B. drop

      C. have dropped

      D. are dropping

      E. None of the above is correct.

_____ 10. What word correctly completes the following sentence?
She is _____ to do well on this diagnostic test.

      A. anxious   B. eager

Part 2. Errors! Fix Them!

Carefully read each sentence in this section. If you think the sentence has
an error (or errors), select the best choice for correcting it (or them) from
the options offered. If you think the sentence is correct as written, select D.

_____ 11. A reporter should always try to protect their sources.

      A. Change *try to* to *try and.*

      B. Either change *their* to *his or her* or make the subject
plural.

      C. Insert a comma after *reporter.*

      D. There are no errors.

_____ 12.   The fire that struck the warehouse district last night
completely destroyed three buildings and injured six
people.
A.   Change *that* to *which.*
B.   Eliminate the redundancy *(completely destroyed).*
C.   The corrections in both A and B are necessary.
D.   There are no errors.

_____ 13.   She is a well-known scholar who understands academic
committment.
A.   Eliminate the hyphen from the compound modifier
(well-known).
B.   Change *who* to *that.*
C.   *Committment* should be spelled *commitment.*
D.   There are no errors.

_____ 14.   You're never going to believe who we saw today at the
mall!
A.   Change the exclamation point to a question mark.
B.   Change *you're* to *your.*
C.   Change *who* to *whom.*
D.   There are no errors.

_____ 15.   Each of her movie scripts have great box office potential.
A.   Change *have* to *has.*
B.   Change *scripts* to *scripts'.*
C.   Insert a comma after *scripts.*
D.   There are no errors.

_____ 16.   Seriously, I don't think that the prosecution has proved its
case.
A.   Change *proved* to *proven.*
B.   Change *its* to *their.*
C.   The corrections in both A and B are needed.
D.   There are no errors.

_____ 17.   Billy said he was loath to describe how his experience as a
            community volunteer compared to his later work as a
            nonprofit executive.
            A. Change *loath* to *loathe.*
            B. Change passive voice to active.
            C. Change *compared to* to *compared with.*
            D. There are no errors.

_____ 18.   The woman whom detectives suspected of committing the
            so called "summer of love" robberies has been arrested.
            A. Change *whom* to *who.*
            B. Change *committing* to *commiting.*
            C. Insert hyphen between *so* and *called.*
            D. There are no errors.

_____ 19.   The council approved the parking ordnance, but the
            auditorium bond proposal was defeated by it.
            A. Create parallel structure by making voice consistent.
            B. Change *ordnance* to *ordinance.*
            C. The corrections in both A and B are needed.
            D. There are no errors.

_____ 20.   How has the defendant's behavior effected the defense's
            ability to persuade the jury?
            A. Change *defendant's* to *defendants.*
            B. Change *effected* to *affected.*
            C. The corrections in both A and B are needed.
            D. There are no errors.

Part 3. Good Grief! Spelling!

Choose the correctly spelled word from each group of three words. Write
the letter of your selection in the space provided. **If all spellings are
incorrect, write an *I* in the space.** Alternate or secondary listings in a
standard dictionary are *not* considered correct. Relax and give this a try!

_____ 21.   A. admissable   B. judgment   C. relavant

_____ 22.   A. gauge   B. embarassed   C. resistent

_____ 23.   A. fraudaulent   B. dillema   C. premier

_____ 24.   A. pasttime   B. pronounciation   C. premiere

_____ 25.   A. accessible   B. weild   C. seperate

_____ 26.   A. accommodate   B. accummulate   C. reccommend

_____ 27.   A. tarriff   B. versus   C. superintendant

_____ 28.   A. procede   B. preceed   C. recede

_____ 29.   A. sophmore   B. supersede   C. definate

_____ 30.   A. seige   B. sieze   C. occurred

Part 4. Parts of Speech

Identify the part of speech of the <u>underlined</u> word from the options offered in the first five sentences. Then answer the questions posed in numbers 36–40.

_____ 31.   <u>She</u> demands unwavering loyalty from her employees.
          A. noun   B. pronoun   C. adjective   D. adverb

_____ 32.   <u>Tripping</u> over the fence, he tore his pants.
          A. adjective   B. gerund   C. noun   D. noun

_____ 33.   Churchill <u>attended</u> a concert the night of the election.
          A. linking verb   B. transitive verb
          C. intransitive verb

_____ 34.   <u>Who</u> wrote this incredible essay?
          A. relative pronoun   B. interrogative pronoun
          C. coordinating conjunction

_____ 35.   This is the silliest <u>exercise</u> ever foisted on humanity.
          A. noun   B. pronoun   C. adjective   D. adverb

_____ 36. How many <u>prepositions</u> are in the following sentence?
Between you and me, this plan should be discussed only
among your closest friends; please keep this information
inside your close circle.
A. two
B. three
C. four
D. five
E. There are no prepositions in the sentence.

_____ 37. What kind of verb is *seems* in the following sentence?
Tom <u>seems</u> concerned about his company's future.
A. transitive
B. linking
C. intransitive
D. conjunctive
E. None of the above is correct.

_____ 38. What part of speech is the word *crying* in the following
sentence?
<u>Crying</u> your heart out won't get you this job.
A. noun (used as an infinitive)
B. noun (used as a gerund)
C. adverb
D. adjective
E. conjunction

_____ 39. What kind of pronoun is the word *this* in the following
sentence?
<u>This</u> is a movie you shouldn't miss.
A. relative   B. adjectival   C. possessive
D. conjunctive   E. demonstrative

_____ 40. How does the word *that* function in the following sentence?
This is one of those sentences <u>that</u> never make sense to
students.
A. personal pronoun   B. relative pronoun
C. demonstrative pronoun   D. coordinating conjunction
E. subordinating conjunction

Part 5. Oh, No! More Spelling!

Carefully examine each group of three words and identify the misspelled word, if any, in each group. If you think a word is misspelled, spell it correctly in the blank provided. If you think that all words in a group are correct, write *correct* in the blank.

_____ 41. definate   adolescent   occasion

_____ 42. aide   aid   tenets

_____ 43. detect   legitimate   withold

_____ 44. roommate   misspell   wield

_____ 45. stationery   stationary   similar

_____ 46. wiener   existance   vengeance

_____ 47. leisure   noticeable   likeable

_____ 48. reservoir   villain   villify

_____ 49. hinderance   sizable   maneuver

_____ 50. acquitted   cancelled   omitted

Part 6. Word Use

Now let's see how well you understand the definitions and uses of the words. Choose the word that best fits the intended meaning of each of the following sentences from the choices offered.

_____ 51.   Nathaniel enjoys reading _____ novels.
             A. historic   B. historical

_____ 52.   Please _____ the book on the table.
             A. lay   B. lie

_____ 53. Let's examine this issue _____ at our next meeting.
      A. farther   B. further

_____ 54. She is an _____ to Senator Woodbridge.
      A. aid   B. aide

_____ 55. Quit acting _____ you are the boss!
      A. like   B. as if

_____ 56. Honestly, I'm not _____ to your point of view.
      A. adverse   B. averse

_____ 57. Her plan is _____ of three distinct parts.
      A. composed   B. comprised

_____ 58. I like bananas more _____ tangerines.
      A. than   B. then

_____ 59. That professor has been _____ a manic composer.
      A. compared to   B. compared with

_____ 60. This debate could use _____ critics and more
      diplomats.
      A. fewer   B. less

Part 7. Sentence Parts and Types

Carefully examine the following sentences and select the correct answer
to the questions posed about them.

_____ 61. What is the grammatical term for the underlined portion
      of the following sentence?
      He drove <u>through the night</u> in blinding rain.
      A. direct object
      B. prepositional phrase
      C. predicate nominative
      D. participial phrase
      E. dependent clause

_____ 62. What is the grammatical term for the underlined portion
of the following sentence?
This is one of those sentences <u>that drive me crazy</u>.
A. independent clause
B. participial phrase
C. subordinate phrase
D. dependent clause
E. infinitive phrase

_____ 63. Okay, let's get more detailed: What type of sentence is in
question 62?
A. simple
B. compound
C. complex
D. compound–complex
E. fragment

_____ 64. Here's another: What type of sentence is this?
Having the courage to face adversity and the fortitude to
defeat it, no matter the obstacles.
A. simple
B. compound
C. complex
D. compound–complex
E. fragment

_____ 65. How many subjects are in the following sentence?
The Senate has approved its version of the bill, but the
House appears to be deadlocked over a provision that may
take weeks to resolve.
A. none
B. one
C. two
D. three
E. four

Part 8. A Long Dash to the Finish Line

Think these questions over carefully and select your answers from the choices offered. Note the variety of grammatical areas covered in this large section. You'll be dealing with these issues throughout the exercise book.

_____ 66. Which of the following lettered items is *not* a complete
sentence?
   A. Watch yourself on that slick sidewalk!
   B. Stop!
   C. That which you covet may one day be your millstone.
   D. He contended his was the superior invention, which
       proved to be untrue.
   E. Killing me softly, ever so softly.

_____ 67. What is the error in the following sentence?
Houstons biggest environmental problem is its sprawling
highway system.
   A. *Houstons* should be punctuated as a possessive.
   B. *Environmental* is misspelled.
   C. A comma should follow *problem.*
   D. *Its* should be *it's.*
   E. The sentence is correct as written.

_____ 68. Which word correctly fills the blank?
Edith is more qualified to do this assignment than _____.
   A. he
   B. him

_____ 69. Which of the following underlined nouns is also a gerund?
   A. The recently <u>completed</u> building is ready for inspection
   B. Gambling on his future can be a costly <u>mission</u>.
   C. <u>Things</u> that go bump in the night can be scary.
   D. <u>Building</u> on your failures makes you stronger.

_____ 70. Which is the correct punctuation from the choices provided?
The stock market continued its startling decline today
_____ trading exceeded 100 million shares.
   A. ,
   B. ;

_____ 71. The following sentence contains what type of verb?
He seems very uncomfortable in his new role.
A. linking
B. intransitive
C. transitive

_____ 72. What's the error in the following sentence?
Working through the night to battle the stubborn blaze.
A. two misspellings
B. sentence fragment
C. wrong verb
D. punctuation
E. dangling modifier

_____ 73. Which of the following sentences is correctly punctuated?
A. Firefighters repelled the flames on the ridge but a
sudden windburst helped the blaze jump the fire lines.
B. Firefighters repelled the flames on the ridge; but a
sudden windburst helped the blaze jump the fire lines.
C. Firefighters repelled the flames on the ridge...but a
sudden windburst helped the blaze jump the fire lines.
D. Firefighters repelled the flames on the ridge, but a
sudden windburst helped the blaze jump the fire lines.

_____ 74. Which word correctly completes the sentence?
The witness _____ police believe lied to the grand
jury has disappeared.
A. who
B. whom

_____ 75. Your answer in question 74 serves as the _____.
A. direct object of the transitive verb
B. subject of the dependent clause
C. subject of the independent clause
D. object of the prepositional phrase

_____ 76. None of your theories _____ sense.
A. makes
B. make

_____ 77.   Question 76 deals with what grammatical topic?
       A.   pronoun–antecedent agreement
       B.   subject–verb agreement
       C.   restrictive clauses
       D.   nonrestrictive clauses

_____ 78.   In the following sentence, how would you classify the underlined verb?
       Jericho <u>won</u> easily.
       A.   linking
       B.   transitive
       C.   intransitive

For the following items, select the word in the parentheses that correctly completes the sentence.

_____ 79.   I don't understand (A. your   B. you) campaigning for someone who is so narrow-minded.

_____ 80.   Please return that rhinoceros to (A. its B. it's) owner.

_____ 81.   Security forces detained (A. we B. us) reporters at the border.

_____ 82.   (A. Her's B. Hers) is the office at the end of the hall.

_____ 83.   What sources have you (A. cited B. sited) to support your thesis?

_____ 84.   Among the recently discovered documents from the apartment of the former clerk of courts (A. is B. are) several shoe boxes full of undeposited campaign contribution checks.

_____ 85.   The news media (A. is   B. are) under attack again.

_____ 86.   Have you finished your project on "Stopping by Woods on a Snowy (A. Evening?"   B. Evening"?)

_____ 87. The county commission has decided to revise (A. its B. their) charter.

_____ 88. Carly has a (A. good-natured B. good natured C. good, natured) personality.

_____ 89. Yesterday she hiked (A. farther B. further) than ever before.

_____ 90. This discussion is going (A. farther B. further) than I intended.

_____ 91. The officer (A. that B. who C. which) stopped his car was professional and polite.

_____ 92. Geometry is a course (A. that B. which) depends heavily on theorems.

_____ 93. He failed his (A. drivers B. driver's) exam because he didn't park correctly.

_____ 94. (A. Who's B. Whose) going to the store tonight?

_____ 95. (A. Three fourths B. Three-fourths C. Three forths D. Three-forths) of the shipment is missing.

_____ 96. The story of his battle with addictions has been (A. well documented B. well-documented).

_____ 97. The mayor called her opponent _____
     A. , "a feeble minded bureaucrat."
     B. "a feeble-minded bureaucrat."

_____ 98. Her opponent responded _____
     A. , "That makes me twice as smart as you."
     B. "That makes me twice as smart as you."

_____ 99. Climbing over the barbed wire fence, (A. his pants tore B. he tore his pants).

_____ 100. You won't find a better grammarian than (A. she B. her).

OK, let's discuss those answers!

Part 1

1.   E—All of the above are correct. The present tense for *sent* is *send*; yes, it is this sentence's only verb (a transitive one, providing action), which is key to making the sentence complete.

2.   B—company. *Team* is the direct object; *investigators* is the object of the preposition, as is *scene*. All of these choices, by the way, are nouns.

3.   C—two. The verbs are *wants* and *has*. *To attend* is an infinitive, which does not act as a verb.

4.   D—threw. Your dictionary is a trusty source for determining principal parts of verbs.

5.   A—The verb does not agree with its subject in number. The true subject is *The number,* which is singular. *Bank failures* is the object of a preposition.

6.   B—really. It's an adverb, never an adjective. An adverb modifies an adjective (in this case, the adjective *bright*). The other choices in this question are adjectives—note that they all modify nouns.

7.   B—Homophones have different meanings and different spellings, though the words (e.g., *bear, bare*) have similar pronunciations. Always keep a dictionary near!

8.   C—pique. Love that dictionary!

9.   A—drops. The true subject of this sentence is *The number* (singular), not *airline flights* (plural). Hence we use a singular verb.

10.   B—eager. As you will see in Part II of *When Words Collide,* you want to use *eager* here. You can only be anxious *about* something.

Part 2

11.   B—Either change *their* to *his or her* or make the subject plural. The sentence contains what is called an antecedent agreement error.

12.   B—Eliminate the redundancy. Something cannot be partially destroyed. If it is not destroyed, then it has some level of damage.

13.   C—The correct spelling is c-o-m-m-i-t-m-e-n-t.

14.   C—Change *who* to *whom*. The sentence contains what is called a case error.

15.   A—Change *have* to *has*. *Each* is the true subject of the sentence.

16.   D—There are no errors.

17.   C—Change *compared to* to *compared with*. *Compared with* shows a side-by-side comparison.

18.   C—Insert hyphen between *so* and *called*. This is correct punctuation for a compound modifier. And, yes, *whom* is correct in that sentence!

19.   C—The corrections in both A and B are needed. The sentence improperly mixes active and passive voices. In addition, *ordnance* (weaponry) is not what the sentence intended.

20.   B—Change *effected* to *affected*. This is a silly and unfortunately common error. When in doubt about word use, look it up!

Part 3

Correct spellings follow.

21.   B—judgment

22. A—gauge

23. B—premier

24. C—premiere (Yes, *premier* and *premiere* are different words!)

25. A—accessible

26. A—accommodate

27. B—versus

28. C—recede

29. B—supersede

30. C—occurred

Part 4

31. B—pronoun

32. A—adjective (It's part of a *participial phrase*.)

33. B—transitive verb (It has a direct object: *concert*.)

34. B—interrogative pronoun (Note that the sentence ends with a question mark.)

35. A—noun

36. B—three prepositions *(between, among, inside)*

37. B—linking verb (Not all linking verbs are forms of *to be*.)

38. B—noun (as a gerund)

39. E—demonstrative pronoun

40. B—relative pronoun

Part 5

41.   definite

42.   correct

43.   withhold

44.   correct

45.   correct

46.   existence

47.   likable

48.   vilify

49.   hindrance

50.   canceled

Part 6

Use your dictionary and refer to Part II of the "When Words Collide" text for a thorough explanation of the differences between the word pairs in this segment of Exercise 1.

51.   B—historical

52.   A—lay

53.   B—further

54.   B—aide

55.   B—as if

56.   B—averse

57.   A—composed of

58.   A—than

59.   A—compared to

60.   A—fewer

Part 7

61.   B—prepositional phrase

62.   D—dependent clause (Although this part of the sentence has its own subject and verb, it cannot stand alone; it is subordinate (or dependent) on the main clause.)

63.   C—complex (The sentence contains two clauses—one independent, one dependent.)

64.   E—fragment (This is not a complete sentence. It contains neither a subject nor a verb.)

65.   D—three subjects *(Senate, House, that)*

Part 8

66.   E—Killing me softly, ever so softly (No subject, no verb, right? So, what is *killing?*)

67.   A—*Houstons* should be *Houston's,* a possessive.

68.   A—he (It is a comparative clause, as in "more qualified…than he [is qualified"].)

69. D—Building (The entire phrase, *Building on your failures,* is the subject of the sentence.)

70. B— ; (The semicolon separates the two independent clauses.)

71. A—linking (*Uncomfortable* is the verb's predicate adjective.)

72. B—sentence fragment (There is neither a subject nor a verb.)

73. D— (A comma is sufficient to separate the two independent clauses.)

74. A—who (who lied)

75. B—subject of the dependent clause

76. A—makes (In most cases, think of *none* as *not one.*)

77. B—subject–verb agreement

78. C—intransitive (There is no direct object.)

79. A—your (Use possessive case to modify *campaigning.*)

80. A—its (Use simple possessive, not a subject–verb contraction.)

81. B—us (Must be in the objective case to modify *reporters,* the direct object of the sentence.)

82. B—Hers (Possessive pronouns don't need apostrophes.)

83. A—cited

84. B—are (True subject is *shoe boxes.*)

85. B—are (*Media* is the plural of *medium.*)

86. B—(The quotation marks are part of a title, not of the question itself.)

87. A—its (*Commission* refers to the organization—not the individuals in the organization.)

88. A—good-natured

89. A—farther (Refers to physical distance.)

90. B—further (Refers to degree rather than measured distance.)

91. B—who (*That* and *which* do not refer to people.)

92. A—that (See the discussion of restrictive and nonrestrictive clauses in "When Words Collide.")

93. A—driver's (It is a possessive noun.)

94. A—who's (*Whose* is a possessive pronoun—it can't be both a subject and a verb, as is the case with *who's [who is]*).

95. B—three-fourths

96. B—well-documented

97. B—"a feeble-minded bureaucrat." (There is no need for a comma before a partial quotation.)

98. A— ,"That makes me twice as smart as you." (You *do* need a comma to introduce a quotation that can stand as a complete sentence when it is inserted into an existing sentence.)

99. B—he tore his pants (Dangling modifiers can tear up the logic of your writing, too!)

100. B—her (Compare this answer with that of question 68. Do you see the difference?)

So. What does it mean?

Although it was not intended as a test, Exercise 1 is an important diagnostic for you. You should feel good at this point if, on each section, you scored 75 percent or better. You should be concerned if you scored below 50 percent. In any case, these results will point out weaknesses you may have in certain grammatical areas. And, as you continue work in this exercise book, you will have plenty of opportunity to improve!

EXERCISE 2 • CORE COMMUNICATION: THE SUBJECT
AND ITS VERB

Purpose   To correctly identify the subject; to correctly identify
                subjects as actors always paired with verbs; to
                understand subject–verb combinations as the basic
                unit of all sentences.

Reference   "When Words Collide" (8/e), Chapters 4 and 5

Directions: Select the correct answer from the options provided,
                or fill in the blanks as directed.

_____ 1.   Which noun, acting as the subject, is linked to the verb in
            this sentence?
            At noon, the sound of the choir carried through the
            cathedral.
            A. noon
            B. sound
            C. choir
            D. cathedral

2.   What is the verb in sentence 1?

_____

_____

_____ 3.   How many verbs are in this sentence?
            I went to the chiropractic offices yesterday, but the first
            specialist ignored my urgent knocking, and the second was
            at a regional conference.
            A. one
            B. two
            C. three
            D. four

4. List the verbs you identified in question 3.

_____

_____

_____ 5. How many subjects are in this sentence?
My friend complained loudly about the new hit movie
because, throughout, the music drowned out the actors'
voices.
A. one
B. two
C. three
D. four

_____ 6. What are the subjects in this sentence?
My neighbor is internationally known for the violins he
makes in his backyard carriage house.
A. neighbor, violins, he
B. neighbor, violins
C. neighbor, he

7. Why is *Sophia, Kyle and Prita* considered the subject of this
sentence?
Sophia, Kyle and Prita coordinated the university blood drive again
this year.

_____

_____

_____ 8. How many verbs are in the following sentence?
She enjoyed her museum group trip to San Francisco, and
she hopes she will have the opportunity to participate in
another one soon.
A. one
B. two
C. three
D. four

9. In the following sentence, *to tell* sounds like an action word.
    Succinctly, and using grammar terms you already know, explain
    why it is *not* a verb.
    The writer called her father in Paris to tell him about her new job
    in New York.

    _____

    _____

10. Underline and identify all the subjects and verbs in the following
    sentence.
    The water in that part of the desert tastes terrible.

11. Underline and identify all the subjects and verbs in the following
    sentence.
    My mother said I should add whole milk instead of cream to that
    recipe to avoid unnecessary calories.

12. In one clear sentence, using grammar terms you already know, tell
    how to recognize the subject of a sentence.

    _____

    _____

_____ 13. How many verbs are in this sentence?
            Shahala lost her thumb drive, rewrote seven pages and still
            managed to turn her article in on time.
            A. one
            B. two
            C. three
            D. four

14. What is/are the subject(s) of the verbs in sentence 13?

    _____

    _____

15. In the following sentence, *completing* sounds like an action word. Succinctly, and using grammar terms you already know, explain why it is *not* a verb.

    After completing his first marathon, Zachary suddenly collapsed.

    _____

    _____

16. Underline and identify all the subjects and verbs in the following sentence.

    Ahmad's recently published research on the flow of sediment in streams was widely accepted by his peers.

_____ 17. How many subjects are in the following sentence?
             After the student driver gripped the steering wheel, she closed her eyes and slammed her foot on the brake to prevent her front wheels from falling into the ditch.
             A. one
             B. two
             C. three
             D. four

18. List the subjects in sentence 17.

    _____

    _____

19. List the verbs in sentence 17.

    _____

    _____

20. What is the subject of this sentence?
    Please present the hero his award.

    _____

    _____

EXERCISE 3 • FIND THE VERB!

Purpose   To develop mastery of verb conjugation; to recognize auxiliary verbs as part of verb strings with main verbs; to recognize verbs, even when they are separated from their subjects.

Reference   "When Words Collide" (8/e), Chapters 4 and 5

_____ 1.   What is the complete verb in the following sentence?
The actors have been rehearsing their lines for five hours.
A. have been rehearsing   B. have
C. rehearsing   D. have been

2.   What is/are the verb(s) in the following sentence?
The doctors insisted that treating the tumor with chemotherapy was the only viable solution.

_____

_____

3.   What is/are the verb(s) in the following sentence?
The passenger was jostled by the bumps of the speeding train and fell into the old woman's lap!

_____

_____

_____ 4.   What constitutes the verb(s) in this sentence?
The two sisters have been noisily begging for a new dog since March, and now their father is expected to make a decision by Sunday.
A. have been noisily begging, is expected
B. begging, is expected, to make
C. have been begging, is expected
D. have been, is

5. What is the complete verb in this sentence?
    Will anything persuade Jill not to take a kayak over Niagara Falls?

    _____

    _____

6. What is/are the verb(s) in the following sentence?
    Winds of at least 74 mph are classified as hurricanes.

    _____

    _____

7. What is/are the verb(s) in the following sentence?
    The workers rejected the contract, despite the company's
    counteroffer, and announced a strike for the next day.

    _____

    _____

8–20 Directions

Complete the following sentences by supplying the proper conjugation
of the infinitive form of the verb provided under each blank space.

Although he _____ his job as a beat reporter for the local
          8. *to enjoy* (present tense)
newspaper, he _____ always uncomfortable with the
          9. *to be* (present perfect)
wreckage he _____ of automobile accidents.
          10. *to see* (present tense)

Many seniors graduating from college _____ to move back in with
                              11. *to plan* (present tense)
their parents.

The shop owner _____ the professional dog walker who _____
       12. *to sue* (present progressive)   13. *to begin* (simple past)
providing services last month in the next door building over damages
to his storefront by

some of the dogs he _____ _____ out of control.
       14. *to say* (present tense)   15. *to be* (present tense)

Six friends, whose relationship _____ back as far as kindergarten,
             16. *to go* (present tense)
_____ the unique and lively music of the new high school band,
17. *to create* (present tense)
Go Back to School.

Antique violins _____ his passion, and he _____ several trips
       18. *to be* (present tense)   19. *to take* (present perfect)
to Italy to study the craft.

She shuns ice cream while training for marathons and

instead _____ lots of yogurt.
      20. to substitute (present tense)

EXERCISE 4 • NOUNS AND PRONOUNS AS SUBJECTS
AND OBJECTS

Purpose   To connect understanding of nouns and pronouns
                     with sentence elements.

Reference   "When Words Collide" (8/e), Chapters 4 and 6

Directions: Indicate the letter of the correct answer.

_____ 1.   Robert Louis Stevenson is classified as what part of speech?
              A. common noun   B. proper noun
              C. personal pronoun   D. relative pronoun

_____ 2.   What is the subject in the following sentence?
              According to Billy, Sarah is the best choice for the job.
              A. Billy   B. Sarah
              C. choice   D. job

_____ 3.   How many subjects are in the following sentence?
              It's a tough call, but I think Helen is the best choice for the
              job.
              A. none   B. one
              C. two   D. three

4.   List those subjects.

_____

_____ 5.   Of all the subjects in sentence 3, how many are pronouns?
              A. none   B. one
              C. two   D. three

6.   List those pronouns, if any.

_____

_____ 7. What is the direct object in the following sentence?
Billy gave Tommy a dirty look after the presentation.
A. Billy   B. Tommy
C. look   D. presentation

8. Sentence 7 contains two other grammatical "objects." List them
below according to their grammatical terms.
Indirect object _____
Object of preposition _____

_____ 9. How many pronouns are in the following sentence?
Who told you that I turned down both of the Hollywood
offers?
A. one   B. two
C. three   D. four

10. Okay—what are the pronouns in sentence 9?

_____

_____ 11. How many nouns are in the following sentence?
Are you excited about this incredibly innovative program?
A. none   B. one
C. two   D. three

_____ 12. What is the possessive form of the personal pronoun *she*?
A. she's   B. her's
C. their   D. her

_____ 13. Why is *homicides* in the following sentence not its subject?
The rate of homicides in the county is dropping rapidly.
A. It is the direct object.
B. It is the indirect object.
C. It is the object of the preposition.
D. Actually, it *is* the subject!

_____ 14. We know that some verbals can act as nouns. Which ones?
A. linking verbs and participles
B. gerunds and infinitives
C. participles and adverbs
D. subjunctives and conjunctives

_____ 15. What kind of verbal serves as one of the subjects in the
           following sentence?
           It's clear to me that recognizing verbals is an important
           grammatical skill.
           A. participle
           B. gerund
           C. infinitive
           D. conjunctive

_____ 16. The preceding sentence has _____ subject(s) and _____
           direct object(s).
           A. one...one
           B. two...no
           C. one...no
           D. two...one

_____ 17. What kind of pronoun is *anybody?*
           A. interrogative
           B. limiting
           C. relative
           D. indefinite

_____ 18. How many nouns are in the following sentence?
           You seem very quiet; are you okay?
           A. none
           B. one
           C. two
           D. three

_____ 19. Why is the word *friendly* in the following sentence not a
           noun or a pronoun?
           He seems like a friendly person, don't you think?
           A. Actually, it *is* a noun!
           B. It's a descriptor—or a modifier—not a person, place,
               or thing.
           C. It can't be a noun because *friendly* is the subject of the
               sentence.
           D. It is a pronoun, however, because *friendly* is a
               substitute for the noun *he.*

_____ 20.   How many subjects are in the following sentence?
The assailant fled the scene, dropping his gun in an alley.
A.   There is no subject—it's a fragment, not a complete sentence.
B.   one
C.   two
D.   three

21–25 Directions

Complete the following sentence by supplying an appropriate noun or pronoun, as listed, for each blank.

_____ gave the _____ to the _____ ,

21. personal   22. common   23. common
    pronoun   noun   noun

_____ quickly ran into an alley _____ contained an

24. relative pronoun   25. relative pronoun

unmarked police car.

EXERCISE 5 • SUBJECT, VERB, OBJECT, PLUS...

Purpose To develop mastery of sentence components through accurate identification of sentence subjects, verbs and objects (direct, indirect, objects of prepositions, predicate nominatives and predicate adjectives).

Reference "When Words Collide" (8/e), Chapters 4 and 5

Directions: Select the correct answer from the options provided, or fill in the blanks or underline as instructed.

_____ 1. What is the subject of the following sentence?
According to state officials, three-fourths of the filbert crop was destroyed in the freak storm.
   A. state officials
   B. three-fourths
   C. crop
   D. storm

_____ 2. The verb in sentence 1 is *was destroyed*. What kind of verb is it?
   A. transitive
   B. linking
   C. intransitive
   D. It's not a verb; it's a gerund.

3. Underline and mark all the subjects, verbs and objects in the following sentence, indicating the kind of verbs and objects as well.

You gave Tom the book, but it amazes me that he left without thanking you.

_____ 4.   What is the direct object in the following sentence?
           Tripping over the sleeping dog, Bethany twisted the ankle
           that she broke last year.
           A. dog   B. Bethany
           C. ankle   D. year

_____ 5.   Why does the preceding sentence have a direct object?
           Because the main clause has:
           A. a transitive verb   B. an intransitive verb
           C. a linking verb   D. a helping (auxiliary) verb

_____ 6.   What is the subject of the following sentence?
           There are at least 10 reasons for changing the bylaws of this
           organization.
           A. There   B. reasons
           C. bylaws   D. organization

_____ 7.   What is the direct object in the following sentence?
           Tommy gave Billy a dirty look after the game.
           A. Tommy   B. Billy
           C. look   D. game

8.   Sentence 7 contains two other grammatical "objects." List them
     below according to their grammatical terms.
     Indirect object _____
     Object of preposition _____

_____ 9.   How many subjects are in the following sentence?
           People who live in glass houses shouldn't throw stones.
           A. one   B. two
           C. three   D. none

_____ 10. Same question for this sentence.
           Right there, lying on the table, is your ticket for your
           vacation in Bali.
           A. none   B. one
           C. two   D. three

_____ 11. By the way, what kind of verb is that in question 10?
A. transitive   B. intransitive
C. linking

_____ 12. What is the verb in the following sentence?
Training for three months and sacrificing almost
everything for a chance to qualify for the 2016 Olympics.
A. training
B. sacrificing
C. qualify
D. The sentence does not contain a verb.

_____ 13. Why is _homicides_ in the following sentence not its subject?
The rate of homicides in the county has dropped rapidly
this year.
A. It is the direct object.
B. It is the indirect object.
C. It is the object of the preposition.
D. Actually, it _is_ the subject!

_____ 14. Which verbal—or verbals—can be the subject of a sentence?
A. participles
B. gerunds
C. infinitives
D. Both B and C are correct.

_____ 15. What do we call the underlined word in the following sentence?
It's clear to me that recognizing verbals is an important
grammatical _skill_.
A. direct object
B. indirect object
C. linking verb
D. predicate nominative

_____ 16. There are two verbs in the preceding exercise sentence.
They are both
A. transitive
B. fragmentary
C. intransitive
D. linking

_____ 17. What grammatical term suggests a "mirror reflection" of a
           sentence's subject?
           A. indirect object
           B. predicate nominative
           C. direct object
           D. gerund

_____ 18. What are the only two parts of speech that can serve as the
           subject of a sentence?
           A. nouns and pronouns
           B. nouns and gerunds
           C. nouns and adverbs
           D. pronouns and verbs

_____ 19. What is the complete direct object of the following
           sentence?
           I simply can't believe that the project is finished.
           A. believe
           B. can't believe
           C. the project
           D. that the project is finished

_____ 20. How many subjects are in the following sentence?
           Dropping his gun in an alley after running from the bank.
           A. None. It's a fragment, not a complete sentence.
           B. It may be a fragment, but it still has one subject.
           C. It *is* a complete sentence, with one subject.
           D. It has two subjects.

21–25 Directions

Complete the following sentence by supplying an appropriate word for
each blank.

_____ gave the _____ to the _____ ,
21. subject   22. direct object   23. object of preposition

_____ seemed _____ to receive it.
24. subject   25. predicate adjective

EXERCISE 6 • SINGULARS AND PLURALS

Purpose   To develop mastery of verb conjugation; to recognize singular subjects and plural subjects; to recognize that *s* at the end of a verb form does not denote plural conjugation of the verb.

Reference   "When Words Collide" (8/e), Chapters 4, 5 and 6

1–5 Directions: Choose the correct conjugation of the verb from the answers provided.

_____ 1.   Diabetes _____ wear and tear of several major organs as sufferers of the disease age.
   A. hasten
   B. hastens
   C. hastening

_____ 2.   His new dog Luca and the older puppy Lila _____ fetch together.
   A. plays
   B. play
   C. plays'
   D. playing

_____ 3.   Many experts _____ some of the negative campaigning _____ run its course.
   A. believes, has
   B. believe, have
   C. believes, have
   D. believe, has

_____ 4.   The students in that new course in folklore _____ the teacher is one of the best at the university.
   A. says
   B. say
   C. saying

_____ 5.   Carly's interest in ballet, music and art _____ she is a
           focused child.
           A. proves
           B. prove
           C. proving

6–10 Directions

Complete the following sentences by supplying the proper conjugation
of the infinitive form of the verb provided under each blank space.

6.   Shelby, Spider and Lee _____ several shows a week in the
                            to play (present tense)
     San Francisco area.

7.   Surveys and interviews of the people who went on the cruise more
     than once _____ a preference for lavish meals over expensive
               to reveal (present tense)
     entertainment.

8.   Those two large farms by the foothills of the mountain outside of
     town _____ owned by the same landholder.
        to be (present perfect)

9.   The book, translated into three languages and made into several
     movies, _____ scheduled for a worldwide release after this
            to be (present perfect)
     year's Academy Awards ceremony.

10. A glut of movies using computer animation _____ cooled
                                                to have (present perfect)
     audience interest in the once-novel format.

11–15 Directions

In each of the following sentences there is a verb conjugation error. Circle the incorrect verb form and write the correct one on the line provided underneath the sentence. **Note:** There is only one conjugation error and there are no other errors to find in the sentence.

11. His doors was always open to his students.

_____

_____

12. A pair of the brightest Madras shorts you ever have seen are hanging in my favorite boutique on Fifth Avenue today.

_____

_____

13. Measles are one of the diseases pediatricians warn parents about most.

_____

_____

14. To the annoyance of her friends, she often give away the plot of new movies in her blog posts.

_____

_____

15. His wife often said she could never asks him his advice on domestic doings before he drank his first cup of morning coffee.

_____

_____

EXERCISE 7 • VERB TYPES

Purpose   To correctly identify all verb forms and to show their relationship to other parts of the sentence.

Reference   "When Words Collide" (8/e), Chapter 5

Directions: Underline the verb or verbs in each sentence. It's possible that there will be more than one verb type in the sentence. In the space provided at the left, indicate whether the verb is transitive (T), intransitive (I), or linking (L). If the verb is transitive, circle its direct object. If the verb is linking, circle its predicate nominative or predicate adjective. **Note:** If a numbered item does not contain a verb, mark SF (sentence fragment) in the space.

Example   Snow and high winds <u>closed</u> the Denver airport this morning.
(T—Verb is transitive. It has a direct object, *Denver airport*.)

_____ 1.   Sacramento is the capital of California.

_____ 2.   Thank goodness the rain has stopped!

_____ 3.   The appeals court upheld the lower court decision.

_____ 4.   Driven by violent winds, the storm struck the coast with great fury.

_____ 5.   I constantly dream of great fame and fortune.

_____ 6.   Dreaming of chocolate all day long.

_____ 7.   Tripping over the sleeping dog, he fell down and lost consciousness.

_____ 8. Swimming, running and cycling are parts of a demanding triathlon.

_____ 9. To win this prestigious race, an important goal for him.

_____ 10. Emily Anderson, who won the Des Moines Marathon, will run the Charlotte Marathon on April 29.

_____ 11. You'll never guess whom Tito is dating!

_____ 12. Do you know how to build a den for a platypus?

_____ 13. Please stop!

_____ 14. You are on the grounds of the University of Oregon, heralded as one of the most beautiful campuses in the United States.

_____ 15. She is researching the impact of "blog" journalism.

_____ 16. Wait!

_____ 17. Because of rapidly declining profits, the board decided to fire its chief executive officer.

_____ 18. Icy conditions sent drivers skidding off the highway.

_____ 19. Jericho seems quite friendly, don't you think?

_____ 20. The newly appointed commissioner appears concerned about her new role.

21–25 Directions

Provide the appropriate verb type and tense as indicated in the
parentheses.

21. The city's budget _____ doomed, according to press
                              (linking verb, present tense)
    reports.

22. A new vote on the budget _____ soon, the councilors
                              (intransitive verb, future tense)
    hope.

23. Her agent _____ the station's offer of contract renewal.
                  (transitive verb, past tense)

24. _____!
    (intransive verb, present tense)

25. Voters _____ the parking resolution but
                  (transitive verb, present tense)

    _____ the public safety budget.
    (transitive verb, present tense)

EXERCISE 8 • PROPER USE OF VOICE

Purpose   To identify active and passive voice; to identify the
                   constructions that are better suited to passive voice;
                   to learn to write more forcefully and crisply by using
                   active voice constructions.

Reference   "When Words Collide" (8/e), Chapters 4 and 5

1–5 Directions

Select the correct answer from the options provided, or fill in the
answer as directed.

_____ 1.   Which of the following choices places this sentence in
              active voice?
              The sugar water _____ the hummingbirds.
              A. was relished by
              B. satiated

_____ 2.   Which of the following choices places this sentence in
              passive voice?
              The student body _____ the trees would be cut down.
              A. was not informed
              B. protested that

_____ 3.   Which sentence construction do you think is the best
              choice, given the information?
              A. This weekend, as expected, the decrease in student
                  studying was due to the warm, unseasonable weather.
              B. The decrease in student studying this weekend,
                  because of the warm, unseasonable weather, was to be
                  expected.
              C. Professors at the school said they had expected that
                  students would study less during the unseasonably
                  warm weekend weather.
              D. The warm, unseasonable weather, which was expected,
                  caused students to study less.

4. What voice does the sentence use that you chose in question 3?

_____

_____

5. Why did you choose the sentence you did in question 3?

_____

_____

6–18 Directions:

Active voice makes the subject of the sentence perform. In most
writing, the subject acts rather than is acted upon. In the following
passive voice sentences, underline the agent who (or that) performs the
action. Then, unless passive voice is more effective, rewrite the sentence
in the active voice. If you make no change to a sentence, explain your
decision. If necessary, "tighten" any wordy constructions.

Example   In the final seconds of the game, there was an
                         astonishing dunk shot made by Christy
                         Newland.

Rewrite   Christy Newland made an astonishing dunk
                         shot in the final seconds of the game.

(The actor or agent *[Christy Newland]* now is more prominent in the
sentence, and the action is more direct.)

6. The mayor could not be persuaded by any council member to
    change her vote on the zoning change.

_____

_____

7. The Hastings Museum treasure, the so-called Magic Chalice, was stolen from the museum twenty years ago.

_____

_____

8. At dawn, the pitiful moaning of a wildebeest, which was wounded, was heard.

_____

_____

9. The meeting was gaveled to order by Jennifer Miles, who was serving as interim council president.

_____

_____

10. Tons of deadly plutonium particles were carried over the city by brisk winds.

_____

_____

11. Former Providence mayor Robert "Big Bob" Harrison was arrested last night for drunken driving.

_____

_____

12. A defense appropriation measure to guarantee the funding of "drone" spy planes will be considered tomorrow by the House Armed Services Committee.

_____

_____

13. The negative effect on your class performance because of text-messaging every class period has been noticed by your professors.

_____

_____

14. The elderly man was robbed by a mob of knife-wielding teenagers.

_____

_____

15. The 200-pound marlin was wrestled to the deck by four burly fishermen.

_____

_____

16. The Thompson murder trial got underway today, and it is being presided over by Judge Alicia Evans.

_____

_____

17. The football was rifled 70 yards from the quarterback, John Warner, to the wide receiver, Billy Bob Jackson.

_____

_____

18. The largest tobacco settlement in the history of the United States was won today by a 54-year-old Lawrence man, who says he was a heavy smoker for more than 30 years.

_____

_____

19. Read the following passage. Rewrite the ideas in active voice,
    eliminating wordiness and awkward constructions if necessary.

    The new federal nutrition regulations for schools were designed to
    help end the obesity epidemic in America, but just because school
    districts have to create regulations on the availability of junk food
    does not mean children will not have access to it.

    _____

    _____

    _____

20. Rewrite the following sentence to be more direct and less wordy.

    At the community meeting with the legislator, there was a heated
    argument between two of the community members attending that
    legislators should enforce stricter dangerous dog codes, such as
    breed-specific bans or a zero tolerance bite policy, to reduce the
    amount of preventable dog attacks.

    _____

    _____

    _____

    Based on your rewrite, your readings, and any class discussion on
    defensible uses of passive voice, explain your decision to use either
    active or passive voice. Why is the one you chose better than the
    other?

    _____

    _____

    _____

EXERCISE 9 • GIVING POWER AND FOCUS TO VERBS

Purpose   To improve verbs that are weak and imprecise; to
                    choose the correct verb to match intended meaning;
                    to improve sentence clarity and conciseness.

Reference   "When Words Collide" (8/e), Chapter 5

1–10 Directions

Rewrite each of the following short (but weak) sentences with one
strong, precise, and more meaningful verb. Be careful in your rewrite
not to change the meaning conveyed in the original sentence.

Examples

Original Sentence: She imitated the actions of her brother.

Rewrite: She mimicked her brother.

Original Sentence: He shut off debate after 10 minutes.

Rewrite: He silenced debate after 10 minutes.

1.   She was possessed of the courage to win.

_____

2.   He read lightly the notes for the test.

_____

3.   They complained constantly about the noise.

_____

4. The potter hit hard and repeatedly the new clay.

_____

5. She stared at him angrily.

_____

6. He quietly but firmly expressed his anger.

_____

7. The doctor lessened the effect of the procedure by numbing the muscle.

_____

8. The council put a check on discussion for the new park.

_____

9. The employee made a point in support of more vacation days.

_____

10. He worked to get around driving through the new subdivision.

_____

11–20 Directions

These sentences suffer from the same malady: underpowered verbs. However, they are now surrounded by wordy constructions. Strengthen (and shorten) them by making the verb more straight forward and truly descriptive.

Example   The mayor treated her suggestion with disrespect.

The verb *treated* is weak because it is too general; we can do much better, especially because we know the mayor had a disrespectful tone.

The mayor *scoffed* at her suggestion.

11. The loud rock music from the apartment next door really affected his nerves; it made him very nervous.

_____

_____

12. I approached you after class with a notification of my basketball competition dates.

_____

_____

13. He ate the spinach salad quite quickly, almost in a single devouring gulp.

_____

_____

14. The Smiths were very sorry about the destruction of their neighbor's lawnmower.

_____

_____

15. The sailor walked drunkenly down the alley, hitting one wall after the other.

_____

_____

16. These junk bonds have really caused damage to the company's pension fund in a devastating way.

_____

_____

17. The floodwaters ran over the banks in a violent surge.

_____

_____

18. The university president spoke in an extremely loud voice as he
     yelled, with an angry tone, at students who were protesting outside
     his office.

_____

_____

19. Bill's sports car slid over the icy road in a dangerous skid.

_____

_____

20. Sarah held back her thoughts about the staff reorganization, even
     though she was bursting to express her anger.

_____

_____

EXERCISE 10 • IT WAS A _____ BOX: LEARNING
TO LOVE ADJECTIVES

Purpose   To explore the descriptive and limiting talents of
                     adjectives.

Reference   "When Words Collide" (8/e), Chapter 6

1–5 Directions

Underline all of the adjectives in these sentences. Below your
underlinings, indicate whether the adjectives are descriptive (D) or
limiting (L). If the adjective describes a subject noun connected to a
linking verb, list it as a predicate adjective (pred. adj.).

Example The <u>weary</u> rescuers hiked <u>eight</u> miles to reach the <u>lost</u> hunter.
                     D   L   D

1. This meeting is quickly turning into a depressing spectacle.

2. Erin became upset when the new coach told her to sit out the game
    for 10 minutes.

3. His speech was met with almost universal condemnation, but that
    criticism hardly fazed him.

4.   The mayor, barely containing her temper, said the city was "perilously close" to bankruptcy.

5.   Depressed at the painful prospect of another surgery, Richard sought advice from a surgeon in New York.

6–10 Directions

In the space provided below each sentence, list all adjectives and indicate which words they modify. Also indicate the part of speech of each word that is modified.

Example   You are fabulous; you are going to be a great success!

> *Fabulous,* a predicate adjective, modifies the pronoun *you.*
> *Great,* a descriptive adjective, modifies the noun *success.*

6.   Anderson, who seemed rather shy at first, is the most talkative dentist I ever met.

7.   This is not the wisest decision you have made this year!

8.   Five miles of strenuous hiking into that remote wilderness is no problem for me!

9.   Twenty is my lucky number; which one is yours?

10. I like a crisper crust, so it would be great if you could make it more crisp.

11–20 Directions

Supply an adjective appropriate to the function indicated for each blank in these sentences.

Example   _____ meeting won't result in a _____outcome.
              (limiting)   (descriptive)

        This meeting won't result in a positive outcome.
        (limiting)   (descriptive)

11. A _____ truck hit a _____ barrier and rolled over.
      (limiting)   (descriptive)

12. Trust me: _____ option is not _____.
              (limiting)   (pred. adj.)

13. This has to be the _____ idea I've encountered in a
                       (descriptive superlative)

    _____ time.
    (descriptive)

14. Harriet finally won the lottery on her _____attempt.
                                            (limiting)

15. Your _____ criteria for judging the contest are strangely _____.
         (limiting)   (pred. adj.)

16. _____ until the _____ crowd settled down, she
    (descriptive, as part   (descriptive)
    of a participial phrase)

    began to speak.

17. _____ time she tried to speak, the crowd hurled
    (limiting)

    _____ insults.
    (descriptive)

18. The _____, _____ vampire vanished quickly
        (descriptive)   (descriptive)

    into the _____ night.
            (descriptive)

19. Please give our _____ report to _____ board member.
                    (descriptive)   (limiting)

20. The rescue team was _____ , _____, and _____
                        (pred. adj.)   (pred. adj.)   (pred. adj.)

    after its _____ hours in the _____ wilderness.
            (limiting)   (descriptive)

EXERCISE 11   PARTS OF SPEECH: THOSE VERY
INTERESTING ADVERBS

Purpose   To build recognition and use of adverbs.

Reference   "When Words Collide" (8/e), Chapter 6

1–15 Directions

Identify the part of speech of the underlined word in each of the
following sentences. Write the letter that corresponds to the correct
answer in the space at the left of each sentence.

_____   1.   Coyote and Friends' new CD is <u>amazing</u>, don't you think?
                 A. noun   B. adjective   C. adverb

_____   2.   The robber ran out of the bank and <u>down</u> the street.
                 A. adjective   B. adverb   C. preposition

_____   3.   Baseball is fun, but basketball is <u>physically</u> challenging.
                 A. noun   B. adverb   C. conjunction

_____   4.   The lieutenant ordered Gustavo and me to peel <u>5,000</u> potatoes.
                 A. adverb   B. pronoun   C. adjective

_____   5.   The bobcat ran <u>wildly</u> around its cage.
                 A. adverb   B. adjective   C. interjection

_____   6.   <u>This</u> option works for me.
                 A. adjective   B. pronoun   C. adverb

_____   7.   I <u>absolutely</u> will never be late for class again.
                 A. adverb   B. adjective   C. conjunction

_____ 8. I hope I never see <u>another</u> zucchini!
   A. adverb   B. noun   C. pronoun

_____ 9. <u>Our</u> women's soccer team is magnificent.
   A. adjective   B. adverb   C. noun

_____ 10. <u>Please</u> seat Tina Turner next to me.
   A. preposition   B. adverb   C. conjunction

_____ 11. <u>Prancing</u> merrily down the lane, she encountered the evil troll.
   A. adverb   B. adjective   C. noun

_____ 12. <u>Now</u> it can be told!
   A. adverb   B. preposition   C. adjective

_____ 13. Do you believe you are <u>well</u>-educated?
   A. adjective   B. preposition   C. adverb

_____ 14. I am not convinced that Sara is smarter <u>than</u> he.
   A. conjunction   B. adverb   C. preposition

_____ 15. Negotiations have broken down <u>between</u> labor and
   management.
   A. adverb   B. preposition   C. conjunction

16–25 Directions

The following questions ask you to identify adverbs correctly and to know how to use them properly in sentences. Select the correct answer from the choices provided.

_____ 16. What is the adverb in the following sentence?
   Building the high-rise waterfront condominiums was more demanding than Werner had remembered from past projects.
   A. high-rise
   B. more
   C. remembered
   D. past

_____ 17. Which of the following choices is true about adverbs?
A. They always appear before the word they modify.
B. They always end in –ly.
C. They never modify the subject of a sentence.
D. They always indicate direction or place.

_____ 18. Which of the following underlined items is *not* an adverb?
A. <u>definitively,</u> the smartest student
B. a <u>really</u> bright student
C. the <u>tallest</u> building on the block
D. a <u>truly</u> principled decision

_____ 19. Which is the correct punctuation from the choices provided?
Heavy rains are delaying what is left of the grape harvest _____ clear weather is forecast for next week.
A. , however,
B. ; however,

_____ 20. What is the adverb in the following sentence?
The store manager made an announcement over the loudspeaker that he planned to close the store earlier the day after Thanksgiving.
A. made
B. over
C. earlier
D. after

_____ 21. In which sentence is the adverb used incorrectly?
A. Sara hurriedly changed her plans before her boss changed his mind.
B. She quit her job at the nursing home immediately after she won the high jump event.
C. He thought eating 17 hot dogs in five minutes was a real good plan for earning $50.
D. You know very well that I must have a late afternoon nap if I don't get my coffee early enough.

_____ 22.   In which sentence is the adverb *good* used correctly?
   A.   The bread smells good.
   B.   He whittled good.
   C.   He felt good after two hours of yoga.
   D.   After seven communications workshops, the council still doesn't run good.

_____ 23.   Adverbs generally answer all but the following.
   A.   who
   B.   when
   C.   why
   D.   how

_____ 24.   Which of the following uses correctly the superlative form of the adverb *cohesively*?
   A.   Of all the proposals they considered, the first worked more cohesively.
   B.   Of all the proposals they considered, the first worked most cohesively.
   C.   Of all the proposals they considered, the first worked cohesivlier.
   D.   Of all the proposals they considered, the first worked cohesivliest.

_____ 25.   Which of the following may an adverb *not* modify?
   A.   a verb
   B.   an adverb
   C.   an adjective
   D.   a noun

EXERCISE 12 • VERBALS: THEY'RE NOT IN THE DRIVER'S SEAT!

Purpose   To correctly identify all verbal types and to distinguish them from verbs.

Reference   "When Words Collide" (8/e), Chapter 5

1–5 Directions

Choose the correct response from the choices offered.

_____ 1.   Which one of the following parts of speech cannot be a verbal?
  A. noun
  B. adverb
  C. adjective
  D. preposition

_____ 2.   Which one of the following verbals cannot be the subject of a sentence?
  A. gerund
  B. participle
  C. infinitive
  D. A verbal cannot act as the subject of a sentence.

_____ 3.   Which verbal is always a noun?
  A. participle
  B. gerund
  C. infinitive

_____ 4.   Which of the following three sentences does not contain a verbal?
  A. Working on the project all night took its toll.
  B. The company is dedicating all of its resources to this new project.
  C. I really enjoy solving difficult crossword puzzles.

_____ 5.   What is the only verb in the following sentence?
           A severe rainstorm lashed the South Carolina coast last
           night, followed today by the heaviest snowfall to hit that
           state in the last 30 years.
           A. lashed
           B. followed
           C. heaviest
           D. hit

Bonus Question

How many verbals are in sentence 5? What are they?

6–15 Directions

Each of the following 10 sentences contains one verbal phrase. Indicate
the correct verbal using this code:

   G   Gerund phrase

   P   Participial phrase

   I   Infinitive phrase

_____ 6.   He finished his class project in three days, barely pausing
           to eat or sleep.

_____ 7.   The former CEO volunteered to work with Habitat for
           Humanity.

_____ 8.   Is it really that difficult to identify a verbal?

_____ 9.   Well, recognizing verbals can be a real challenge.

_____ 10. Crushed by the realization that her collegiate career was over, Samantha nevertheless focused intensely on her final academic term.

_____ 11. Buffeted by gale-force winds, he barely managed to cross the street.

_____ 12. Isn't it about time to question his authority?

_____ 13. I hope you now appreciate your focusing on the most recent notes for the midterm exam.

_____ 14. You are on the grounds of the University of Oregon, long heralded as one of the most beautiful campuses in the United States.

_____ 15. He refuses to release the documents on moral grounds.

Bonus Question

Write one sentence that contains all three verbal forms. Just one sentence—you can do this!

_____

_____

_____

16–20 Directions

This final section deals with subject–verb agreement and proper use of modifiers involving verbals. Choose the correct answer from the choices offered.

Example   Restoring old houses (A. is B. are) both her hobby and her business.

Answer: A. is. The subject of this sentence is the gerund *Restoring.* Gerunds always take a singular verb. The gerund's object, *houses,* does not control the number of the verb.

_____ 16. What is the participial phrase in the following sentence?
Returning from a six-week trip, Paul now promises never
to embark on such an incredibly tiring marathon again.
A. now promises
B. incredibly tiring
C. never to embark
D. Returning from a six-week trip

_____ 17. And what does that participial phrase modify in sentence 16?
A. trip
B. Paul
C. marathon
D. promises

_____ 18. Running three marathons in two weeks (A. has   B. have)
taken a heavy toll on Richard's knees.

_____ 19. What does the participial phrase in the following sentence
modify?
Working around the clock, his project was finished three
hours before the deadline.
A. hours
B. deadline
C. clock
D. project
E. Actually, the phrase "dangles." It doesn't logically
connect with any word in the sentence.

_____ 20. Sending complaints to several executives (A. was   B. were)
part of her long-term strategy.

EXERCISE 13 • A GERUND IS NOT A PARTICIPLE (AND VICE VERSA)!

Purpose   To correctly identify *–ed* and *–ing* words according to their part of speech in increasingly complicated sentences; to distinguish gerunds from participles.

Reference   "When Words Collide" (8/e), Chapters 5 and 6

1–6 Directions

Choose the correct response from the choices offered. When asked to rewrite sentences, use the space provided to do so.

_____ 1.   In this sentence, what kind of verbal is contained in the underlined phrase?
Melissa was arrested while <u>protesting with her friends</u>.
A. infinitive
B. gerund
C. participle
D. adverbial

_____ 2.   What part of speech is the verbal in the sentence above?
A. noun
B. pronoun
C. adverb
D. adjective

_____ 3.   Why is the underlined word in the following sentence *not* a participle?
Tom was <u>hoisted</u> onto the platform by two burly volunteers.
A. It is part of an infinitive phrase.
B. It is a predicate nominative.
C. It is part of the transitive verb.
D. It is part of the intransitive verb.

_____ 4.   What is the role of the underlined word in this sentence? Runners <u>jogging</u> down the wooded path did not see the lion waiting in the grass.
     A.   With *did not see*, it is the second action word, or verb, of the sentence.
     B.   It is an adjective that provides a description of the runners.
     C.   It is the noun subject of the clause that begins *jogging down the wooded path.*
     D.   It is the beginning of a participial phrase.
     E.   It is both B and D.

_____ 5.   What's the error in this sentence? After throwing a 96-mph curve ball, the batter was struck out by the pitcher.
     A.   dangling modifier
     B.   word usage
     C.   passive voice
     D.   both A and C

6.   In the space provided, rewrite the sentence in item 5 to correct the error(s).

_____

_____

7–10 Directions

Each of these sentences has three *–ing* words. In the space provided, write the part of speech of the word and its function in the sentence.

Example   After traveling to a remote corner of the Oregon desert, the hiking team attached a huge tarp to the rocks, creating a large enclosure that protected them from the elements.

     traveling: noun; object of the prepositional phrase beginning with *after hiking:* adjective; a modifier of the noun *team*

creating: adjective; begins the participial phrase that ends with *enclosure*

7. Jeff was kicking himself for persuading his mother to convert her savings into gold futures.

    kicking: _____

    persuading: _____

    savings: _____

8. As a way of hiding her disdain for compromise, Yuki often goes searching for blame in others, effectively alienating them.

    hiding: _____

    searching: _____

    alienating: _____

9. Avoiding her friends who lived by the marina was Jessica's way of dealing with her trepidations about deep-sea diving.

    avoiding: _____

    dealing: _____

    diving: _____

10. Shuji decided that avoiding sick people and taking his vitamins were two strategies this season for preventing too many colds.

    avoiding: _____

    taking: _____

    preventing: _____

11–13 Directions

In each of the following sentences, there are three –ed words. In the space provided, write the part of speech of the word and, briefly, the purpose of the word as a function of its part of speech.

11. The manager's convoluted instructions frustrated his employees, creating palpable tensions in the meetings between him and already overworked workers.

    convoluted: _____

    frustrated: _____

    overworked: _____

12. He decided to leave the movie because the theater was too crowded and the heat system continuously blasted hot air into the room.

    decided: _____

    crowded: _____

    blasted: _____

13. Don't accept that widely circulated and expanded story about the embezzlement unless you have adequately researched it.

    circulated: _____

    expanded: _____

    researched: _____

14–15 Directions

Choose the correct response from the choices offered.

_____ 14. Which of the following sentences contains a dangling modifier?
   A. She's a great athlete, rarely tiring during an event.
   B. Discovering a zero balance in my bank account, a credit card was needed to complete the transaction.
   C. Although he studied for more than a week and literally copied parts of two texts.
   D. Remember everything the professor demanded.

_____ 15. What is the proper term for the underlined section in the sentence that follows?
   Jill enjoys <u>collecting rare stamps</u> from the early 20th century.
   A. gerund phrase
   B. participial phrase
   C. direct object
   D. A and C
   E. None of the above is correct.

EXERCISE 14 • CHECKUP: VERBS, VERBALS, MODIFIERS

Purpose   To strengthen your understanding and use of verbs, verbals and modifiers in effective writing.

Reference   "When Words Collide" (8/e), Chapters 5 and 6

1–5 Directions

Select the correct response from the choices offered.

_____ 1.   Identify the verb or verbs in the following sentence.
            Practicing his downhill ski routine every day gave Lindsay
            the confidence to join the ski team and to eventually win
            an Olympic medal.
            A. practicing, gave
            B. gave, win
            C. win
            D. gave

_____ 2.   What kind of verb or verbs is (are) in sentence 1?
            A. transitive
            B. intransitive
            C. linking

_____ 3.   What kind of verbals are there in sentence 1?
            A. participle and gerund
            B. gerund and infinitives
            C. infinitives and participle
            D. There are no verbals in sentence #1.

_____ 4. What kind of verb is in the following sentence?
Stop!
A. transitive
B. intransitive
C. linking
D. It's not a sentence.

_____ 5. A linking verb can never have a _____ .
A. pronoun as a predicate nominative
B. a past tense
C. direct object
D. predicate adjective

6–10 Directions

In the spaces provided, supply appropriate modifiers as identified below the line.

6. Jerry said he is "_____ excited" about his new job and that he
(adverb)
is _____ looking forward to some new challenges.
(adverb)

7. _____ company has grown _____ in the last _____ years.
(possessive pronoun)   (adverb)   (limiting adjective)

8. Her reputation as a _____ columnist is _____
(descriptive adjective)   (compound modifier—
adverb and adjective)

9. _____, she was struck by a speeding motorcycle.
(participial phrase as an adjective)

10. After a _____ summer in Arizona, he moved to more
(descriptive adjective)
_____ Oregon.
(descriptive adjective)

11–15 Directions

Replace the following underlined phrases with one strong, descriptive verb.

Example instead of: <u>stare at angrily</u> **glare**

11. instead of: <u>look at sullenly</u>   _____

12. instead of: <u>walk heavily and laboriously</u>   _____

13. instead of: <u>enthusiastically give praise to</u>   _____

14. instead of: <u>constantly complain</u>   _____

15. instead of: <u>weep intensely and loudly</u>   _____

16–18 Directions

The following sentences contain two clauses. Use the information in one of the clauses to create a verbal, so that the resulting sentence is more concise—as a simple sentence with only one clause. Underline your verbal and identify its type.

Example   Tom was running to class; however, he tripped and fell.

Revised   <u>Running to class</u>, Tom tripped and fell.
                     participial phrase

16. Tom builds model planes from balsa wood, and this is his favorite hobby.

_____

17. One of the pledges that she gave her constituents is that she will decrease the sales tax very soon.

_____

18. The defendant said he will go to jail, but that he will constantly maintain his innocence while there.

_____

EXERCISE 15 • PREPOSITIONS: THE PARTS OF SPEECH
WITH A PREFERENCE FOR PHRASES

Purpose   To correctly identify prepositions, especially as parts
                   of phrases; to understand the effect prepositional
                   phrases have on meaning.

Reference   "When Words Collide" (8/e), Chapter 6

1–13 Directions

Choose the correct response from the choices offered.

_____ 1.   What is the prepositional phrase in the following sentence?
             The court reporter decided to file a records request for
             information to sue the new district attorney.
             A. to file a records request
             B. for information
             C. to sue the new district attorney

_____ 2.   What is the first of three prepositional phrases in the
             following sentence?
             The old stable, which had been built in the late 1800s over an
             inactive volcano, was burning quickly, to Salvatore's dismay.
             A. in the late 1800s
             B. was burning quickly
             C. to Salvotore's dismay

_____ 3.   Which of the following three sentences does *not* contain a
             preposition?
             A. A precipitous drop in temperature discouraged the
                 hikers from continuing their journey to the summit.
             B. Business leaders say the U.S. economy, which last
                 month had struggled mightily, could be recovering.
             C. Braving a snowstorm in boots and a tank top ranks as
                 one of the top worst ideas, according to Stuart's mom.

_____ 4.   How many prepositions are in this sentence?
Rachel poured water on her sister Sara's head after she
found Sara had stuffed melted marshmallows into her new
superhero pillowcase.
A. none   B. one   C. two
D. three   E. four

5.   In question 4, what are the prepositional phrases? Write them here.
Separate each one with a period.

_____

_____

_____ 6.   How many prepositions are in this sentence?
Denzel disappeared from the campground without a trace,
prompting the police to conduct a four-month
investigation of his family and friends.
A. none   B. one   C. two
D. three   E. four

7.   In question 6, what are the prepositional phrases? Write them here.
Separate each with a period.

_____

_____

_____ 8.   How many prepositions are in this sentence?
One of the ecology students wondered aloud in class
whether there was any effect of biodegradable tableware on
the environment.
A. none   B. one   C. two
D. three   E. four

9.   In question 8, what are the prepositional phrases? Write them here.
Separate each with a period.

_____

_____

_____ 10. How many prepositions are in this sentence?
The withdrawal of troops from the mountain area was the first
maneuver the new general promised his allies to the north.
A. none   B. one   C. two
D. three   E. four

11. In question 10, what are the prepositional phrases? Write them
here. Separate each with a period.

_____

_____

_____ 12. How many prepositions are in this sentence?
My brother asked to leave the dinner table to visit his
friend who was traveling to Thailand next week for a year.
A. none   B. one   C. two
D. three   E. four

13. In question 12, what are the prepositional phrases? Write them
here. Separate each one a period.

_____

_____

14–18 Directions

This section deals with proper placement of prepositional phrases. In
the following sentences, confusions in meaning are caused by
misplaced prepositional phrases. Rewrite the sentences with the
prepositional phrases properly placed.

14. Finneman recently moved to San Francisco from Seattle, where he
owned a magazine that focused on miniature golf competitions for
11 years.

_____

_____

15. The officer spotted the fleeing burglar hiding in the rose bush with his infrared goggles.

_____

_____

16. Alice entertained us with stories about a recent trip to Mexico in her hot tub.

_____

_____

17. Krissy made some pasta for her niece with parmesan cheese.

_____

_____

18. He solved, in just 22 minutes, the crossword puzzled published on Sunday.
(**Note:** Try to make this sentence more concise as you work on the alignment of these phrases.)

_____

_____

Bonus Question

Explain the difference between a prepositional phrase and a participial phrase. Then write a sentence containing an example of each. Circle and identify each of the phrase types.

_____

_____

_____

_____

_____

EXERCISE 16 • VERBALS AS PHRASES
(AND SENTENCE ELEMENTS)

Purpose   To correctly identify verbal phrases and to understand the role of a phrase as a part of speech and, at times, a sentence element.

Reference   "When Words Collide" (8/e), Chapters 4, 5 and 6

1–10 Directions

In the spaces provided under each sentence, write the type of verbal phrase, the complete verbal phrase, its part of speech and its use in the sentence as a sentence element, if appropriate.

Example   She decided never to follow the crowd.

Infinitive; *to follow the crowd;* noun; operating as the direct object of the verb *decided*

1.   Pressing forward despite the gale-force winds, he finally reached his car.

   _____

   _____

2.   Swimming in the ocean today reminded Sara of her trip to the Oregon Coast.

   _____

   _____

3.   The gold miner, frustrated by the lack of gold, quit his search shortly after noon.

   _____

   _____

4. International databases foiled the tax evader's attempt to hide in another country.

_____

_____

5. Mark decided attending graduate school was his best shot at a new career.

_____

_____

6. Working in radio at first was pursued as a whim, but Liz's admiration is now total.

_____

_____

7. Sam supports the initiative to ban smoking in all enclosed public places.

_____

_____

8. For many professional athletes, training every day is necessary for success.

_____

_____

9. I saw the Roller Derby girl hurtling toward me, but I couldn't stop her.

_____

_____

10. Writing for three straight days, the journalist created a vibrant magazine story with historical narratives, first-hand experiences and background research.

_____

_____

EXERCISE 17 • PREPOSITIONS VS. CONJUNCTIONS

Purpose   To continue to build awareness of the specific role
                     prepositions play in introducing phrases, compared
                     with the role of conjunctions, which link words in
                     phrases and clauses.

Reference   "When Words Collide" (8/e), Chapter 6

1–10 Directions

Circle the answer that correctly identifies the underlined portion, and
then in the space provided, briefly explain how the part of speech
functions in the sentence.

Example   The council approved the new ordinance, <u>but</u>
                     councilors could not agree on its effective date.

Answer   *But* is a coordinating conjunction. It joins the two
                     independent clauses.

1. <u>Before</u> the guerillas surrendered to the army, they took a vote.
    A. preposition   B. coordinating conjunction
    C. subordinating conjunction

    _____

    _____

2. The workers will strike <u>unless</u> you meet their demands.
    A. preposition   B. coordinating conjunction
    C. subordinating conjunction

    _____

    _____

3. The community is grateful <u>that</u> her generosity knows no bounds.
    A. preposition   B. coordinating conjunction
    C. subordinating conjunction

_____

_____

4. <u>As</u> he took the fresh sushi in his chopsticks, he imagined the eel
    he'd seen in an exhibit at the aquarium and decided to have a
    California roll instead.
    A. preposition   B. coordinating conjunction
    C. subordinating conjunction

_____

_____

5. The horse came <u>into</u> view on the last lap of the race.
    A. preposition   B. coordinating conjunction
    C. subordinating conjunction

_____

_____

6. Maybe he should put on his coat <u>before he gets wet</u>.
    A. prepositional phrase   B. dependent clause
    C. independent clause

_____

_____

7. <u>Against my better judgment</u>, I was persuaded to join the
    investment club.
    A. prepositional phrase   B. dependent clause
    C. independent clause

_____

_____

8. The soccer team had an amazing win <u>within the last two exciting but bone-chiling minutes</u> of play.
    A. prepositional phrase   B. dependent clause
    C. independent clause

    _____

    _____

9. The new butterscotch-flavored soda bombed on its debut, <u>although it had been thoroughly tested in focus groups</u>.
    A. prepositional phrase   B. dependent clause
    C. independent clause

    _____

    _____

10. When he handed in his homework, <u>he forgot to give the teacher the last page</u>.
    A. prepositional phrase   B. dependent clause
    C. independent clause

    _____

    _____

11–15 Directions

Choose the answer that correctly identifies the number of prepositions or clauses in the sentences that follow.

_____ 11. How many prepositions are in the following sentence? Policies that would direct federal money to Gore's investments in green technology have drawn accusations of profiteering.
            A. none
            B. one
            C. two
            D. three
            E. four

_____ 12.   How many prepositions are in the following sentence?
The teacher and her guest speaker walked into the
classroom, greeted the students, and handed out pamphlets
on the study abroad program.
    A. none
    B. one
    C. two
    D. three
    E. four

_____ 13.   How many clauses are in the following sentence?
Not taking the medicine as prescribed could allow the
infection to re-establish itself in your body and become
more resistant to the drugs later.
    A. one
    B. two
    C. three
    D. four
    E. five

_____ 14.   How many clauses are in the following sentence?
Armed with the best research she could gather, Helen walked
into the meeting room and gave a dazzling presentation.
    A. one
    B. two
    C. three
    D. four
    E. five

_____ 15.   How many prepositions and clauses are in the following
sentence?
The legislation you are proposing for the new budget is
worthwhile and needed, but I'm afraid we won't have the
votes to pass it in the remaining weeks of the current
legislative session.
    A. one preposition, one clause
    B. two prepositions, two clauses
    C. three prepositions, two clauses
    D. two prepositions, three clauses
    E. three prepositions, three clauses

Bonus Question 1

Rewrite the sentence so that a preposition is used to create a more streamlined sentence with a clearer meaning.

His expertise will help shed light on the issues debated by the city government surrounding the use of Tasers.

_____

_____

_____

Bonus Question 2

Rewrite the sentence so that a preposition is used to create a more streamlined sentence with a clearer meaning.

I am writing an article pertaining to a public policy proposal on child health care, and I was wondering whether you would be available for an interview.

_____

_____

_____

EXERCISE 18 • COMPARATIVES AND SUPERLATIVES

Purpose   To continue to build understanding of parts of speech, pronoun use, and the specific role the preposition *than* plays in defining sentences of comparisons (objective pronouns), while the conjunction *than* is linked to subjective pronouns; to correctly identify the proper part of speech for expressing the degree of a superlative; to distinguish between the use of *then* as an adverb and *than*.

Reference   "When Words Collide" (8/e), Chapters 6 and 7

Directions: Circle the correct choice in each of the following sentences. On the line underneath, write the part of speech of the circled word, or if a question is asked, provide an answer.

1. Do you think she is a better golfer than (A. I B. me)?

   _____

2. Are you sure that Tom is a better writer than (A. her B. she)?

   _____

3. No one is more accomplished than (A. her B. she), the hiring committee said.

   _____

4. I'd rather eat a doughnut covered in ants (A. than B. then) submit to your criticism about my fashion sense.

   _____

5.   Oscar thinks you are less qualified to write the story than
     (A. he   B. him).

     _____

6.   No one is funnier than (A. she   B. her), my mother used to say.

     _____

7.   My roommates say that I'm much neater than (A. they   B. them).

     _____

8.   Tami hung up the phone, and (A. than   B. then), only one hour
     later, the package was in her mailbox!

     _____

9.   The crowd could barely contain its surprise because, without a
     doubt, Jake and his partner were much better dancers than
     (A. they   B. them).

     _____

10. His condition was (A. much worser   B. much worse) than doctors
     had expected.

     _____

     What part of speech is *much* in the above sentence?

     _____

11. Your chocolate muffins taste better (A. than any   B. than any
     others) I've eaten.

     _____

12. Give a reason for your answer in question 11. Why is your choice
    correct and the other answer incorrect? What is the difference in
    meaning?

    _____

    _____

    _____

    _____

    _____

13. (A. More often   B. More oftener) than not, we find online
    introductions can create misunderstandings and be awkward.

    _____

14. She complained that her salary and benefits were lower than
    (A. her assistant B. her assistant's).

    _____

15. Give a reason for your answer in item 14. Why is your choice
    correct and the other answer incorrect? What is the difference in
    meaning?

    _____

    _____

    _____

    _____

EXERCISE 19 • INDEPENDENT AND DEPENDENT CLAUSES

Purpose   To learn how to identify and construct effective
clauses by recognizing the differences between
phrases and clauses.

Reference   "When Words Collide" (8/e), Chapter 4

1–5 Directions

Examine each sentence and respond to each question below by
selecting the correct option.

_____ 1.   What kind of clause is *that struck the low-lying islands* in
this sentence?
The cyclone that struck the low-lying islands was
responsible for more than 1,000 deaths.
A. independent
B. dependent
C. insubordinate
D. It's not a clause; it's a participial phrase.

_____ 2.   How many clauses and how many phrases are in sentence 1?
A. one and none
B. one and one
C. two and none
D. two and one

_____ 3.   Fill in the blanks.
An independent clause must have a _____ and must
contain a _____.
A. modifier…subordinate meaning
B. verb…predicate nominative
C. subject…direct object
D. verb…complete thought

_____ 4.   How many prepositional phrases are in the following
            sentence?
            For more years than I can recall, Vanessa has been the best
            speller in our class.
            A. none
            B. one
            C. two
            D. three

_____ 5.   What is the subject of the independent clause in sentence 4?
            A. years
            B. I
            C. Vanessa
            D. speller

6–10 Directions

Underline the complete independent clause(s) in each sentence.

Example   The fire that destroyed the Sherwood Apartments has
                       been confirmed as arson.

(In this example, note that a dependent clause separates the subject of
the main [independent] clause from its verb and following phrase.)

6.   After the storm subsided, we all went for a walk on the beach.

7.   I ran the marathon in less than four hours, but I paid the price
     when my right knee finally gave out.

8.   Hillary wants to run the marathon in less than three hours!

9.   He waited for what seemed like an eternity for that train, which
     arrived only an hour late.

10. Do you understand that grammar can be fun?

11–15 Directions

Combine each pair of sentences into one, creating a sentence that contains a main (independent) and a subordinate (dependent) clause. Such a combination shows that the independent clause you choose will be the main part of the sentence, and the dependent clause will be secondary.

After you write the sentence, underline the dependent clause. In some cases, you may want to incorporate a phrase into the sentence, depending on the amount of information included. This is an opportunity to create more concise sentences.

Example   Dan lost the TweetMeHoney account. It was because the agency didn't provide adequate research support.

Rewrite   Dan lost the TweetMeHoney account <u>because the agency didn't provide proper research support.</u>

11. An airline passenger went through a secured door at JFK airport Tuesday morning, and this caused the Transportation Security Agency to shut down the terminal. This delayed flights for more than five hours.

_____

_____

_____

12. Rescue workers removed 10 tons of rock from the shaft. Then they drilled a secondary tunnel through five feet of rock, and then they found the trapped miners.

_____

_____

_____

13. The district attorney gave his summation to the jury this morning, but he appeared agitated and also confused while doing so. His name is Frank Anderson.

_____

_____

_____

14. The analysts' conclusions were original and thought-provoking. However, none of the board members agreed with them.

_____

_____

_____

15. The books are lying on the table. They must be returned to the library today.

_____

_____

_____

16–20 Directions

Using the information provided, create one complete sentence according to the sentence type indicated. In some cases, you will use both phrases and clauses to use all the information. Underline the independent clause or clauses for each sentence you create.

Example   Write a compound sentence using the following information: There was an election Tuesday in the city of Circleville. In that election, city voters approved a bond issue to build a new fire station. However, they rejected a bond issue for a new convention center.

<u>Circleville voters Tuesday approved a bond issue to build a new fire station</u>, but <u>they rejected a bond issue for a new convention center</u>.
(two independent clauses joined by the coordinating conjunction *but*)

16. Write a simple sentence with this information: Heavy rains hit Circleville last night. That rain was mixed with hail, and that combination made for dangerous driving.

_____

_____

_____

17. Write a complex sentence with this information: Striking machinists will return to work tomorrow. They agreed tonight to do so. They have been on the picket lines for three months.

_____

_____

_____

18. Write a compound sentence with this information: The women's basketball team of Bentley College was seeking its ninth straight victory. However, it lost to Conan College in overtime by a score of 88–87.

_____

_____

_____

19. Write a compound-complex sentence (at least two independent clauses, with at least one dependent clause) with this information: I used to love airline travel. However, I prefer to use the train now. That's because it is more hassle-free.

_____

_____

_____

20. Write a simple sentence with this information: Henderson County Food Bank volunteers did the following in an eight-hour period today: They packaged more than 500 school lunch packs. They also delivered 200 hot meals to homebound senior citizens. In addition, they stored more than 1,000 canned goods from donors.

_____

_____

_____

EXERCISE 20 • THAT/WHICH/WHO AND
RESTRICTIVE/NONRESTRICTIVE CONSTRUCTIONS

Purpose   To learn the difference between restrictive and
nonrestrictive constructions; to choose correct
relative pronouns and punctuation for them.

Reference   "When Words Collide" (8/e), Chapters 4, 6 and 8

PART ONE: RESTRICTIVE OR NONRESTRICTIVE?

1–15 Directions

Identify the underlined section according to the following code.

> A = restrictive clause   B = nonrestrictive clause
> C = restrictive phrase   D = nonrestrictive phrase

_____ 1.   The dirt <u>that is piled behind Rick's house</u> is for his new
vegetable garden.

_____ 2.   This year's election, <u>which has attracted an unprecedented
number of campaign contributions,</u> features incredibly
close races for nine Senate seats.

_____ 3.   <u>Trying to reach the summit by nightfall,</u> the expedition
pushed forward.

_____ 4.   His digital animation process, <u>patented only two years ago,</u>
is being eagerly sought by all the major studios.

_____ 5.   Sarah, <u>my former high school prom date,</u> challenged me to
an arm wrestling match at my high school reunion.

_____ 6.   Runners <u>passing the wooded path</u> did not see the lion
waiting in the grass.

_____ 7.   Every spring, Harold, <u>a failed efficiency expert</u>, moves all
the boxes and trunks from one side of the attic to the other.

_____ 8.   The violinmaker made five trips to Italy in one year <u>after
becoming obsessed with the violins made by 16th century
craftsmen.</u>

_____ 9.   The mechanic, <u>who tried multiple times to explain to me
the purpose of a timing belt,</u> stormed out of the shop in
frustration.

_____ 10. Presidential campaigns, <u>which receive substantial federal
financial support</u>, are not for the faint of heart.

_____ 11. Cellular phones <u>fitted with high-end digital cameras</u> are
becoming popular.

_____ 12. We need more executives <u>who place ethics over financial
gain</u>.

_____ 13. The students learned <u>they can mount a well-organized
campaign.</u>

_____ 14. The new tenant <u>who called the police over every little noise</u>
was confronted by other condo owners at the most recent
association meeting.

_____ 15. The device <u>triggering the explosion</u> is from a company in
Idaho.

PART TWO: THE TROUBLE WITH *THAT!*

16–20 Directions

The word *that* can be used three ways: as a limiting adjective, as a conjunction and as a relative pronoun. Using structure as your guide, identify the part of speech for the use of *that* in the following sentences.

_____ 16. No one thought the primary race would last until the summer, but it looks as if that may be the case.
  A. conjunction
  B. adjective
  C. relative pronoun

_____ 17. My parents keep telling me to drive their sedan, but I want that new sports car advertised in popular magazines.
  A. conjunction
  B. adjective
  C. relative pronoun

_____ 18. The handball team that dominated the informal neighborhood leagues more than 50 years ago is gathering for a reunion at Erasmus Hall High School.
  A. conjunction
  B. adjective
  C. relative pronoun

_____ 19. Brendan won the first grade spelling bee the second year in a row with *uncooperative,* a word that he first learned during his "Terrible Twos."
  A. conjunction
  B. adjective
  C. relative pronoun

_____ 20. I forgot to tell you that this is a nonrefundable purchase.
  A. conjunction
  B. adjective
  C. relative pronoun

PART THREE

21–30 Directions

Select the correct pronoun (with appropriate punctuation and subject–verb agreement) from the choices offered.

_____ 21.   The budget _____ the president vetoed has received heavy support in national polling.
    A.   that
    B.   which

_____ 22.   Diane _____ is a motivational speaker by trade.
    A.   , that has become a tireless advocate for the homeless,
    B.   that has become a tireless advocate for the homeless
    C.   , who has become a tireless advocate for the homeless,
    D.   who has become a tireless advocate for the homeless

_____ 23.   Are you sending this package of news clippings _____ to Boise?
    A.   , that has been sitting here and gathering dust for two weeks,
    B.   which has been sitting here and gathering dust for two weeks
    C.   , which has been sitting here and gathering dust for two weeks,
    D.   that has been sitting here and gathering dust for two weeks

_____ 24.   As more water is exposed to sunlight, more heat is stored in the water, _____ warms and melts some of the ice.
    A.   that
    B.   which

_____ 25.   An export slowdown _____ is contributing to the shutdown of factories in several countries.
    A.   , which has been magnified by the global financial crisis,
    B.   that has been magnified by the global financial crisis
    C.   which has been magnified by the global financial crisis

_____ 26.   What is your opinion of the commentary _____ was
             published in our neighborhood newsletter?
             A.   that
             B.   which

_____ 27.   Stock certificates _____ are counterfeit.
             A.   that have a pink watermark
             B.   which have a pink watermark
             C.   , which have a pink watermark,

_____ 28.   The protesters _____ refused to disperse have been
             arrested and jailed.
             A.   that
             B.   who

_____ 29.   I asked you three times to take all those magazines
             _____ have been gathering dust to the recycling bin!
             A.   that
             B.   who
             C.   which

_____ 30.   Robin is one of those obsessive workers _____ never
             learned the value of a vacation.
             A.   who
             B.   that
             C.   which

PART FOUR

31–34 Directions

Using the information presented below, write four sentences: one with
a nonrestrictive clause, one with a restrictive clause and two with a
nonrestrictive appositive phrase.

Diabetic acidosis is a life-threatening condition. It can occur in people with type 1 diabetes. Type 2 diabetics also can get it, but it's less common with them. Diabetic acidosis is referred to by doctors as *ketoacidosis*. Ketoacidosis is caused when insulin is deficient or lacking. A lack of insulin leads to high blood sugar levels and the presence of what are known as *ketones* in the blood and also the urine. Ketones are byproducts or waste products; they are produced when the body burns fat for energy. And then there is a build-up of acids. The build-up is of certain acids. Those acids are called *ketoacids*.

31. Sentence with a nonrestrictive clause:

_____

_____

_____

32. Sentence with a restrictive clause:

_____

_____

_____

33. Sentence with an appositive phrase:

_____

_____

_____

34. Sentence with an appositive phrase:

_____

_____

_____

EXERCISE 21 • APPOSITIVES

Purpose   To improve understanding and use of appositives in your writing.

Reference   "When Words Collide" (8/e), Chapters 7 and 8

Note: Pay particular attention to how appositives (used as single words, phrases or clauses) can add helpful, complementary information to a sentence. Note also the importance of proper punctuation and pronoun case in their use.

1–10 Directions

Select the correct answer from the choices offered.

_____ 1. What is the appositive in the following sentence?
Harriet Thompson, editor of the new Browning Book series, will speak to our students this afternoon at three o'clock.
A. Harriet
B. Thompson
C. editor
D. series

_____ 2. What is the appositive in the following sentence?
Tommy's aunt, Sarajean, often tells the story of coming to America with her sisters.
A. aunt
B. Sarajean
C. story
D. America

_____ 3. In the previous sentence, why is there a comma after _aunt_
and _Sarajean?_
   A. _Sarajean_ is a restrictive construction, denoting a
      particular aunt.
   B. Appositives are always set off with commas.
   C. _Sarajean_ is used in a nonrestrictive or looser sense.
   D. It is obvious that Tommy has more than one aunt, and
      it is likely that more than one aunt tells this story.
   E. Both C and D are correct.

_____ 4. Is the appositive in the following sentence a phrase or
a clause?
Jared Sumpter, president of Tri-County chemicals,
declined comment about the pending toxic waste litigation.
   A. phrase
   B. clause

_____ 5. Is the appositive in the following sentence a phrase or
a clause?
Wendy Bowman, soon to be appointed chair of the United
Way Board, has an inspirational life story.
   A. phrase
   B. clause

_____ 6. Is the appositive in the following sentence a phrase or
a clause?
The paper wrote a glowing story about Billy Andersen, who
will be honored as Smallville's "First Citizen" tonight.
   A. phrase
   B. clause

_____ 7. Identify the appropriate pronoun to use in the following
sentence and whether, based on meaning, punctuation is
necessary.
The company decided that the three of us, Sara, Henry and
_____ will represent it at the conference.
   A. me,
   B. I,
   C. me
   D. I

_____ 8. Name the two nouns that are followed by two nearby
appositives in the following sentence.
One of the largest calderas in the world, Ngorogoro, is in
Tanzania, a republic in East Africa.
A. calderas...Ngorogoro
B. world...Ngorogoro
C. calderas...republic
D. calderas...Tanzania

_____ 9. Does the following sentence contain an appositive? Why
or why not?
Steve Martin is a comedian as well as a great banjo player.
A. Yes. *Comedian* and *banjo player* complement and add
helpful information to the subject, *Steve Martin.*
B. Not really. The nouns *comedian* and *banjo player*
follow the linking verb *is,* which makes them
a predicate noun (or nominative).
C. *Banjo player* would be an appositive if *as well as* was
preceded by a comma.

_____ 10. Why is there no comma after the subject in the following
sentence?
The tenor Capezio thrilled Milan audiences with his
performance in *Tosca.*
A. *Capezio* specifies or clarifies the noun *tenor,* which
makes this a restrictive appositive.
B. Commas are not needed in a short sentence.
C. Placing a comma after the subject *Capezio* will harm
the sentence's meter.
D. Both A and B are correct.

11–15 Directions

From the information provided, combine each pair of sentences into
one by turning one clause into an appositive phrase. Underline the
appositive phrase in your answer. Try to make your sentences as
concise as possible.

Example   George Mallory was a famous British explorer. He
                     disappeared in 1924 during a climb of Mount Everest
                     during the winter.

Rewrite   George Mallory, <u>a famous British explorer,</u>
                     disappeared in 1924 during a winter climb of Mount
                     Everest.

11. Sam Johnson's novel is *Windward Passage*, and it has been on the
     best-seller list for six months. Today, it won the annual Bookman
     Prize for best work of fiction.

     _____

     _____

12. The *Kensington Review* is an annual publication, published by the
     Kensington Foundation. Today, it was announced that,
     immediately, the *Review* will cease publication.

     _____

     _____

13. Police say the suspect in the robbery of the First National Bank has
     been identified and arrested. He has been identified as Norman
     Bates, and he has been charged with the crime of first-degree
     robbery.

     _____

     _____

14. Cleveland is an important part of the region's history of
     manufacturing. That region has often been referred to as the
     "Rust Belt."

     _____

     _____

15. First-degree robbery is a felony. In many states, it is punishable by
    a prison term of 10 years, at a minimum.

    _____

    _____

Bonus Question

Write a sentence in which an appositive phrase relates to the object of a
preposition rather than to a subject or a direct object. Underline the
object of the preposition.

_____

_____

_____

_____

_____

_____

EXERCISE 22 • CHECKUP: PHRASES AND CLAUSES

Purpose   To assess your understanding of phrases and clauses, as well as your understanding of sentence construction.

Reference   "When Words Collide" (8/e), Chapters 4, 5 and 6

Directions: Select the correct answer from the choices offered.

_____ 1.   Identify the participial phrases in the following sentence. Completing her second triathlon in two weeks proved that Rebecca, though hampered by a shoulder injury, could overcome incredible obstacles.
A. Completing her second triathlon
B. hampered by a shoulder injury
C. overcome incredible obstacles
D. Both A and B are correct.

_____ 2.   How many dependent clauses are in the following sentence? He waited all morning for the mysterious stranger, but no one appeared; at two o'clock in the afternoon, he decided to go home.
A. one   B. two
C. three   D. none

_____ 3.   Why is the following a compound sentence? The hurricane struck the coastline with a fury, but its power diminished during its move westward.
A. It's not a compound sentence; it is a complex one.
B. It is compound because it contains two dependent clauses.
C. It is compound because the clauses are joined by the preposition *but*.
D. It is compound because it contains two independent clauses joined by the coordinating conjunction *but*.

_____ 4.   How many clauses are in the following sentence?
People who live in glass houses must, without a doubt, pay a pretty hefty insurance premium.
A. one   B. two
C. three   D. four

_____ 5.   A gerund phrase, which can be the subject or direct object of a sentence, is always what part of speech?
A. noun   B. pronoun
C. verb   D. adjective

_____ 6.   The following sentence seems to take forever to get to the point. What is the most precise explanation why?
Although he had prepared intensely in the past two weeks, which actually caused him to fall ill, Smith, who had expected to win the competition easily, placed last in the national finals.
A. Actually, it's not a sentence; it's a fragment, which explains the problem.
B. The subordinate clause is buried in a pile of dependent clauses.
C. Passive voice is the obvious culprit.
D. Oversubordination is the problem: The independent (main) clause is interrupted by a host of dependent clauses.

_____ 7.   What type of clause is underlined in the following sentence?
This is one of those sentences <u>that create confusion with subject–verb agreement.</u>
A. dependent   B. independent
C. subordinate   D. Both A and C are correct.

_____ 8.   What's the most accurate label for the underlined section in the following sentence?
Tom Smith, <u>Jordan's uncle,</u> is a famous diplomat.
A. participial phrase
B. sentence subject
C. predicate nominative
D. appositive phrase

_____ 9. The underlined section in the following sentence is called
a(n) _____ clause.
Nonesuch chocolate, <u>which is prepared and packaged in
Portland</u>, has become the darling of the so-called "foodies."
A. independent clause   B. nonrestrictive clause
C. gerund phrase   D. essential clause

_____ 10. A participial phrase is always what part of speech?
A. noun   B. verb
C. adverb   D. adjective

_____ 11. A sentence fragment cannot stand alone as a complete thought.
Which of the following three constructions is a fragment?
A. Not only is this proposal going to fail, but it will do so
miserably.
B. All around the mulberry bush, with the monkey
chasing the weasel.
C. Wait!

_____ 12. Identify and describe the underlined section in the
following sentence.
<u>To be happy</u> is to live well.
A. It's an infinitive phrase serving as the subject of the
sentence.
B. It's the verb in the dependent clause.
C. It's an infinitive clause.
D. It's a gerund phrase, serving as the subject of the sentence.

_____ 13. A verbal can never be a _____.
A. subject   B. adverb
C. phrase   D. clause

_____ 14. The verbal most related to the <u>dangling modifier</u> error is
the _____.
A. participle   B. gerund
C. infinitive   D. conjunctive

_____ 15. Which is the only verbal that can be a noun adjective or
adverb depending on its use in the sentence?
A. participle   B. gerund
C. infinitive   D. conjunctive

_____ 16. What is the appropriate term for the underlined section in the following sentence?

To be eligible for federal funds, the restoration project must be located in a nationally designated historical district.

A. prepositional phrase
B. infinitive clause
C. subordinate clause
D. infinitive phrase

_____ 17. Although the underlined section in question 16 contains a preposition as well as noun, what is its part of speech in that sentence?

A. verb
B. adverb
C. adjective
D. pronoun

_____ 18. How many clauses are in the following sentence?

The Gingerbread Boy ran out of the house, into the yard and toward the town, and then headed toward the lair of Mr. Fox.

A. one
B. two
C. three
D. none

_____ 19. Why is the following sentence a run-on?

You'll really like this new convertible of Volvo's, it's wonderfully sporty yet truly safe.

A. It begins with a dependent clause, which should come last.
B. It should only be written as two separate sentences.
C. It lacks an independent clause.
D. Its two independent clauses are improperly joined; they need to be connected either with a semicolon or with a coordinating conjunction and a comma.

_____ 20. A sentence fragment _____.

A. never contains a subject or verb
B. may contain a clause, but it does not express a complete thought
C. never contains any punctuation
D. is always a phrase

EXERCISE 23 • CASE 1

Purpose   To create consistency within sentences by using the
                   correct case of pronouns.

Reference   "When Words Collide" (8/e), Chapter 7

Directions: Select the correct pronoun choice in each of the
                   following sentences.

_____ 1.   Jamie is a hardworking student, just like you and _____.
             A. I   B. me

_____ 2.   This is a clearcut case of _____ abusing a
             commissioner's authority.
             A. she   B. her

_____ 3.   Say, _____ a blue moon out tonight!
             A. theirs
             B. they'res
             C. there's

_____ 4.   You're never going to believe _____ we saw today at
             the mall!
             A. who   B. whom

_____ 5.   It's quite apparent to _____ writers that this poetry
             competition is rigged.
             A. we   B. us

_____ 6.   That was he, not _____, at the concert.
             A. I   B. me

_____ 7.   Really, _____ not that big a deal.
             A. its   B. it's

_____ 8. I would appreciate _____ getting back to me at your
           earliest convenience.
           A. you   B. your

_____ 9. _____ is the apartment on the third floor.
           A. Hers   B. Her's

_____ 10. _____ incessant coughing infuriated the conductor.
           A. You're   B. Your

_____ 11. To avoid any software conversion issues, we have decided
           to run the update tool for any users _____ have more
           than 10 affected files.
           A. who   B. whom

_____ 12. The article discusses his fall from grace and speaks of
           _____ admission of guilt while he was chairman.
           A. his   B. him

_____ 13a. I asked her to provide me the citation for the research that
            shows children (A. who B. whom) have been
            overprotected often

_____ 13b. become adults for (A. who B. whom) life is difficult
            outside the family circle.

_____ 14. I've always known that _____ is a special relationship.
           A. theirs   B. they'res
           C. there's

_____ 15. The mayor refuted the accusation that she was a power
           broker _____ jumps from one business luncheon to the
           next.
           A. who   B. whom

_____ 16. The woman _____ police believed committed the
           robbery has been released on bail.
           A. who   B. whom

_____ 17. I certainly understand _____ asserting his Fifth
             Amendment rights.
             A. him   B. his

_____ 18. So, _____ up first?
             A. who's   B. whose

_____ 19. _____ dog-eared book is this?
             A. Who's   B. Whose

_____ 20. _____ judges were unimpressed by the new line of
             clothing designed by the celebrity's father.
             A. Us   B. We

_____ 21. Don't you agree that _____ freelance writers should
             form a guild?
             A. us   B. we

_____ 22. The county commission will soon release _____ traffic
             survey results.
             A. their   B. they're
             C. it's   D. its

_____ 23. This is mine; which is _____?
             A. ours   B. our's
             C. ours'

_____ 24. _____ going to be very sorry if you eat that foot-long
             hot dog!
             A. Your   B. You're

_____ 25. I'm going to vote for _____ tells the funniest joke.
             A. whoever   B. whomever

_____ 26. It's official—the lottery winnings are _____!
             A. your's   B. yours
             C. you'res

_____ 27.   Between you and _____ , I don't understand the point
of this exercise.
A.   I   B.   me

_____ 28.   The other delegates and _____ immediately accepted
the resolution drafted by the Senate.
A.   him   B.   he

_____ 29.   Adding Sara and _____ to the members list of the ski
club allowed us to get a group rate.
A.   I   B.   me

_____ 30.   The Free Clown Society of Barcaster will hold _____
annual gathering next week.
A.   their   B.   they're
C.   it's   D.   its

EXERCISE 24 • CASE 2

Purpose   To continue to build an understanding of the proper use of case and to improve editing abilities.

Reference   "When Words Collide" (8/e), Chapters 7 and 8

Directions: Carefully read each of the following sentences. Correct all errors in pronoun case, pronoun selection and noun possessives. Make your edits at the sentence line or just below it. Watch for improper use of subject–verb contractions and possessives (including those for nouns). If the sentence is correct, write *Correct* in the space below.

1. Between you and I, this assignment is going to be difficult for we writers.

2. Do you think that sending Colin and she to the therapist is an idea who's time has come?

3. You volunteering to lead the parade does have it's advantages.

4. Well, it's certainly someone's fault!

5. You should award the prize to whomever wears the silliest hat.

6. She's much smarter than me, but our's is still a competitive relationship.

7. Theres a beautiful moon out tonight; its the kind of evening that remains in ones' heart.

8. She is a celebrity who Truman Capote once described as "a cat with a cold."

9. Their's is a compelling explanation of those poems meanings.

10. She and Tom's advocacy has been influential in improving childrens' safety.

11. I don't think she is a better writer than I, but I agree that she is far more creative than me.

12. Fred Henderson, whose conviction for burglary was overturned last year, was killed last night by an intruder whose still at large.

13. Neither of these men could handle this crisis by themselves'.

14. Its just a matter of time until the finger of suspicion is pointed at us
    who are professional lobbyist's.

15. This is neither yours nor ours; it's theirs.

16. Who did the board elect as their new chair?

17. Shes afraid that the court will reject the attorney generals opinion.

18. Police have arrested a man that they say is responsible for a series
    of fires in the citys' urban renewal district. There lead came from
    an anonymous witness' phone call.

19. The stock markets rally fizzled after the Johnson Corporation
    released their dismal report on fourth-quarter earnings.

20. Your going to be a great grammarian, thats for sure!

NAME _____   SCORE _____

EXERCISE 25 • WORD USE 1

Purpose   To add accuracy and logic to writing by preserving
                     the distinctive meaning of words; to understand word
                     usage as a function of part of speech.

Reference   "When Words Collide" (8/e), Part 2, and a
                     good dictionary

Directions: Choose the correct word from the options offered.
                     Then, on the line below, succinctly explain why your
                     answer is correct based on the word's part of speech
                     and its proper meaning.

_____ 1.   The director has _____ many times that it is the
              principle of the issue that counts, not its fiscal impact.
              A. proven   B. proved

_____

_____ 2.   Have you completed your application for financial
              _____ for next year?
              A. aid   B. aide

_____

_____ 3a.   The chicken casserole smells _____,
              A. bad   B. badly
_____ 3b.   but don't worry—he isn't _____ particular about the
              food he eats.
              C. real   D. really

_____

_____ 4. Her offhand comments _____ wide-ranging reactions
          from the people who were attending the convention.
          A. elicited   B. illicited

_____ 5. The congressional _____ repeatedly referred to a
          "mysterious foreign force" on the political action committee.
          A. aide   B. aid

_____ 6. The landlord agreed to _____ the security deposit.
          A. wave   B. waive

_____ 7. Your persistence has had an _____ on me.
          A. effect   B. affect

_____ 8. Let's try to figure out a way to _____ him a computer.
          A. loan   B. lend

_____ 9. This is no time to _____ your nerve.
          A. lose   B. loose

_____ 10a. One night my sister and I behaved so _____,
           A. bad   B. badly
_____ 10b. we were shocked our mother came into our room, praising
           us for acting _____.
           C. good   D. well

_____ 11.   I _____ your logic and your politics.
A. loath   B. loathe

_____ 12.   You're acting _____ this is a "done deal."
A. as if   B. like

_____ 13.   How will the rise in interest rates _____ your plans?
A. affect   B. effect

_____ 14.   Let's tour the exhibit first, _____ head to the bistro.
A. than   B. then

_____ 15.   A new blog for 30-year-olds says that that the number of
young adults returning home after college is increasing
_____ the recession.
A. because of   B. due to

_____ 16.   I find penguins more fascinating _____ puffins.
A. than   B. then

_____ 17.   The one good piece of _____ the bicycle commuter
took seriously his whole life to was never leave home
without a raincoat.
A. advise   B. advice

_____ 18. After several hours of pleading, he realized his mother had yet to be _____ that getting a puppy was a good idea.
    A. convinced   B. persuaded

_____ 19. The _____ reason for hiring this ad agency is its commitment to new media.
    A. principle   B. principal

_____ 20. Sorry to say, it looks _____ your campaign is going downhill.
    A. as if   B. like

_____ 21. What _____ will this report have on future sales?
    A. affect   B. effect

_____ 22. I don't think he is able to _____ his position on this.
    A. altar   B. alter

_____ 23. The youngest daughter always said she was _____ to go to school even when she needed 10 minutes more to finish her morning routine.
    A. already   B. all ready

_____ 24. After she blew out the candles on her birthday cake, she
told us her wish: to be a writer of _____ by the time she
turned 50.
A. renown   B. renowned

_____ 25. After several hours of deliberation, the city _____ voted
against the library tax measure.
A. counsel   B. council

EXERCISE 26 • WORD USE 2

Purpose   To sharpen precision in meaning by spotting and correcting word choice errors.

Reference   "When Words Collide" (8/e), Part 2, and a good dictionary

Directions: Review the following 40 sentences for any word usage errors; there can be as many as three in each sentence. If you find one, make a correction directly on the page using traditional editing marks. If the sentence is correct, write *Correct* below it.

1. That tie is a nice compliment to your new suit.

2. He's been compared with a furtive ferret.

3. It's only about six miles further to camp.

4. This course should be offered for less credits.

5. Over 300 persons have enrolled in the seminar on preventative snacking.

6. The speeding convertible collided with the stop sign.

7. I listened to those tapes for over 30 hours.

8. I'm not adverse to receiving nice complements from the audience.

9. What are you inferring by that remark?

10. There appointment is scheduled for 3 p.m., but I'll bet you a dime to a donut that they are late for it.

11. She appears reticent to join the group.

12. Helen is anxious to start her new job.

13. The clerk poured over the legal documents for over 10 hours, and she declared that they were the most unique she had ever read.

14. After he laid down for a while, he said he felt like he was a new man.

15. Your sure to land this internship if you can figure out who to contact.

16. This engine is comprised of nine moving parts.

17. His political values have been compared with a decaying tenement.

18. A fowl, stifling odor intimated from the poultry shack.

19. Many potatoes which are grown in Idaho soon make there way to fast-food restaurants.

20. That was quite a compliment you paid him!

21. If you are truly an impartial observer of these talks, than we should be able to say that you are uninterested.

22. The doctors had not expected her averse reaction to the medication.

23. The general lead his troops into battle.

24. His sculpture is the most unique piece of art I have ever seen.

25. Beside you and me, only Tom knows the combination to the safe.

26. Be sure to study those chapters which the professor keeps mentioning in class.

27. Are you certain that you can insure our safety during this raft trip?

28. Hopefully, we will complete this exercise, irregardless of the consequences.

29. So, whose going to bungee-jump first?

30. Shelley compared the drop in stock prices to a free fall from a jet plane.

31. The faculty senate censored the dean for her failure to produce a more convincing tenure package for the young professor.

32. You know, I am really eager about getting to the exam on time.

33. The lynch mob hung an innocent man.

34. Theirs too much to learn in too little time!

35. Let's examine this issue further.

36. Please lie the camera on the counter.

37. What were you inferring in your statement to the city council?

38. He has always lead by example.

39. It's difficult to steer a recreational vehicle on this tortuous mountain road.

40. Why does the speaker keep eluding to something that happened over 100 years ago?

EXERCISE 27 • PUNCTUATION

Purpose   To bring clarity and proper meter to your writing by making correct punctuation choices.

Reference   "When Words Collide" (8/e), Chapter 8

PART ONE

1–25 Directions

Complete the following sentences by selecting the correctly punctuated choice.

_____ 1.   You can talk about this issue all day _____ but you won't change my mind.
    A. long,
    B. long;

_____ 2.   The counterfeit by _____ had been hanging in the Museum of Modern Art is now in the possession of Spanish authorities.
    A. Picasso that
    B. Picasso, that

_____ 3.   Alison is a _____ architect.
    A. well known
    B. well-known

_____ 4.   E. Harrison Smythe is a _____ patron of the arts.
    A. very-influential
    B. very influential

_____ 5. Wow! This is a _____ exercise.
   A. surprisingly easy
   B. surprisingly-easy

_____ 6. A warm front is expected in the region early next _____
   that should also bring rain and high winds.
   A. week, however,
   B. week; however,
   C. week; however

_____ 7. He asked _____
   A. , Where's the television remote?
   B. "where's the television remote"?
   C. , "Where's the television remote?"
   D. , "where's the television remote"?

_____ 8. That speech was a _____ mess.
   A. disorganized irrational
   B. disorganized, irrational

_____ 9. The protestors told the mayor _____
   A. , "to stand for justice and not for business."
   B. "to stand for justice and not for business."

_____ 10. We really missed you during your _____ absence.
   A. three week's
   B. three weeks
   C. three weeks'

_____ 11. The quarterback _____ and rifled a touchdown pass to
   the speedy receiver.
   A. dropped back
   B. dropped back,

_____ 12. This home will soon be _____
   A. ours.
   B. our's.
   C. ours'.

_____ 13. You've crossed my mind many times _____ why is it
           you never stay?
           A. ,
           B. ;

_____ 14. The man _____ is acting strangely.
           A. carrying the tattered briefcase
           B. , carrying the tattered briefcase,

_____ 15. Journalists are only human _____ readers can be harsh
           critics.
           A. , nevertheless,
           B. ; nevertheless
           C. ; nevertheless,

_____ 16. Labor and management _____ have had their share of
           disagreements.
           A. not surprisingly
           B. , not surprisingly,
           C. —not surprisingly—

_____ 17. Have you read _____
           A. "Sense and Sensibility?"
           B. "Sense and Sensibility"?

_____ 18. _____ has damaged his health.
           A. Working around toxic chemicals,
           B. Working around toxic chemicals

_____ 19. _____ the challenger asked the incumbent.
           A. "Where's the beef"?
           B. "Where's the beef?"
           C. "Where's the beef?",

_____ 20. He will return from vacation in three _____ .
           A. week's
           B. weeks'
           C. weeks

_____ 21.   He paid $25,000 for the _____.
A.   200-year old book
B.   200 year-old book
C.   200-year-old book

_____ 22.   Judge Olson will order another investigation _____ she
believes the primary evidence is tainted.
A.   because
B.   , because

_____ 23.   Here's what management proposes to _____ shut
down the production line, retool the machinery and reduce
the shift periods.
A.   do,
B.   do;
C.   do:

_____ 24.   _____ of the county's farmland is under water.
A.   Two thirds
B.   Two-thirds

_____ 25.   Tom bought two suits _____
A.   (the three button kind.)
B.   (the three-button kind).
C.   (the three-button kind.)

PART TWO

26–35 Directions

Read the following sentences to determine whether they contain
punctuation errors. If you think a sentence has an error, choose an
answer that corrects it. If you think the sentence is correct, select C.

_____ 26.   He's a terrific snowboarder but an inept downhill skier.
A.   Insert a comma after "snowboarder."
B.   Change "He's" to "He is."
C.   The sentence is correct.

_____ 27. The torrential rains were unyielding; making driving a
           deadly nightmare.
           A. Delete the semicolon.
           B. Replace the semicolon with a comma.
           C. The sentence is correct.

_____ 28. Long thought to be relatively flat and shaped like Frisbees,
           some galaxies actually are oblong in shape, this has
           prompted some scientists to call for more studies.
           A. A comma splice creates a run-on sentence; insert a
               semicolon after _shape._
           B. A comma is needed between the word _flat_ and the
               conjunction _and._
           C. The sentence is correct.

_____ 29. Did you see that article titled Greening My (City) Alley in
           "Mother Earth" magazine? I did; and believe me, it had a
           tremendous influence on me.
           A. Replace the semicolon with a comma.
           B. Enclose the article title in quotation marks.
           C. The sentences are correct.

_____ 30. Susan Butler says she's ready, "to stand on a stump and
           shout" if that's what it takes to get the city council's
           attention.
           A. A comma is not needed before the partial quotation.
           B. The quotation marks should be deleted.
           C. The sentence is correct.

_____ 31. She enjoys sailing, but prefers to avoid the boating resorts
           that so many well-heeled tourists enjoy.
           A. No comma is needed between _sailing_ and _but._
           B. A hyphen is not needed after _well._
           C. The sentence is correct.

_____ 32. I came to your well-publicized lecture to get the real story
             about the eco-terrorism trial, not to hear a litany of old war
             stories.
             A. Delete the comma between *trial* and *not.*
             B. Delete the hyphen between *well* and *publicized.*
             C. The sentence is correct.

_____ 33. "Fight all unfair taxes!" the candidate urged the audience in
             a strongly-worded attack.
             A. The exclamation point should be outside the quotation
                 marks.
             B. A hyphen is not needed between *strongly* and *worded.*
             C. The sentence is correct.

_____ 34. I refuse to support Anderson, because I oppose his position
             on taxes.
             A. Delete the comma between *Anderson* and *because.*
             B. Replace the comma with a semicolon.
             C. The sentence is correct.

_____ 35. The defendant, fled the courtroom in the midst of his
             sentencing.
             A. Insert a comma after *courtroom.*
             B. Delete the comma after *defendant.*
             C. The sentence is correct.

EXERCISE 28 • EDITING FOR GRAMMAR, PUNCTUATION, WORD USE AND SPELLING

Purpose   To incorporate "When Words Collide" readings and workbook exercises into a comprehensive editing exercise that tests a wide range of grammatical principles.

Reference   "When Words Collide" (8/e), your dictionary

Directions: Review the following sentences and correct all errors in grammar, punctuation, word use and spelling. Look for ways to be more concise. Edit on this sheet. **Look carefully!**

1. Because I disagree with her in principal, I won't try and convince her that this project is pure folley.

2. The lightening which hit several of the trailer homes' was responsable also, for several deaths in Canton.

3. The pirate captain, entertained we sailors with his tales of adventure and lonliness.

4. In my judgement, everyone should complete his financial questionaire before proceding with this investment scheme.

5.   The people that taut that math course need to be fired!

6.   The victory that alluded the team for so long is finally in their grasp.

7.   Tom is one of those workers that never seems to tire of a new

challendge.

8.   The company president has refused to meet with the media today,

however a press conferrence will be called by the public relations

department tomorrow.

9.   Concerned that passage would lead to a rash of lawsuits, the

loitering ordnance was defeated by the council, by a unanimous

vote of 6-0.

10. The police claims that it's anti-drug efforts have had profound affects in the downtown neighborhood.

11. His plan is comprised of seven discreet stages.

12. The board is not anxious to take this new public safty plan any farther.

13. None of these cigarette brands are superior to low-tar M/Pha/Zema, in fact " Zema" is the most unique tobbaco product which I have ever encountered.

14. Due to child resistent caps on pill containers childrens' deaths from aspirin overdose has been reduced by over 80%.

15. Although we failed to acheive concensus on this issue, we certainly can site our collegiality as a marked improvment in our style of deliberation.

16. The City Counsel has postponed it's regular monthly meeting, due

to a power failure which hit the City Hall complex this afternoon.

17. Mayor Helen Jennings was killed, instantly this morning, when the

sport utility vehicle which she was driving collided with a

telephone poll.

18. What the eyes see excite the brain.

19. Inflation is one of those economic evil's which tends to perpetuate

itself.

20. I fail to understand you're rational for this decision; but it's a

decision I will support.

EXERCISE 29 • THIS SENTENCE IS <u>CORRECT</u> BECAUSE...

Purpose   To assess understanding of grammatical concepts, especially agreement, case, parallelism and punctuation.

Reference   "When Words Collide" (8/e), Chapters 4 through 8

Directions: All of the sentences in this exercise are correct. From the three choices offered, select the answer that best explains *why* the sentence is correct.

_____ 1. Lifting all those bricks has injured Harold's back.
    A. The objective case is used properly.
    B. The subject and the verb agree.
    C. The passive voice actually helps this sentence.

_____ 2. We reporters must be vigilant in our pursuit of public records.
    A. This sentence avoids the use of appositives.
    B. The writer scrupulously avoids the use of the dash.
    C. The nominative case is used properly in the subject of the sentence.

_____ 3. Running marathons, creating metal sculptures and volunteering at the food bank keep George and Samira quite busy, thank you.
    A. Parallelism of the subjects creates a nice balance.
    B. The participial phrases are in harmony with subjects of the sentence.
    C. *George* and *Samira* are properly used as indirect objects.

_____ 4. The professor reported that she enjoyed the students'
papers, but she added that much more research needs to be
done.
  A. This complex sentence is correctly punctuated.
  B. This compound-complex sentence is correctly
     punctuated.
  C. The writer keeps all verbs in the past tense.

_____ 5. You're going to enjoy this new play; it's a Tony winner
for sure!
  A. The sentence uses a parallel series of adjectives.
  B. The sentence avoids the passive voice, though this
     would have been as strong as an active construction.
  C. The writer properly uses two subject–verb
     contractions for economy and balance.

_____ 6. Dashing across the uneven pavement, Andrew fell and
broke his collarbone.
  A. The writer skillfully avoids a dangling modifier.
  B. The passive voice works well in this construction.
  C. Linking verbs strengthen this sentence.

_____ 7. He is the kind of writer who never fails to do at least 10
drafts of any story.
  A. The writer avoids the erroneous use of _that_ in picking
     who.
  B. The adverb _never_ is properly placed before the verb.
  C. Most of the prepositional phrases are placed at the end
     of the sentence.

_____ 8. Hillary is one of those artists who use only recycled
materials.
  A. The writer is able to contain all this information in a
     simple sentence.
  B. By using the plural verb in the dependent clause, the
     writer keeps the pronoun and its antecedent in
     agreement.
  C. The strategic placement of the adverb _only_ is the chief
     factor in this sentence's correctness.

_____ 9. It's difficult to understand this year's budget without comparing it with last year's revenues and expenditures.
   A. The sentence successfully eliminates all internal punctuation except apostrophes.
   B. The writer stays in the same verb tense.
   C. The writer properly uses *compared with* instead of *compared to.*

_____ 10. How do you think this decision will affect the next election?
   A. The writer keeps this as a declarative sentence.
   B. The writer makes the correct *affect/effect* choice because a noun, not a verb, is needed.
   C. The writer makes the correct *affect/effect* choice because a verb, not a noun, is needed.

Bonus Question

Examine the following sentence, and in the lines provided, give three potential errors that were avoided in order for it to be correctly written. (By the way, we see five possible pitfalls that were avoided.)

Searching for reliable clients has proved fruitful for the firm; however, there's always a risk in losing old customers.

_____

_____

_____

_____

_____

EXERCISE 30 • THIS SENTENCE IS <u>INCORRECT</u> BECAUSE...

Purpose   To assess understanding of grammatical concepts, especially agreement, case, parallelism and punctuation.

Reference   "When Words Collide" (8/e), Chapters 4 through 8

Directions: All of the sentences in this exercise are incorrect. From the choices offered, select the answer that best explains *why* the sentence is incorrect.

_____ 1.   Do you think that rising tuition costs will result in less students?
   A.   The writer needs to identify and fix the word usage error.
   B.   The possessive form of *students* should be used.
   C.   The auxiliary verb should be *may*, not *will*.

_____ 2.   Her choice of dinner partners are alienating to her closest friends.
   A.   This sentence uses an improper antecedent.
   B.   The comma left out after *to* creates a run-on sentence.
   C.   The sentence contains an agreement error.

_____ 3.   Everyone, including Sam and I, is going to the county fair.
   A.   The words *county* and *fair* should be capitalized.
   B.   The sentence contains a case error.
   C.   The indefinite pronoun should be written as two words.

_____ 4.   The team feels badly about one of its worst seasons ever.
   A.   The *its* should be changed to the contraction *it's*.
   B.   The possessive pronoun *their* should replace *its*.
   C.   The linking verb should be followed by an adjective, not an adverb.

_____ 5.   Among all these competing proposals are a truly
               innovative idea.
               A.   A change in number of the verb will fix the agreement
                    error.
               B.   The sentence should use active rather than passive
                    voice.
               C.   The sentence needs a comma after _truly._

_____ 6.   The board approved the nomination of the new directors,
               but the proposed slate of officers was rejected by them.
               A.   The improper use of the comma creates a run-on
                    sentence.
               B.   Changing from passive to active voice will create
                    proper parallelism.
               C.   Intransitive verbs should be used instead.

_____ 7.   How do you think a university professor should evaluate
               his students?
               A.   The word usage problem creates confusion.
               B.   The adverb _always_ should be inserted before the verb.
               C.   The writer errs in using the possessive pronoun _his._

_____ 8.   Neither of these settlement options, as offered by the panel
               of mediators Monday, seem viable to either party.
               A.   By using the plural verb in the independent clause, the
                    writer creates a subject–verb agreement error.
               B.   The phrase needs to be restrictive, without the commas.
               C.   The time element _Monday,_ as an adverb, should be
                    closer to the verb.

_____ 9.   The traveling circus is one of a dying breed of professions
               which trains the next generation of performers by using
               apprenticeships.
               A.   The writer needs a dash before _which_ for dramatic
                    effect.
               B.   The objective case is used improperly.
               C.   The writer should change _which_ to _that_ to establish
                    restrictive meaning.

_____ 10. Billy walked into the newsroom and immediately he starts
shouting at the city editor.
A. The writer needs to use the same verb tense
throughout the sentence.
B. The sentence needs to add additional commas.
C. The nominative case is used improperly for the subject
of the dependent clause.

EXERCISE 31 • DO I REALLY UNDERSTAND THESE GRAMMATICAL TERMS?

Purpose   To show understanding of grammatical concepts by properly identifying terms associated with them.

Reference   "When Words Collide" (8/e), all chapters

Directions: Select the correct answer from the choices offered.

_____ 1.   A linking verb is never followed by a(n) _____.
    A. predicate nominative
    B. prepositional phrase
    C. predicate adjective
    D. direct object

_____ 2.   What is the proper term for the underlined segment in the following sentence?
This is one of those trivia games <u>that can deflate one's ego</u>.
    A. gerund phrase
    B. dependent clause
    C. independent clause
    D. prepositional phrase

_____ 3.   What is the proper term for the underlined segment in the following sentence?
<u>Climbing over the wire fence</u>, his pants tore.
    A. dangling modifier
    B. infinitive phrase
    C. dependent clause
    D. indirect object

_____ 4.   What kind of verb is contained in the following sentence?
            Despite setting a furious pace at the beginning of the race,
            Tom collapsed near the finish line.
            A. transitive
            B. intransitive
            C. linking
            D. auxiliary

_____ 5.   A complex sentence contains _____.
            A. at least two independent clauses
            B. at least two semicolons
            C. one independent clause and one dependent clause
            D. only one clause

_____ 6.   Which part of speech modifies a verb?
            A. pronoun
            B. adverb
            C. adjective
            D. interjection

_____ 7.   What is the underlined part of speech in the following
            sentence?
            The experimental car performed <u>poorly</u> in road tests.
            A. pronoun
            B. adverb
            C. adjective
            D. interjection

_____ 8.   What is the proper term for _writer_ in this sentence?
            Bonnie is the kind of writer who never misses a deadline.
            A. pronoun
            B. indirect object
            C. proper noun
            D. antecedent

_____ 9. What is the proper term for the underlined segment in the following sentence?

After months of haggling, he finally gave <u>Anderson</u> the trophy.

A. indirect object
B. predicate nominative
C. direct object
D. subject

_____ 10. In the underlined portion of the following sentence, a(n) _____ is linked to a(n) _____ to create a(n) _____.

Teresa is a <u>well-known</u> anthropologist.

A. pronoun...noun...contraction
B. adverb...adjective...compound modifier
C. adverb...adjective...dangling modifier
D. participle...gerund...indirect object

_____ 11. What is the proper term for the following construction?
This is a challenging exercise, it's creating a lot of stress.

A. compound–complex sentence
B. oversubordinated sentence
C. nonrestrictive construction
D. run-on sentence

_____ 12. What is the tense of the verb in the following sentence?
Andrea has written to the mayor five times in the past month.

A. present
B. past perfect
C. subjunctive
D. present perfect

_____ 13. Which verbal is always a noun?
A. gerund
B. participle
C. infinitive
D. interjection

_____ 14.   What is the proper term for the underlined segment in the
following sentence?
<u>Between you and me</u>, I'll never use the subjunctive mood
properly.
   A.   introductory clause
   B.   participial phrase
   C.   prepositional phrase
   D.   adverb clause

_____ 15.   What is the case of the underlined pronoun in the
following sentence?
I'll never understand <u>his</u> devotion to such an illogical
belief.
   A.   nominative
   B.   objective
   C.   possessive
   D.   prepositional

_____ 16.   Some verbs, such as *sit* and *lie,* don't change into past tense
with conventional –*ed* endings. We call these verbs
_____.
   A.   oversubordinated
   B.   progressive
   C.   irregular
   D.   passive

_____ 17.   The verb pair *bear* and *bare* is an example of what?
   A.   acronyms
   B.   homonyms
   C.   dipthongs
   D.   contractions

_____ 18.   You can better understand the difference between *than* and
then when you realize that *than* is often a(n) _____
and that *then* is almost always a(n) _____.
   A.   conjunction…adverb
   B.   adverb…conjunction
   C.   noun…preposition
   D.   adjective…adverb

_____ 19. What is the proper term for the underlined clause in the
           following sentence?
           The upgraded solar panels, <u>which will be shipped from our
           Oregon plant</u>, will increase energy savings by 40 percent.
           A. restrictive
           B. nonrestrictive
           C. redundant
           D. correlative

_____ 20. The words *completely destroyed* and *fatal suicide* are
           _____.
           A. nonrestrictive
           B. redundant
           C. indefinite
           D. relative

EXERCISE 32 • SPELLING 1

Purpose   To quickly recognize (and correct) misspelled words.

Reference   "When Words Collide" (8/e), Appendix A,
                     your dictionary

Directions: In each of the three-word sets below, underline or
                     circle the word that is misspelled. Secondary spellings
                     in dictionaries are incorrect. Correctly spell the
                     misspelled word on the line.

1. accumulate   definately   relevant

_____

2. goverment   occasional   immunity

_____

3. wholly   wholesome   enviroment

_____

4. criteria   criterion   accessable

_____

5. abhor   wintery   hygiene

_____

6. changeable   admirable   useable

_____

7. accommodate   pronounciation   digestible

_____

8. legitimate   reluctant   adolesense

_____

9. dilemma   antecedant   aide

_____

10. concensus   harass   embarrassed

_____

11. battalion   reccommend   canceled

_____

12. discrete   discreet   caffiene

_____

13. corroborate   persistant   tobacco

_____

14. loathe   paralell   apparent

_____

15. maintainence   missile   exaggerate

_____

16. questionnaire　　　　withold　　　　　　advertising

_____

17. rhythm　　　　　　　credability　　　　colossal

_____

18. innuendo　　　　　　concurred　　　　　indefensable

_____

19. wield　　　　　　　　wierd　　　　　　　yield

_____

20. supersede　　　　　　proceed　　　　　　preceed

_____

21. receive　　　　　　　percieve　　　　　　germinate

_____

22. irritible　　　　　　　despondent　　　　minimal

_____

23. pestilence　　　　　　physique　　　　　suggestable

_____

24. epademic　　　　　　misstate　　　　　　innovative

_____

25. mournfull　　　　　　pseudonym　　　　resilient

_____

26. ellipsis   eliptical   harmonic

_____

27. sensatize   benefitted   profited

_____

28. nauseous   changable   excusable

_____

Directions

In the passage below, identify the incorrectly spelled words by
underlining them. Write the correct spelling directly above.

Before Simon left his small hometown and went to university, he was

oblivous that he had grown up with a life of privalege. He had spent his

whole childhood manuevering his way toward college, that he never

even considered the liklihood that he had gained quite a few

"acceptable" habits for survival in a larger, more business-like

environment. He realized later that the number of years it had taken to

accummulate these skills in part had obscured the depth of his

knowlege.

EXERCISE 33 • SPELLING 2

Purpose   To further your mastery of spelling.

Reference   "When Words Collide" (8/e), Appendix A,
your dictionary

Directions: There are 30 spelling errors in this exercise. Review
each sentence, and write the correctly spelled word
for each misspelling. If there are no errors in a
sentence, write *No Errors*. Focus on spelling only;
there are no word use errors in this exercise.

1.   Do you beleive that our athletes have benefitted from seperate
study facilities?

_____

2.   Her favorite pasttime is photographing lightening strikes.

_____

3.   In all liklihood, our goverment's enforcment of our new
enviromental policy will surly fail.

_____

4.   Our school superintendant is responsable for this disasterous mess.

_____

5.   I'm dumbfounded that you thought you could embarrass or harass
me with this silly charade.

_____

6. Thompson said she felt priviledged to work with such a conscientious and commited superviser.

_____

7. The city is being sued for its resistence to providing adequate accessability to its facilities.

_____

8. Do we have an adaquate precedant to procede with our dismissal of the county sherrif?

_____

9. Scott thinks it is weird to wield such power in these desperate times.

_____

10. The company promises a sizeable investmant in the city's power grid.

_____

11. Our bookkeeper has a wonderful temprament for such repetitious work.

_____

12. The counselor recomends more relevent therapy for supervisors suffering from stress.

_____

13. Her curiousity never seems to abate!

_____

14. The intensity of the boss's predjudice is simply stunning.

---

15. "This was an act of incredible desparation," said the obviously irritated police chief.

EXERCISE 34 • AWK!

Purpose   To detect, understand and correct awkward writing.

Reference   "When Words Collide" (8/e)

Directions: Rewrite the sentences below to eliminate awkward
                     constructions and to improve clarity and conciseness.

Example   There has this term been a very dramatic increase in
                     the number of citations for disturbing the peace,
                     according to the campus police who have reported
                     this information.

Rewrite   Campus police have reported a dramatic increase in
                     citations for disturbing the peace this term.

1. So, this is going against my better judgment, but anyways I am
    going to give my permission for the class to attend the Def
    Wombat concert that will be held tonight.

    _____

    _____

    _____

2. The Food and Drug Administration, an agency of the federal
    government, says it is planning to take steps to increase its
    oversight of a number of medical radiation procedures—the three
    most potent forms, exactly—which includes CT scans that are
    becoming increasingly popular.

    _____

    _____

    _____

3. The subcommittee has, for the past five months, struggled to
    achieve a consensus of opinion on changes to the agency's charter.

    _____

    _____

    _____

4. The Senate Judiciary Committee will, for the next two weeks, hold
    hearings, which will be closed, on changes to election rules for
    primary elections.

    _____

    _____

    _____

5. Heather Britt has a new novel, and it has been topping the best-
    seller charts for the last two months; and just yesterday, she has
    been named as recipient of the annual Platinum Pen Award.

    _____

    _____

    _____

6. The man, who is from Smithfield and is 28 years old, has two
    drunken driving citations already in the last two years, and now he
    has received his third such citation.

    _____

    _____

    _____

7. Calvin started his job, which was as a receptionist in the front office, but just two days after beginning work he suffered his first panic attack, which hadn't happened for the past three years.

_____

_____

_____

8. Writers who don't pay attention to detail, and those who don't prepare for interviews, as well as those who miss deadlines—they are just the kind of writers whom Editor Patricia Brown dislikes.

_____

_____

_____

9. Harrison worked for 10 hours to correct all the errors and omissions in his speech, and then he even spent four more hours changing the opening of the speech, but later that evening, a power surge so badly damaged the hard drive of his computer, which resulted in his losing every document in that computer.

_____

_____

_____

10. Just minutes after she descended down the ladder from the roof of her condominium, after having completed some roof repair, lightning struck and set Donna's building on fire.

_____

_____

_____

EXERCISE 35 • RHYTHM!

Purpose   To focus and combine ideas in sentences; to create order, prominence, and subordination in sentences; to create rhythm by crafting sentences of varying length.

Reference   "When Words Collide" (8/e), Chapters 4 and 5

Directions: Write two sentences based on each group of facts. In your sentences, create the proper order and prominence of information. Sentence 1 should be complex; sentence 2 should be simple. The purpose of this alignment is to show the different pacing (rhythm) created by using different sentence types to present your information.

Example   A sudden blizzard hit the western part of Colorado last night. It stranded hundreds of motorists on highways and led to cancellation of all flights at the Denver Airport through 11 this morning. The snowstorm resulted in accumulation of 17 inches of snow and was a factor in several landslides.

Rewrite Sentence 1 (complex): A sudden blizzard that hit western Colorado last night dumped 17 inches of snow and was a factor in several landslides.

Rewrite Sentence 2 (simple): It caused cancellation of all flights at the Denver airport and stranded hundreds of motorists.

(**Note:** You don't need to use all the information given in your sentences. Just be sure that sentence 1 has one independent clause and at least one dependent clause and that sentence 2 has only one independent clause.)

1. A movie reviewer for the Claremount Times (his name is Geoff
    Hedges) proclaimed "A Witness Named Spot" the "worst" film he
    had seen in his life in his weekly column this morning. Several
    hours later, Hedges was found shot to death in an alley on Franklin
    Avenue, near his newspaper. Police say they are looking for a
    "person or persons of interest" in the slaying of Hedges.

    Sentence 1 (complex): _____

    _____

    Sentence 2 (simple): _____

    _____

2. Three people have died and 11 are injured in a fire in east
    Evanston. Fire officials think it is arson-related. It is the third fatal
    fire of the year. It occurred at the Woodbine Apartments this
    morning.

    Sentence 1 (complex): _____

    _____

    Sentence 2 (simple): _____

    _____

3. Striking aerospace workers have agreed to return to work
    tomorrow. They approved a new contract. The pact is for a three-
    year period. The vote was 450-17. The Seattle local has been in a
    work stoppage for the past three months.

    Sentence 1 (complex): _____

    _____

    Sentence 2 (simple): _____

    _____

4. Elvis Presley was special. He was, many would say, a musical titan. He had a troubled life, however. It was a life marked by drug use.

Sentence 1 (complex): _____

_____

Sentence 2 (simple): _____

_____

5. Nehru and Gandhi were two names that upset the quietude of the British in embattled India. Clearly, India was nearing a state of revolution, at a time when the British colonists spent a great deal of time attending garden parties.

Sentence 1 (complex): _____

_____

Sentence 2 (simple): _____

_____

6. An unlicensed Rhode Island social club was packed with people Sunday morning at 3. At that time, a fire destroyed the club. Screaming people trying to find relatives hampered efforts by firefighters to rescue people and to fight the fire. In the fire, 22 people were killed.

Sentence 1 (complex): _____

_____

Sentence 2 (simple): _____

_____

7. A heat wave is in its third week throughout the Midwest. It has produced record high temperatures, and as a result has claimed the lives of 13 people. According to a report by the Illinois Farm Bureau, thousands of acres of corn and soybean crops are in a state of ruin.

Sentence 1 (complex): _____

_____

Sentence 2 (simple): _____

_____

8. An overloaded passenger ferry capsized in a lake during a severe hailstorm. This happened in Finland today. A government spokesperson announced today that more than 200 people drowned in this incident. The spokesperson also said there were no survivors.

Sentence 1 (complex): _____

_____

Sentence 2 (simple): _____

_____

EXERCISE 36 • FINAL GRAMMAR, SPELLING AND WORD-USE EXAM

Purpose To evaluate your performance and progress with a comprehensive examination of grammatical principles. Sorry—no answers provided this time; your instructor has them!

NAME THAT ERROR!

1–10 Directions

Use the following code to identify the error in each of these sentences. (In a later section, you'll have an opportunity to identify the proper "fix" for an error.)

A = Subject–verb or antecedent agreement
B = Punctuation
C = Case
D = Dangling modifier
E = Spelling

_____ 1. Scanning the horizon carefully, the ship still hit the towering iceberg.

_____ 2. Struggling with a mountain of debts have taken its toll on the Smith Brothers.

_____ 3. It was him who reported the embezzlement.

_____ 4. The corporation has lost sight of their priorities.

_____ 5. Can you believe what Tom used as a slogan on his campaign stationary?

_____ 6. The company will abandon its new venture because of its exhorbitant cost.

_____ 7. Between you and I, this idea for a movie will rock the industry.

_____ 8. The typhoon lashed the beleaguered island all night, it left great devastation in its wake.

_____ 9. I'm truly sorry, but Carlos and I cannot accomodate your request.

_____ 10. She was stunned at him insisting on a cleaning deposit for the apartment.

AGREEMENT

11–20 Directions

Make the correct selection from the choices provided.

_____ 11. The number of mortgage foreclosures _____ increased dramatically in the last two months.
     A. has   B. have

_____ 12. This is one of those types of movies that _____ the daylights out of me.
     A. scares   B. scare

_____ 13. The rate of influenza cases _____ dropping, according to county health officials.
     A. is   B. are

_____ 14. Between a rock and a hard place with sharp edges _____ where they are today.
     A. is   B. are

_____ 15. Five million board feet of plywood _____ been shipped to the war-torn country.
   A. has   B. have

_____ 16. The United Auto Workers says that _____ will set a strike deadline tonight.
   A. it   B. they

_____ 17. None of your excuses _____ going to be accepted.
   A. is   B. are

_____ 18. This is a tough assignment for _____ students.
   A. us   B. we

_____ 19. Two-thirds of the office building _____ under water.
   A. is   B. are

_____ 20. Building all those national monuments _____ given her a monumental ego.
   A. has   B. have

CASE

21–25 Directions

Make the correct selection from the choices provided.

_____ 21. The candidate _____ the newspaper endorsed was arrested last night on charges of embezzlement.
   A. who   B. whom

_____ 22. Corey and _____ are getting married next month.
   A. her   B. she

_____ 23.   This is the candidate _____ the party faithful believe
will be the next state treasurer.
      A.   who   B.   whom

_____ 24.   Do you think that Sarah is smarter than _____?
      A.   he   B.   him

_____ 25.   The university is deeply interested in _____ alumni.
      A.   its   B.   their

ANTECEDENTS

26–30 Directions

Make the correct selection from the choices provided. Look carefully
for the proper antecedent!

_____ 26.   Economics is one of those courses that really _____ him.
      A.   bores   B.   bore

_____ 27.   I found Harold's report to be very interesting, but I'm afraid
that the panel of judges was not impressed by _____.
      A.   it   B.   him

_____ 28.   She is only one of the snowboarders who _____ have a
sponsor.
      A.   don't   B.   doesn't

_____ 29.   Neither of the women has admitted _____ involvement
in the land-swap scandal.
      A.   her   B.   their

_____ 30.   I understand why you chose those criteria; I just don't
agree with _____.
      A.   it   B.   them

IDENTIFICATION OF SENTENCE ELEMENTS

31–35 Directions

Identify the underlined sentence element by indicating the correct choice.

_____ 31. Among the many reasons I love this book is the author's sense of <u>humor</u>.
   A. object of preposition
   B. subject
   C. direct object
   D. predicate nominative

_____ 32. <u>Fearing the creation of a dangling modifier</u>, she quickly rewrote the sentence.
   A. independent clause
   B. adjectival clause
   C. dependent clause
   D. participial phrase

_____ 33. This is one of those sentences <u>that drive me crazy</u>.
   A. dependent clause
   B. participial phrase
   C. gerund phrase as subject
   D. independent clause

_____ 34. Police surrounded the compound in early morning while helicopters <u>hovered</u> directly overhead.
   A. gerund
   B. linking verb
   C. transitive verb
   D. intransitive verb

_____ 35. The auditors, who contend they were misled, are seasoned corporate <u>veterans</u>, with a combined 60 years' experience.
   A. predicate nominative
   B. predicate adjective
   C. direct object
   D. indirect object

SPELLING

36–50 Directions

Underline the misspelled word in each item. In the line provided, write its correct spelling. If all spellings are correct, write *Correct* on the line.

_____	36.	A. existance	B. environment	C. procedure
_____	37.	A. similar	B. commitment	C. superintendant
_____	38.	A. proceed	B. precede	C. recede
_____	39.	A. imminent	B. eminent	C. definate
_____	40.	A. hygeine	B. fierce	C. weird
_____	41.	A. resistant	B. tremendous	C. irresistible
_____	42.	A. accommodate	B. accumulate	C. dilemma
_____	43.	A. aid	B. forteen	C. aide
_____	44.	A. harassment	B. embarass	C. morass
_____	45.	A. questionnaire	B. deterrent	C. consensus
_____	46.	A. skillful	B. reccomend	C. accessible
_____	47.	A. forcible	B. sherrif	C. dependable
_____	48.	A. seize	B. seige	C. legitimate
_____	49.	A. privilege	B. perserverance	C. withhold
_____	50.	A. plausable	B. succeed	C. permanent

PUNCTUATION

51–65 Directions

Complete the following sentences by making the correct punctuation choice.

_____ 51. She's leaving the theater troupe _____ she cannot get along with the artistic director.
  A.   because   B.   , because

_____ 52. I've done all my research _____ completed all my fact-checking.
  A.   and   B.   , and

_____ 53.   _____ has accused the judges of favoritism.
     A. The pageant runner-up
     B. The pageant runner-up,

_____ 54.   _____ going to the game tonight?
     A. Whos'   B. Who's
     C. Who'se

_____ 55.   Are you going to support the _____ health bill?
     A. children's   B. childrens'

_____ 56.   You are going to regret this _____ decision.
     A. last minute   B. last-minute

_____ 57.   Tommy enjoys what his mom used to _____
     A. call, "comfort food".
     B. call "comfort food".
     C. call "comfort food."

_____ 58.   She _____ "I have nothing to hide."
     A. said   B. said,
     C. said:

_____ 59.   The lovesick lamprey _____ "You picked a fine time to leave me, you eel."
     A. said;   B. said,
     C. said—

_____ 60.   The new trucks are ready for _____ the freight company is behind schedule.
     A. delivery; however,
     B. delivery, however
     C. delivery, however,

_____ 61.   The chef enjoys making vegetarian chili _____ dislikes preparing anything that contains tofu.
     A. but he   B. , but he
     C. ; but he

_____ 62. "How would you feel if someone talked to you like
_____ asked the counselor.
A. that,"   B. that?"
C. that"?

_____ 63. The three most famous Marx Brothers were _____.
A. Groucho, Harpo, and Chico
B. Groucho, Harpo and Chico

_____ 64. She solved the puzzle in _____.
A. three hour's time
B. three hours time
C. three hours' time

_____ 65. That seems to be _____ favorite song these days.
A. everyones
B. everyone's
C. everyones'

WORD USE

66–80 Directions

Select the correct answer from the choices offered.

_____ 66. The government authorized massive _____ to the
war-torn country.
A. aid   B. aide

_____ 67. Hendrickson admits that he _____ Internet dating.
A. loaths   B. loathes

_____ 68. Don't you think we should seek legal _____ on this issue?
A. council   B. counsel

_____ 69. Wilson is one of those politicians _____ you love to hate.
A. that   B. who
C. whom

_____ 70. The town council expressed outrage about his _____ activities.
    A. elicit   B. illicit

_____ 71. Columnists have compared his rambling speech _____ a blindfolded walk down a busy street.
    A. to   B. with

_____ 72. Are you _____ about this new opportunity?
    A. anxious   B. eager

_____ 73. Yours is one of the most _____ presentations I have heard in a long time.
    A. affective   B. effective

_____ 74. The project plan is _____ five distinct stages.
    A. comprised of   B. composed of

_____ 75. The critics seem _____ excited about this new animation technique.
    A. real   B. really

_____ 76. It looks _____ we're in for a harsh winter.
    A. like   B. as if

_____ 77. His new marketing plan surely will be a _____ success.
    A. proven   B. proved

_____ 78. Have you noticed the man _____ has been loitering near the tobacco shop?
    A. that   B. who

_____ 79. The volunteer group has raised _____ $2 million for the playground projects.
    A. more than   B. over

_____ 80. I sense that she is _____ to go to the reunion.
    A. reluctant   B. reticent

IDENTIFICATION AND CORRECTION OF GRAMMATICAL ERRORS

81–100 Directions

Read the following sentences and determine whether they contain grammatical errors. If a sentence contains an error, select the lettered item that suggests how to correct the error. Note that the suggested answers use grammatical terms, so stay focused. If the sentence is correct, select D, no error.

_____ 81. Please return this woebegone wombat to it's owner.
   A. Correct spelling of *woebegone.*
   B. Change *it's* to *its.*
   C. Insert comma after *wombat.*
   D. No error

_____ 82. I don't think that the prosecution has proved their case.
   A. Change *proved* to *proven.*
   B. Change *their* to *its.*
   C. Both changes—A and B—are needed to correct this sentence
   D. No error

_____ 83. Buckle up as soon as you get in the car, it's the best way to protect yourself.
   A. *It's* should be *its.*
   B. Correct the comma splice.
   C. *Yourself* should be replaced with *yourselves.*
   D. No error

_____ 84. Their's a harvest moon out tonight.
   A. Replace the comma with a semicolon.
   B. The entire sentence needs to be in quotation marks.
   C. Change *their's* to *there's.*
   D. No error

_____ 85. Theirs is a tender and incredible love story.
   A. Insert comma after *tender*.
   B. Change *theirs* to *their's*.
   C. Correct spelling of *incredible*.
   D. No error

_____ 86. The man who police say they arrested for the crime has an airtight alibi; however, police aren't willing to drop the charges.
   A. *Who* should be replaced with *whom*.
   B. Improper punctuation has created a comma splice.
   C. *Aren't* is an improper contraction.
   D. No error

_____ 87. Wow! Your advice for taking tests has really yielded dividends.
   A. Change *advice* to *advise*.
   B. Correct the antecedent agreement error.
   C. Correct the subject–verb agreement error.
   D. No error

_____ 88. Struggling to make ends meet by working three jobs.
   A. Eliminate comma.
   B. Correct the sentence fragment.
   C. Correct subject–verb agreement error.
   D. No error

_____ 89. To Meryl Streep Oscar is a deliciously familiar name.
   A. Insert hyphen after *deliciously*.
   B. Insert comma after *Streep*.
   C. Correct spelling of *familiar*.
   D. No error

_____ 90. Us reporters filed more than 500 stories on the foreclosure crisis.
   A. Insert hyphen after *foreclosure*.
   B. Change *us* to *we*.
   C. Change the passive voice to active.
   D. No error

_____ 91. The argument which I am going to pursue in my closing statement is going to be risky, indeed.
  A. Correct the one misspelling.
  B. Eliminate the unnecessary *indeed.*
  C. Replace *which* with *that.*
  D. No error

_____ 92. How has the defendant's behavior effected the defense's ability to persuade the jury?
  A. Change *defendant's* to *defendants.*
  B. Change *effected* to *affected.*
  C. Both corrections—A and B—are needed.
  D. No error

_____ 93. They're bound to make a mistake sooner or later, and there error will come back to haunt them.
  A. Replace *there* with *they're.*
  B. Delete the comma.
  C. Replace *there* with *their.*
  D. No error

_____ 94. None of the stockholders is going to press for a proxy battle, but the board knows they can mount a well-organized buy back campaign.
  A. The compound modifier doesn't need a hyphen.
  B. Correct the error in subject–verb agreement.
  C. Change *they* to *it.*
  D. No error

_____ 95. Now really: Can you justify she going outside official channels to solve this contentious issue?
  A. The colon is not needed.
  B. Correct the one misspelling.
  C. Change *she* to *her.*
  D. No error

_____ 96.   She is the only one of the writers who truly understand what sells in this self-help era.
    A. Correct the subject–verb agreement error.
    B. Change *who* to *that.*
    C. Insert comma after *who.*
    D. No error

_____ 97.   Traveling unaccompanied through the Kenyan bush, he was ever on the alert for ivory poachers.
    A. Correct the spelling of *Traveling.*
    B. Eliminate the dangling modifier.
    C. Replace the comma with a semicolon.
    D. No error

_____ 98.   I can't tell you how wholly dependent I've become on my dictionary; it's heavy, but it's definitely a lifesaver!
    A. Correct the one misspelling.
    B. Correct the two misspellings.
    C. Correct the three misspellings.
    D. No error

_____ 99.   Managing the avalanche of financial crises has given her a well deserved reputation for mental toughness.
    A. Correct spelling of *avalanche.*
    B. Insert proper punctuation to make *well deserved* a compound modifier.
    C. Change *has* to *have.*
    D. No error

_____ 100. You're going to be a truly fabulous grammerian!
    A. Correct the one misspelling.
    B. Insert hyphen between *truly* and *fabulous.*
    C. Correct the two misspellings.
    D. No error